DR. JOHNSON'S PRINTER
The Life of William Strahan

DR. JOHNSON'S PRINTER

*The Life of
William Strahan*

by

J. A. COCHRANE

ROUTLEDGE & KEGAN PAUL
London

First published 1964
by Routledge and Kegan Paul Ltd
Broadway House, 68–74 Carter Lane
London E.C.4

Printed in Great Britain
by Butler and Tanner Ltd
Frome and London

© *J. A. Cochrane 1964*

Contents

Illustrations

Preface

IT is dangerous for any collector, whether of biographical materials or postage stamps, to believe that his specimens are of more general interest than they in fact can command. Courtesy as well as prudence point the need of an explanation for the writing of this book about an eighteenth-century tradesman.

It was and is no ordinary trade in which William Strahan exercised his abilities. It is practised by men no more intelligent than those engaged in other lines of business; its rewards are, commercially, trifling in relation to the industry and shrewdness it calls into play; as an occupation it entails fully as much of the humdrum drudgery, the pettiness of detail, as is exhibited in any manner of earning a living. But the book trade is distinguished from any other by the fact that its fundamental staple is ideas, even though the tangible expression of those ideas is bought and sold much like other commodities. This is the reason for its intrinsic interest and for the fascination it exerts upon those who work in it and so rarely desert it; this is what gives the market place its curious atmosphere, in fluctuating proportions, of idealism and commercial practicality.

The mid-eighteenth century was not distinguished in Great Britain by its fine printing, with such few exceptions as the work of Baskerville and the Foulis brothers. No technical advances were made until the end of the century and in consequence printers were generally faced with a demand for output rather than quality; as Strahan told Benjamin Franklin, 'Here all our Pressmen are spoilt by the hasty and slovenly manner in which our numerous Newspapers and Magazines are printed; nor is there the least Encouragement for any one to carry the Art to any farther Degree of Perfection.' In the history of the book trade as a whole, however, it was a formative period. It inherited from the seventeenth century a lively tradition of the expression and circulation of general ideas. It produced a growing middle class with the means and the leisure to buy books and read them, and it put very little restriction on what the trade could print and sell to this new public. It saw the final emancipation of the writer from the position of an amateur or a hack to that of an often highly paid professional. In response to these needs and pressures the book trade developed an efficient organization. As a result, incidentally, it was equipped to exploit to the full the expansion made possible by the increase of literacy and by the steam press in the next century.

The trade was still sufficiently fluid to enable William Strahan to engage in several sides of its work. He was of course primarily a printer, and one of the leading men in his craft even before he became King's Printer. He was the publisher of some of the most notable books of the century and, more, was in many cases the friend of their writers. As a wholesaler and exporter of books he had large interests in the American market. His letters inform us of problems that still vex the trade—discounts and prices, books that 'stick' and others that sell too fast for the stock, payments to authors, rival or pirated editions, the iniquities and the loyalties of fellow-printers and publishers, anxieties over capital and credit.

Reynolds's portrait of him when he was sixty-five shows the successful man of business; a face without humour, rather insensitive, firm to the point of sternness, with a bold eye and a not ungenerous mouth. Unlike most of his rich contemporaries in the City, he owed his wealth to a craft of which he was himself a master. The somewhat podgy hands in the painting had set many thousands of ens before they kept account of the profits made from organizing other men's handiwork. His life displays a talent for friendship as well as a propensity to quarrel, even within his own family, over what seemed to him points of principle; a 'good hater', he was slow to forgive an injury. He had few intellectual pretensions, often seeking the advice of others on the publication of new works, but once his mind was made up he was loth to admit an error of judgement.

His life, from 1715 to 1785, spanned an era that can too easily from this distance look like a golden age; he was born after the Hanoverian succession had been settled and he died before revolution swept the old Europe away. But to him the times were anything but easy, with almost constant war or alarm of war, faction and rioting at home and the convulsion of the War of American Independence abroad. Long before he became a member of Parliament his interest in public affairs was intense, and his political correspondence provides a background to his business.

As King's Printer and M.P., as the publisher of such works as *The Decline and Fall of the Roman Empire* and *The Wealth of Nations*, as the close friend of men so disparate as Samuel Johnson and David Hume and Benjamin Franklin, Strahan was much more than an ordinary tradesman.

Acknowledgements

FOR his friendly encouragement and guidance to much material that I should not otherwise have discovered, I am deeply grateful to Whitfield J. Bell, Jr. I have drawn heavily upon a busy scholar's fund of patient kindness and never found it wanting.

For their courteous permission to make use of manuscripts or texts as indicated in my footnotes, my thanks are owed to many persons, institutions and publishers. They include Mrs. R. A. Austen-Leigh, Mrs. Dick-Cunyngham of Prestonfield and Mr. J. Bennett Nolan: the American Philosophical Society; University Library, King's College, Aberdeen; Library of Congress; Fordham University Library; Haverford College Library; the Huntington Library, San Marino, California; Pierpont Morgan Library; John Rylands Library; William Salt Library, Stafford; Salem County Historical Society, New Jersey; the Royal Society of Edinburgh: George Allen & Unwin Ltd.— Plant, *The English Book Trade*; Clarendon Press—Balderston, *Thraliana*; Chapman, *Letters of Samuel Johnson*; Hill, *Letters of David Hume to William Strahan*; Hill, Powell, *Boswell's Life of Johnson*; Turberville (ed.), *Johnson's England*; Cornell University Press—Sale, *Samuel Richardson, Master Printer*; Cresset Press—Van Doren, *Benjamin Franklin's Autobiographical Writings*; Oxford University Press—Thompson, *A Scottish Man of Feeling*; Yale University Press—*Papers of Benjamin Franklin*; Yale University

Press, McGraw-Hill Book Company, Inc. and William Heinemann Ltd.—the Isham Collection of *Boswell Papers*.

I should also like to express my thanks to the National Portrait Gallery for permission to reproduce Sir Joshua Reynolds's portrait of William Strahan, and to the Trustees of the British Museum for the same courtesy in respect of various title pages.

The original punctuation and spelling of quoted documents have been retained wherever possible. Dates before September 1752 are Old Style.

J. A. C.

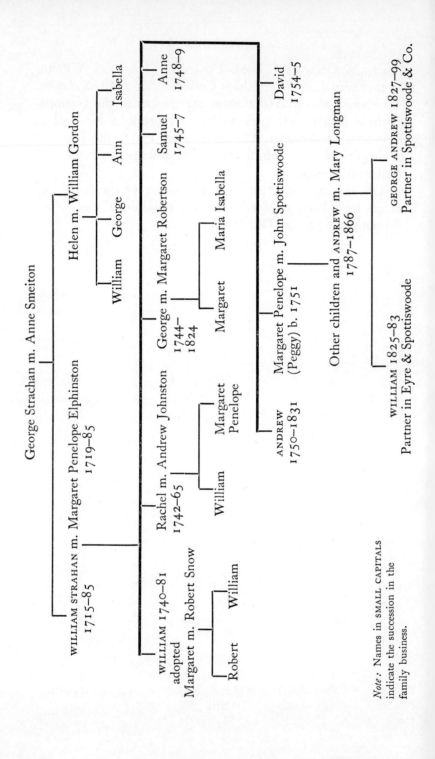

Note: Names in SMALL CAPITALS indicate the succession in the family business.

1

Apprentice to Master

WILLIAM Strachan, or Strahan as he spelled his name when he moved to London, was born in Edinburgh on 24 March 1715. As far as can be learned, this is the only scrap of information he himself has left of his early years. He was to become a voluminous correspondent; he was sufficiently a man of method to note in detail the dates of birth, and too often death, of his children, but of his parents and upbringing there is barely a mention. This is probably fortuitous, and if other letters or papers had survived his biographers might have been spared some pains. As it is, they have been compelled to rely upon an obituary notice which appeared in an Edinburgh magazine, *The Lounger*, on 20 August 1785, and has been drawn upon without comment by various authorities from Timperley's *Encyclopaedia* to the *Dictionary of National Biography*. The obituary was inaccurate, though never corrected by Strahan's son, Andrew: this may perhaps indicate that William had not been reluctant to leave his forebears behind him.

He was born in the exciting year of the '15 of a father who was well on the side of the Hanoverian settlement. George Strachan was a douce citizen with respectable friends, a professional man. He was educated at Edinburgh University, whence he appears to have graduated on 12 May 1704, and then followed the law. He became a writer, or solicitor, but presumably his practice was not a very successful one since he secured, some time after 1716, a position as a clerk of the Customs at Leith.

His wife was Anne Smeiton. They had two children, William and a daughter Helen, who was born on 9 May 1716. The witnesses to William's baptism were 'Mr. John Goodall, professor of Hebrew, Mr. Alexander Primrose, student of Divinity, and Mr. Thomas Herriott, Schoolmaster of Herriotts Hospital'. George Strachan had maintained his university connections; Professor Goodall and another divinity student were witnesses to Helen's baptism the following year.

As was natural in his father's circumstances, young William was sent to the old High School, not yet the Royal High School of Edinburgh. However he did not follow his father to the University; he was apprenticed to a printer. There was no loss of caste in a professional man's binding his son to a trade. A parallel occurs in the case of William Davenport, a clergyman's son, whom Dr. Johnson was instrumental in placing as an apprentice in Strahan's office in 1775. 'I have placed young Davenport', he wrote to Taylor, 'in the greatest printing house in London, and hear no complaint of him but want of size, which will not hinder him much. He may when he is a journeyman always get a guinea a week'—the same prospect, no doubt, which led to the young Strahan's apprenticeship. His success as a printer was such that he must often have blessed his father's decision. There is no trace of his indentures, but by his own account he was apprenticed to John Mosman and William Brown, the King's Printers in Scotland (p. 60). If things followed their normal course he was apprenticed in 1729 at the age of fourteen and became a journeyman in 1736.

The Edinburgh in which he was brought up was the old city, its rookeries huddled in tiers along the slopes below the Castle and along the Royal Mile to Holyrood. It was the city in which, years later, Boswell could not prevent Johnson's 'being assailed by the evening effluvia of Edinburgh' and led that great visitor to grumble 'I smell you in the dark!' Edinburgh was greatly altered to the eye, if not the nose, in Strahan's lifetime. The extent of the changes appears in an article in the form of a letter addressed by Strahan to *The Mirror*, an Edinburgh periodical edited by his friend Henry Mackenzie. It was printed in the issue of April 1780, and was dated from London on 13 March.

> . . . You must know I am a native of *Edinburgh*, where I passed my youth and received my education, but have long been settled in this place. Some years ago I was impelled by a very natural desire to visit my native country,[1] and I now sit down to communicate to you the sensations I felt upon that occasion . . . Even the improvements that had been made during my long absence displeased me. The cornfields on the south side of the town were quite covered with substantial buildings; *Barefoots Parks*, where I have had many a retired and pleasant walk, converted into a splendid city and, in the old town, many ruinous buildings, the scenes of some of my youthful amusements, now rebuilt with equal solidity and elegance . . .
>
> I will acknowledge, however, that I had the satisfaction to find many places that did not hurt me by any alteration or improvement. Your *wynds* and *closes* were nearly in the state I had left them; and where, in some parts of the streets, you have got new pavements, the good people who live at the sides of them take care that there shall be no innovation in point of cleanliness. Your *Theatre* and *Concert-Hall* are new buildings, but your *Assembly Rooms*, where people of the highest fashion resort, is just as paltry as ever . . .
>
> The *High School*, and its environs, I found unaltered, though the yards appeared to me to be much diminished in their extent. The *College*, too, remained the same plain, mean, unadorned building it was half a century ago and seemed to me, after having seen the splendid palaces of *Oxford* and *Cambridge*, more homely than ever.

Strahan did not practise his new trade very long in Edinburgh. He cannot have worked as a journeyman there for more than eighteen months, if that, for by the summer of 1738 he was in London. We do not know the date of his

---

[1] Strahan revisited his native country on several occasions; he was certainly in Scotland in 1749, 1759, 1760 and 1768.

3

father's death, save that it occurred before 1742 when Helen Strachan married William Gordon. There is no trace of George Strachan's will, and we cannot tell whether young William left home in his father's lifetime and with his father's blessing or with a small inheritance to set him up. He had means of some sort, enough at least to tide him over a trading loss in his first year of business; in 1743, five years after leaving Edinburgh, he was anxious to help a friend 'as far as my small Fortune would allow me'. On the other hand, he told Boswell that 'If he had had £100 a year, he never would have left Scotland'.

From the point of view of his prospects in trade he had sound reasons for emigrating to England, as can be seen from an analysis of entries in Plomer's *Dictionary of Booksellers and Printers 1726–1775*. In the period 1735–40, when Strahan had to debate the choice between staying in his native city and moving to London, there were twenty-seven printers at work in Edinburgh, ten in Glasgow and four elsewhere in Scotland. It would be rash to conclude that these were all master printers, since the entry of 'printer' in deeds, wills or marriage certificates may often denote a journeyman. At this same time there were forty-one printers active in London, with only another thirty-seven in the rest of England. Again, a proportion of these is probably composed of journeymen or jobbing printers with a single press, but the figure includes some houses of considerable size. According to Benjamin Franklin who worked there both as compositor and pressman, there were fifty men in Watts's office in Lincoln's Inn Fields. In the 1730s Samuel Richardson had about thirty journeymen and four or five apprentices, and by 1750 he had forty employees in three offices.[1]

Thirty-five years later, in the period 1770–5, the number of printers in London had, surprisingly, only risen to forty-four, although the book trade had been prospering and both the number and the circulation of newspapers and periodicals had increased. It is a fair presumption that there had been

[1] Sale: *Samuel Richardson, Master Printer*, Cornell, 1950.

a general growth in the size of individual houses to meet the demand for greater output and speed. In 1764 Strahan told David Hume, in reply to a question, 'It is not easy to say how many presses there are in London, but as near as I can guess they are from 150 to 200—150 is pretty near the truth, I mean such as [are] constantly employed'.[1]

At the same time it is true that by this second period London no longer held such a pre-eminent place in relation to the rest of the kingdom, for when we turn to the provinces the position has become very different. The number of printers at work more than doubled, from thirty-seven to seventy-seven. Admittedly most of them were in a small way of business and combined their trade with that of book-selling or some other occupation; in one case there occurs the conjunction of printer and publican. Still, cities like Newcastle, Birmingham, Bristol and Norwich were producing a growing number of books and pamphlets, while the establishment of local newspapers meant that one or two presses were at work in many country towns. In the 1730s, however, the capital held the greatest concentration of the printing industry and offered the richest rewards to energy and ambition.

Strahan did not remain solitary in London for very long. On 20 July 1738 at the church of St. Mary le Bow he married Margaret Penelope Elphinston. She was the daughter of William Elphinston, an Episcopalian clergyman of Edinburgh, and cannot have brought much in the way of dowry to her bridegroom if we may judge from the fortunes of her younger brother James, an eccentric schoolmaster and very minor man of letters. Strahan was twenty-three and his bride only nineteen when they wed; marriage was a bold and confident step for a young man just beginning to find his feet in the strange wilderness of London. The

---

[1] Hill: *Letters of David Hume to William Strahan*, Oxford, 1888. A Star Chamber decree of 1637 limited the number of master printers in London to 20, excluding the King's Printers, each master to have only two presses unless he had been Upper Warden or Master of the Stationers' Company, when he could have three.

day before his wedding Strahan became a freeman of the City of London 'in contemplation of my marriage', so binding himself to the then statutory disposal of his personal estate in her favour in the event of his death. He took another step forward on 3 October of the same year when he took up the freedom of the Stationers' Company by redemption.

Beyond these facts, there is a good deal of mystery about his early life in London. Richardson in the same position worked for some years as a journeyman before venturing on the risk and capital outlay involved in becoming a master printer. We do know that for a short time Strahan was in partnership with a T. Hart at Bury Court, Love Lane, Wood Street. Hart was a printer and typefounder who had worked for William Bowyer and later spent twenty years working under Strahan. Hart and Strahan issued a type specimen but unfortunately did not date it.[1] Plomer dates their partnership as 1740–2, a conjecture fortified by the fact that in 1742 Strahan moved to new premises, the presumption being that he then parted from Hart and set up on his own. On the other hand the late R. A. Austen-Leigh dates the partnership with Hart as 1737–9, immediately on Strahan's arrival in London.[2] There are difficulties here in the dates suggested for Hart's employment elsewhere, but strong evidence in favour may be found in Strahan's account books, in which entries begin in 1739 with no mention of a partnership. We may assume with some degree of certainty that by then William Strahan was launched on his career as a master printer.

The expenses of his first year in business were increased by the birth of his eldest son William on 9 March. (For a table of his family, see p. xiv.) By the time the next child, Rachel, was born on 20 June 1742 the printing house had moved to Wine Office Court, an alley off Fleet Street which had been graced by Congreve and was to accommodate

[1] *Library*, Fourth Series, 1923.
[2] *The Story of a Printing House: being a Short Account of Strahans and Spottiswoodes*, London, 1912.

Goldsmith; it is probable that the Strahans lived over the shop. Other children followed; George on 24 March 1744 and Samuel on 15 September 1745, the latter only living for eighteen months. 'Though he married early', says Strahan's obituarist, 'and without such provision as prudence might have looked for in the establishment of a family, he continued to thrive, and to better his circumstances. This he would often mention as an encouragement to early matrimony; and used to say that he never had a child born, that Providence did not send some increase of income to provide for the increase of his household.'

It is time to observe Providence at work. We are fortunate in having a detailed record of Strahan's business life. From 1739 he kept meticulous accounts of his expenses and receipts. His ledgers remained in the possession of the printing house he founded, Messrs. Spottiswoode, Ballantyne, and are now in the British Museum.[1] The items which are of particular interest in tracing Strahan's early career are:

(*a*) What Austen-Leigh calls his 'rough book', a small ledger[2] containing odd accounts with booksellers and typefounders, a list of the thirty-four apprentices bound to him from 1739 to 1771, notes of the birth of his eight children—and the death of four of them—and various persons' birthdays, including those of Millar, Cadell and Johnson.

(*b*) A General Expenses Book[3] in which, in a series of tables starting in 1739, Strahan recorded his outgoings under a number of heads: Journeymen's Wages, Printing Materials, Paper, Books, etc., Household Expenses, Household Furniture, Wearing Apparel, For the Children, and Money Lent.

(*c*) A Ledger running from 1739 to 1768 listing accounts with individual customers, booksellers and partnerships. The record is continued to his death in 1785 in another volume.[4]

[1] Add. MSS. 48800–48919: *Ledgers and other Business Papers of William Strahan ... and his Successors in the printing trade ... 1739–1857.*

[2] Add. MSS. 48802A.

[3] Add. MSS. 48801.   [4] Add. MSS. 48800 and 48803.

(*d*) A book recording the 'copies taken'—that is, the shares he bought in various books and publications—from 1751 to 1775.[1]

These account books are models of exactitude and clarity. Strahan wrote a hand that was more than neat; it is still a pleasure to read today, and it reflects his orderly and methodical mind. Dr. Philip Gaskell suggests with justice that they afford at least part of the reason for his success. 'They were kept with such scrupulous care that Strahan must always have been aware of his precise financial position, so that he could both allow for the disadvantages of the long credit he was generally obliged to give and of the uneconomically large editions that he sometimes had to print, and also take the fullest advantage of the friendly, well-organized trade and of a reading public that was continually increasing.[2]

As has been noted, the ledgers open in 1739. The first account I can trace is dated 24 March of that year and is to Charles Davis; *To printing two Sheets of Spectacle de la Nature*, £4. In the following month he opened his account with Andrew Millar. He was to work more closely with Millar and with his successor Thomas Cadell than with any other booksellers; they were to prove Strahan's link with Johnson, Hume and Gibbon. The first item is dated 12 April; *To printing Political Reflections upon the Finances. 23 Sheets Pica Octavo with Notes and Tables, at £1 1s. p. Sheet, 750 Copies £24 3s.* Millar settled with four pounds' worth of Chambers's *Dictionary*, bound, on 20 August and with the balance in cash on 10 December. On 25 January 1740 Strahan invoiced Millar £39 for *Printing the Principles of Moral Philosophy 32½ Sheets Large Pica Octavo with Foot and Side Notes, 750 Copies at £1 4s. p. Sheet.* This was settled more promptly, on 2 February, by a *Bill from Mr. Noon for £39.* Strahan had begun printing for Noon in July 1739 (Hayes's *Modern Book Keeping*) and received cash from him until 1741 when he began to accept books in part payment.

[1] Add. MSS. 48805.   [2] *Times Literary Supplement*, 5 October 1956.

Strahan was undoubtedly helped in these early years
by having business put in his way by his fellow-Scot, the
famous bookseller. Andrew Millar had been born in Edinburgh in 1701 and by 1729 was established at 141 the
Strand, from which he moved to Tonson's old shop, the
Shakespeare's Head, opposite Catherine Street in the Strand.
Millar rechristened it the *Buchanan's Head* in native pride
and built up there a flourishing business. He had a nose for
a good book and was not afraid to back his fancy in liberal
terms. 'I respect Millar, Sir,' said Johnson, 'he has raised the
price of literature.' Nichols says that Millar 'had a nice dis-
crimination in selecting his literary counsellors; amongst
whom it may be sufficient to mention . . . the late William
Strahan Esq., the early friend and associate of Mr. Millar
in private life and his partner in many capital adventures
in business'.[1] He also says that Millar 'was *not extravagant*, but contented himself with an occasional regale of
humble port at an opposite tavern, so that his wealth ac-
cumulated rapidly'. The regale can scarcely have been
occasional if Millar really was the bookseller described by
Johnson as one who 'was so habitually and equably drunk
that his most intimate friends never perceived that he was
more sober at one time than another'.

July 1739 had seen the opening of several new accounts,
one of which, with Thomas Longman, was like Millar's to
grow to great size. On the 14th Strahan charged Longman
£19 12s. *for printing the last* 14 *sheets of Chambers's Dictionary
No.* 1,000 *at* £1 8s. *p. sheet.*[2] This was paid in cash seven
months later. On the 20th he charged Charles Wesley
£10 3s. for 1,500 of the *second edition of the Hymns*, and thereafter did a considerable amount of bookwork for him. An
account with *John Wesley & Br.* opens on 1 August 1741:

---

[1] *Literary Anecdotes*, III, 387. Millar is one of the very few publishers com-
memorated by a monument in London; a provident man, he erected it in his own
lifetime in what used to be the New Burial Ground of Chelsea Old Church and is
now a public garden on the King's Road.

[2] This was the 3rd edition, published in 1739.

a year later the Wesleys paid part of Strahan's bill by *a Receipt for South Sea Stock—£39 5s. 6d.*

Strahan seems to have had a religious connection in his early days of business; indeed in later years volumes of sermons were among his most profitable publications. As well as working for the Wesleys, he printed for George Whitefield and for James Hutton, the Moravian who acted as an agent for Whitefield while the latter was conducting his Methodist missionary campaign in Pennsylvania. Strahan had an account with Hutton from 1740 to 1742 for printing sermons by Whitefield. With Whitefield himself the account ran from August 1739 to November 1753 to a total amount of over £460. Payment was very slow—see p. 69. When Whitefield advertised in the London Press for subscriptions for a new tabernacle to be built in Philadelphia, one of the persons nominated to receive money was 'William Strahan, Printer in Wine Office Court, Fleet Street'.[1]

An interesting item in this ledger is the account with 'Mr. George Strahan', presumably the bookseller of that name at the Golden Ball in Cornhill. He was the son of the Reverend John Strahan, and it is tempting to posit a relationship between him and the young printer; there is no evidence to support the theory. He had begun publishing about 1699 and prospered sufficiently to be one of the booksellers who contracted to work for The Society for the Encouragement of Learning. If he were related to the printer, his help was not reflected in the way of business. His account opens on 8 September 1739 with *To Printing No. 48 and 49 of the Rehearsal* 100 *Copies*—16s.; most of the items in his account are very small. Indeed the ledger shows that in his first year of trade Strahan was glad to undertake any jobbing work, e.g. 1,000 *half-sheets for Cordial Tincture* 10s. and 700 *Copies with Paper, Advertisement of a Robbery* 6s. By 1742 he may have been financially involved in George Strahan's publications as well as printing them. In August that year he records:

[1] Nolan: *Printer Strahan's Book Account*, Reading, Pa., 1939.

	£	s.	d.
For printing Appendix to the Report of St. Augustine 5¼ Sheets Small Pica 8vo. No. 250 at £1 3s. per Sheet	6	1	0
For 2R3/4 Paper for Do. at 10s. 6d. per Ream	1	8	10½
Paid for Stitching 50 of Do.		1	3
For printing the Report concerning St. Augustine 7¼ Sheets at £1 6s. p. Sheet No. 1,000	9	8	6
For 14½ Reams of Paper for Do. at 10s. 6d. p. Ream	7	12	3

Sadly the contra entry states *Lost upon the Report*—
£10 7s. 4½d. Given the amounts charged, it is hard to see
how this relatively large loss could have occurred upon
the printing only; there was probably a publishing loss as
well. On the other hand, he told Hall in 1745 that he was
'now beginning to print a little for myself . . . The first thing
I tried was a Pamphlet, which I shall clear a Dozen pounds
by . . .' It appears that Strahan distinguished between 'printing for myself' and 'taking copies'. The former presumably
entailed sole ownership of a copyright, the latter part-
ownership of a substantial and expensive work.

Strahan's General Expenses Book shows that his receipts
in his first year ranged from £18 a week to nothing at all.
His wages bill rose and fell from £1 16s. to £4 10s. 6d. a
week, which represents roughly the employment of four
journeymen, and by July 1740 reached £9 2s. a week. His
total expenses for 1739, personal as well as business,
amounted to £737 17s. 6d. while his total 'Received for
Work' was only £444 14s. 6d. How he tided himself over
his first year we do not know; but he felt sufficient confidence in his prospects to bind his first apprentice in November 1739. The 'rough book' lists 34 between this date and
1771; many paid no premium, others paid sums ranging
between £20 and £50. He seems to have been careful in his
recruitment of apprentices, in contrast to some masters who
took on boys for the sake of cheap if unskilled labour during
their apprenticeships, but did not want to keep them on at
journeymen's wages when they had completed their time. A

hint of this shabby practice occurs in a letter Strahan wrote to David Hall in Philadelphia: '. . . From Scotland I have no news. A Race of Printers have now sprung up there to whom we are unknown, except by Report. Since poor Marmy[1] died I scarce hear anything of them; but I am told the young ones among them often talk of you and I as Prodigies of good Fortune. This the old ones, you know, will endeavour to inculcate, to set them adrift at the End of their Times.'

[1] Marmaduke Dallas, printer in Edinburgh. The letter, dated 14 June 1753, is in the Library of the American Philosophical Society, Philadelphia.

2

Printing in the Eighteenth Century

TODAY, the production of the printed word is only one of the functions of the printing industry, a great part of which is engaged in turning out posters, cartons, packages, tickets, cards, letterheads, forms, maps, calendars and every sort of pictorial image, as well as the stamps that send many of them through the letterbox, and the currency that pays for them. To all intents and purposes this variety of work was unknown to the printer in the eighteenth century; apart from a demand for trade cards and handbills, his main and almost his only customers were the publishers of books, newspapers and periodicals, his only output reading matter. The market expanded during the century, and printing grew with it; but restricted as it was to this single field, it was even more of a hand-to-mouth industry than it is today. The printer cannot manufacture and then market his product. He is selling a service to his customer and has to wait until that service is required. There were only three ways in which the eighteenth-century printer could break out of this dependence upon another's initiative, and it is a mark of William Strahan's acumen that he pursued all three with great success.

The first, a method hallowed by custom, was to secure one of the patents, such as the King's Printing Patent or the Law Printing Patent; or an appointment like that of Printer of the Votes of the House of Commons or Printer

13

of the Journals of the House of Lords and the Rolls of Parliament.

The second method, and a more risky one, was the publication of a newspaper—the risk being not only financial but personal, since the Commons was still touchy about its privileges and Ministries were slow to learn that criticism, however resented, must be borne. This accounts for the alacrity with which printers produced uncontroversial periodicals like the *Spectator, Tatler, Guardian, Rambler, Adventurer, Idler, Connoisseur* and *World*. Except in the case of a country newspaper, the printer himself would rarely be the proprietor and publisher, but by taking a substantial share in the venture he could ensure regular work for his presses as long as the journal survived.

The third method, examined in the next chapter, was to become publisher or part-publisher (to use the word in its modern sense) of the books one printed. Strahan claimed that this step had first been taken by him, which may well have been true of his own period, though even here Samuel Richardson may have been ahead of him. But in no sense was he the first printer to own copyrights: in the sixteenth century the registering of copies at Stationers' Hall was principally in the name of printers, and even in the following century, when booksellers had become the main owners of 'copies', a successful printer like Miles Flesher also bought them.[1]

The printer then was concerned with only one method of reproduction, letterpress; that is, the transfer of the image from raised and inked surfaces to the paper under pressure. It was the method used by Gutenberg three hundred years earlier and had suffered only minor refinements in the meantime. The press was now designed for the purpose instead of being an adapted wine or cider press, and its force was exerted by a system of levers rather than by turning a screw. But it was still made of wood, until Lord Stanhope introduced an iron press towards the end of the century, and it

[1] Blagden: *The Stationers' Company*, London, 1960.

14

was anything but an instrument of precision. There had been an immense improvement, however, in the quality and availability of type. In the troubled seventeenth century, when the task of the press had been the production of political and religious propaganda, it had been strictly controlled as a doubtful ally if not an enemy, and the number of typefounders in England had been limited to four. The result was the importation of Dutch type in large quantities. Since imported type was expensive and difficult to acquire, printers tended to use old type long after it was battered and malformed.

In 1734 William Caslon, the greatest of English typefounders, issued his first sheet of specimens. He had the backing of two eminent printers, Bowyer and Watts, for his new letter, which was modelled on Dutch originals; its popularity was great and endures today. Twenty years later John Baskerville turned his experience as a writing master and tombstone cutter to the design of type and produced a more rounded and sharply defined letter than Caslon's. A third type-founder of distinction was Alexander Wilson, who with a partner called Bain opened a foundry in 1742. He moved it, after his appointment as Professor of Practical Astronomy at Glasgow, to a site on College property, and it was here that he produced the superb types used by the Foulis brothers at their famous Glasgow press. Strahan bought much of his type from Wilson, and took one of his sons as an apprentice.[1]

The capital required to set up as a master printer was not great, although enough to present difficulties to a young man. Apart from premises, a press cost about fifteen or sixteen guineas. Strahan's accounts[2] show that a pair of cases could be bought for 7s. 6d., a galley tray for 6d., a composing

---

[1] In 1775 Hume was interested in forwarding the claim of a candidate for the vacant Chair of Divinity at Glasgow, and wrote to Strahan to enlist Wilson's help: 'The Place is filled by a vote of the Professors: You are understood to have great influence with Wilson, the Professor of Astronomy. . .' (Hill, op. cit.). Wilson's partner Bain emigrated and set up a type foundry in Philadelphia, in which was cast in 1797 the first $ in America.

[2] Austen-Leigh, op. cit., and Add. MSS. 48800.

stick for 6*s*.—though the compositor was expected to provide his own—and a chase for 4*s*. Strahan's account with Wilson for type averaged between £50 and £100 a year; he paid 1*s*. 9*d*. a pound for bourgeois, 2*s*. 9*d*. for brevier, 11*d*. for english and 1*s*. 5*d*. for long primer.

Paper was usually supplied to the printer by the bookseller (or publisher), but the printer would have to buy it for jobbing work. Richardson told the House of Commons in 1742 that good English paper could be bought for between 12*s*. and 20*s*. a ream. A ream consisted of 20 quires, each of 24 sheets, but the outside quires of the ream were spoilt and fit only for proof-pulling. This meant buying two additional quires for every ream, plus a further two sheets per quire to bring the ream up to 500 usable sheets. Roughly 23 quires were bought to produce one good ream. 'Consequently when he (Richardson) quoted the paper at 15*s*. a ream, he meant he was buying paper for which he paid the merchant about 13*s*. a ream.'[1] All paper was of course hand made in sheets measuring about 15 inches by 20—the standard crown size —or 12 inches by 16.

Strahan's paper merchant at this period was Stephen Theodore Janssen. Between 1743 and 1746 he sold Strahan paper to the value of £245 2*s*. 6*d*. and between 1746 and 1748 to the value of £188 15*s*. 9*d*.; these were small amounts used for jobbing work and such bookwork as was not worth the bookseller's while supplying paper for. But in 1746, for example, Janssen supplied him with 400 reams for one book alone, Jameson's *Commentary*, on account of the partners in that publication—Millar, Knapton, Hodges, Hitch, Longman, Davis and Rivington.

The wages paid in the printing industry seem more or less constant throughout the century and were, comparatively speaking, fairly high. A good journeyman's wage was a guinea a week. In 1719 Thomas Gent was earning 20*s*. a week as a journeyman, and in 1759 Walpole contracted to pay a guinea a week to a printer for his Strawberry Hill press.

[1] Sale, op. cit.

16

In 1724 Benjamin Franklin was warned by an old workman in Palmer's printing house not to warm his case of type before the fire in cold weather, 'telling me I might lose the use of my hands by it, as two of our companions had nearly done; one of whom, that used to earn his guinea a week, could not then make more than ten shillings, and the other, who had the dangles, but seven and sixpence'.[1] In a letter written in 1745, Strahan observes 'Geo. Reid I have also recommended to a Place in Somersetshire to do a Country Newspaper. He is to have 25 Shillings p. Week and his Lodging, and it is a very cheap Country.'[2]

Richardson paid his compositors 8s. a sheet for setting straightforward text in octavo; for quarto the rate was 5s. 2d. a sheet, for folio 12s. and duodecimo 10s. 6d. A double column folio with marginal notes seems to have been paid at about 13s. 8d. a sheet, while folio of tables might come to 17s. a sheet.[3] To earn a guinea, then, a compositor would have to set about two and a half sheets, or forty pages, of straight setting in octavo. In 1744 piece work was introduced for compositors, the rate being set at '4d. a thousand letters'; this rate is also stated as being a standard payment in London in 1756, in a memorandum written by Daniel Prince, Printer to the University of Oxford.[4]

Strahan appears to have charged his customers the same price whatever the size of type used; Richardson on the other hand tells a friend that the cost of reprinting a book in 12mo will be greater, as one would expect, than in 4to. 'Small print is dearer than large.'

The proof reader or corrector of the press was paid 2d. in the shilling on the price paid to the compositor. Press work

[1] Letter to Benjamin Vaughan, 31 July 1786: Library of Congress.

[2] To Hall, 22 June 1745: American Philosophical Society. Strahan told Hall in 1753 'George Reid has not worked with me these six Years; and I have seldom seen him since. We disagreed about the Price for a Piece of Work, in which I thought him unreasonable, and as he was very apt to drink, and often for a Week together, I was not displeased to part with him.'

[3] Sale, op. cit. But see p. 27 for a charge of 24s. for half a sheet in brevier.

[4] Philip: *William Blackstone and the Reform of the O.U.P. in the Eighteenth Century*, Oxford, 1955.

was paid at the rate of 1s. 2d. for 250 perfected sheets, i.e. printed on both sides; but this sum was shared by two men, one to ink and one to pull. Between them the two pressmen could print their token of 250 sheets in two hours, which must have entailed strength as well as skill since it means a rate of more than four impressions a minute. They might thus each earn about 15s. or 17s. a week. There seems to have been no firm dividing line between compositors and pressmen, despite the wage differential, for Franklin was transferred from the composing room in Watts's office to the pressroom with no ill-effect beyond having to pay a second set of chapel dues.

These wages must be compared with the general level. According to Josiah Tucker's *Instructions for Travellers*, in 1757 'it may be affirmed in general that the Wages of Men is, for the most part, from 1s. to 2s. 6d. per day; and the Wages of Women from 4d. to 1s. throughout the Kingdom'. About the same period meat could be bought for 3d. a pound and bread for 1¼d. a pound. The printer's wage was high, then as now; a London weaver, for instance, earned on average 15s. a week.

The fact that all press work was by hand meant that there was little benefit from printing long runs, or a large number of copies of the same sheet, except that it spread the cost of composition over more copies and reduced the per copy cost —but to a negligible extent. There was naturally no 'run-on rate' in Strahan's printing charges. The comparatively high cost of type meant that it was 'dissed' (the pages broken up and the type distributed for re-use) as soon as possible; indeed unless a printer was extraordinarily well-equipped, he would have to print off the earlier sheets of a long book in order to release the type for setting the remainder.[1] Type was very seldom kept standing from one edition to another. The author could thus make corrections and additions to his

---

[1] There was probably little hardship for the master printers in the Stationers' regulation in 1587—designed for the benefit of journeymen—that impressions should not exceed 1,500 and that reprints should not be taken from standing type.

heart's content in a second edition without upsetting his printer or publisher, since the new edition would in any case have to be entirely re-set. He could even make corrections to the sheet while it was being printed, without greatly holding up production but at the cost of much pain to modern bibliographers.

It has been suggested that authors were prone to make extensive alterations because, under many contracts, they were thereby entitled to a further fee. There can be few writers, however, who can resist a multitude of second thoughts if given a free hand. There is a memo for 1778 in James Beattie's Day Book[1] which refers to a revisal of 'my three new Essays . . . for a new edition now in the Press. I have made about 300 corrections.' This was the second edition of his Essays printed by Strahan. David Hume was another of Strahan's friends and authors who was everlastingly revising his works and harrying his publisher over corrected editions.[2]

There is a good deal of evidence available on the prices which printers charged their customers, much of it from Strahan's own ledgers. Richardson worked on the 'thirds' system of costing, a rough-and-ready rule of thumb which is still sometimes used in the book trade, though not by printers. To the total of costs incurred, half as much again was added to cover materials and overheads. On the basis of the wage rates given above, if an edition of 1,000 copies of an octavo book was required, the composition would cost 8s. a sheet, the reading 1s. 4d. and the presswork 4s. 8d. The wage bill is thus 14s., 'half of which is a third of the whole'—that is, 7s. would be added and the job invoiced at 21s. a sheet. In such a case the paper would be charged separately if it had not been supplied by the publisher, but the 50 per cent

---

[1] Walker: *James Beattie's Day-Book 1773–1798*, Aberdeen, 1948.

[2] Hume went so far as to tell Strahan that the 'Power, which Printing gives us, of continually improving and correcting our Works in successive Editions, appears to me the chief Advantage of that Art. For as to the dispersing of Books, that Circumstance does perhaps as much harm as good: Since Nonsense flies with greater Celerity, and makes more Impression, than Reason . . .'

surcharge would have to cover rent and rates, and the cost of ink, type, equipment and plant, as well as profit.

What of the quality of eighteenth-century printing? It was sometimes deplorable: battered or worn type, badly spaced, unevenly inked and hurriedly printed with hit-and-miss impression. But—leaving aside limited or special editions—the average book can at least claim a decent dignity lacking in the work of the previous age and too often hard to find in the mechanical wonders of the nineteenth century. The reader's comfort was guarded by the use of large types with liberal leading. The effect of the press work is sometimes spoiled by the fading of the ink to a rusty brown, so that there is often more sparkle about a modern reproduction of an eighteenth-century page than there is in the original in its present state. At least the publisher of those days could remind us that the paper in his books is still stoutly carrying the impression, even if faded; and that is a good deal more than will be said about most twentieth-century books in another two hundred years.

3

The Dictionary

IN a few years Strahan was on the way to becoming a printer of some substance and standing. On 1 June 1742 he took a step forward on being 'admitted to the Cloathing' of the Company of Stationers, and at midsummer he moved into his new office—and probably dwelling house as well—in Wine Office Court. In the next few years he began to handle a certain amount of American export business, to be examined in some detail later. At home his growing turn-over enabled him to embark on more ambitious projects, the size of which indicates both that he was regarded as a sound enough printer to be entrusted with the work and that he was in a position to afford the longer credit necessary for these large publications.

In addition to the growing number of individuals for whom he now started to print, such as Robert Dodsley in 1743 (*5th Vol. of a Collection of Old Plays, 15 Sheets, No 1,000 at £1 8s. p. Sheet, £21*), we find him working for part-nerships. The first appears to have been that of William Innys and Partners in 1742. In 1744 he charged Messrs. T. Osborne, A. Millar & Co. (the Co. included Richardson) £24 8s. for 16 sheets of the General Index to the *Universal History*, which was settled by a note payable in six months. He was to continue printing the *Universal History* itself; between February 1747 and February 1749 his account for it amounted to £813 7s. 3d. and by February 1751 to £1,086 17s. 2d. The bill was paid by instalments. Again, in 1744 he charged Thomas Osborne and Co.:

	£	s.	d.
For printing the Letters R & S of the Medicinal Dictionary, containing 70 sheets No 1,000 at £1 8s. p. Sh.	98	0	0
For Recomposing Sheet J of do.	1	0	0
For Extraordinary Corrections in the said 70 Sheets	2	18	0

Strahan was paid with 26 *Setts of James's Dictionary* [the same work] *which was full settlement of £118 1s. 1d. account.* It was Samuel Johnson who wrote James's dedication of his Dictionary to a Dr. Mead, but this of course fell outside the 70 sheets which Strahan printed.

Almost certainly the first of Johnson's works which Strahan printed was his Dictionary, and quite certainly it was in connection with its printing that the two men met and established a friendship which lasted, with a single short break, until Johnson's death. The contract for the undertaking, dated 18 June 1746 according to Hawkins, was between Johnson and five bookselling firms, those of Robert Dodsley, Charles Hitch, Andrew Millar, J. and P. Knapton and T. and T. Longman.

Johnson received £1,575 for his work, which it was hoped he would complete in three years, although it was nearly nine before the folio volumes were published. 'When the expence of amanuenses and paper, and other articles are deducted, his clear profit was very inconsiderable', Boswell comments. 'I once said to him, "I am sorry, Sir, you did not get more for your Dictionary". His answer was, "I am sorry, too. But it was very well. The booksellers are generous liberal-minded men." '[1]

Elsewhere Boswell mentions 'the necessary expence of preparing a work of such magnitude for the press', expense which included taking the house in Gough Square and

---

[1] Hill, Powell: *Boswell's Life of Johnson*, Oxford, 1934, I, 304.

fitting up the upper room for his copyists; and adds, 'I remember his telling me, that a large portion of it having, by
mistake been written upon both sides of the paper, so as
to be inconvenient for the compositor, it cost him twenty
pounds to have it transcribed upon one side only'.

According to Murphy, it was 'for the purpose of carrying
on his arduous undertaking, and to be near his printer and
friend, Mr. Strahan, he ventured to take a house in Gough
Square, Fleet Street'.[1] This is possible, for in 1748 Strahan
began to rent 10, Little New Street, off Shoe Lane, a few
minutes' walk from Gough Square. On the other hand we
do not know when the first sheets of the Dictionary began
printing; 70 sheets had been completed by December 1750,
when Strahan received a first payment on account, and it
seems unlikely that he could have been composing and printing for much more than a year before being paid something.

It says much for Strahan's standing that within ten years
of setting up on his own he could afford a rent of £200 a
year for his Little New Street house, on top of a further
£200 for repairs, and that he should have been entrusted
by such a distinguished consortium of booksellers with the
printing of the Dictionary. Boswell says that Millar 'took the
principal charge of conducting the publication' and it may
well have been through Millar that Strahan got the work.

The earliest certain connection between Johnson and
Strahan occurs in the following year when Johnson wrote
to James Elphinston, Strahan's brother-in-law, one of his
noblest letters, in condolence for his mother's death; 'I read
the letters in which you relate your mother's death to Mrs.
Strahan; and think I do myself honour when I tell you that
I read them with tears; but tears are neither to me nor to you
of any further use, when once the tribute of nature has been
paid'.[2] Elphinston was later to earn Johnson's gratitude by
supporting and supervising an Edinburgh edition of *The
Rambler*, with translations by himself of the mottoes.

[1] Hill: *Johnsonian Miscellanies*, Oxford, 1897, I, 382.
[2] Chapman: *Letters of Samuel Johnson*, Oxford, 1952, I, 30.

Although Millar acted on behalf of the other partners in the Dictionary, it is clear that Strahan was employed as their intermediary with Johnson, as perhaps was only natural since the two men lived near to each other and must have been in almost daily contact while the copy was produced for composition. An early note, dated by Chapman about April 1750, indicates this liaison:

Dear Sir,

I must desire you to add to your other civilities this one, to go to Mr. Millar and represent to him our manner of going on, and inform him that I know not how to manage, I pay three and twenty shillings a week to my assistants, in truth without having much assistance from them, but they tell me they shall be able to fall better in method, as indeed I intend they shall. The point is to get two Guineas for

Your humble Servant Sam: Johnson[1]

Another letter written on Friday 1 November 1751 shows that the position of go-between had its difficulties. Johnson had fallen behind schedule in delivery of the copy and the booksellers had presumably threatened to stop payment without reflecting that the author, in such a half-completed enterprise, had the whip hand.

The message which You sent me by Mr. Stuart[2] I do not consider as at all your own, but if you were contented to be the deliverer of it to me, you must favour me so far as to return my answer, which I have written down to spare you the unpleasing office of doing it in your own words. You advise me to write, I know with very kind intentions, nor do I intend to treat your counsel with any disregard when I declare that in the present state of the matter 'I shall *not* write'— otherwise than the words following—

'That my Resolution has long been, and is *not* now altered, and is now *less* likely to be altered, that I shall *not* see the Gentlemen Partners till the first volume is in the press which they may forward or retard by dispensing or not dispensing with the last Message.'

Be pleased to lay this my determination before them this morning, for I shall think of taking my measures accordingly tomorrow evening,

[1] Chapman: *Letters of Samuel Johnson*, Oxford, 1952, I, 38.
[2] One of the copyists.

only this that I mean no harm, but that my citadel shall not be taken by storm while I can defend it, and that if a blockade is intended, the country is under the command of my batteries, I shall think of laying it under contribution tomorrow Evening.[1]

By speaking of the first volume's being in the press Johnson must have meant the completion rather than the start of printing, for 70 sheets of Volume I had been printed by December 1750. No eighteenth-century printer, whatever his resources, could have delayed the printing until the whole of such a large book had been composed; it was essential to print off a number of sheets as they were set and corrected—four folio pages to the sheet—in order to release the type. Hence delay in checking the proofs held up the whole process, as Strahan must have pointed out: 'What you tell me I am ashamed never to have thought on—I wish I had known it sooner—Send me back the last sheet; and the last copy for correction. If you will promise me henceforward to print a sheet a day, I will promise you to endeavour that you shall have every day a sheet to print, beginning next Tuesday.'[2] On at least one occasion Strahan took upon himself to make corrections. 'You know, Sir,' said Johnson to Boswell, 'Lord Gower forsook the old Jacobite interest. When I came to the word *Renegado*, after telling that it meant "one who deserts to the enemy, a revolter", I added, *Sometimes we say a GOWER*. Thus it went to the press; but the printer had more wit than I, and struck it out.'[3]

In the course of the work Johnson came to know Strahan sufficiently well to borrow books from his wife: he wrote to Millar, 'When I sent back your books I returned by mistake to you a *Young upon Opium*, which I had from Mrs. Strahan; please to let me have it back'.[4] He also began to employ Strahan as his man of affairs when he was out of London, as well as his banker when he was at home. But their transactions were not purely financial. Strahan is recorded by

---

[1] *Letters*, I, 35. It was presumably on Saturday evening that he was paid, and in turn paid his staff.
[2] *Letters*, I, 37 (undated).   [3] *Life*, I, 296.   [4] *Letters*, I, 44.

Frank Barber, Johnson's negro servant, as one of those who 'visited him at that time' after Tetty's death in 1752.

The first entry in Strahan's ledger relating to the Dictionary is dated 1750. The account runs as follows:

Partners in Johnson's Dictionary

	£	s.	d.
1750			
Decr. For Printing the first 70 Sheets, No 2,000 at £1 18s. 0d.	133	0	0
1752			
May For 50 Sheets more of Do	95	0	0
1753			
Octr For 100 Sheets more of Do	190	0	0
	£418	0	0

The contra entries run:

		£	s.	d.
1750				
Decr. 20	By Cash of Mr. Millar	26	12	0
1751				
Jan 1	By Do of Mr. Dodsley	26	12	0
8	By Do of Mr. Longman	26	12	0
	By Do of Mr. Hitch	26	12	0
1752				
May 28	By Do of Mr. Millar	19	0	0
	By Do of Mr. Dodsley	19	0	0
June 12	By Do Messrs. Knapton	45	12	0
	By Do Mr. Hitch	19	0	0
	By Do Mr. Longman	19	0	0
1753				
Octr 4	By Do Mr. Millar	38	0	0
	By Do Mr. Hitch	38	0	0
19	By Do Mr. Dodsley	38	0	0
Nov 9	By Do Messrs. Knapton	38	0	0
1754				
Jan 15	By Do Mr. Longman	38	0	0
		£418	0	0

From the account one can see the amount of credit which Strahan had to give. One can also see that some publishers were not so punctual as others in their remittances; the Knaptons contributed nothing to the first round of payments. The account continues to the same partners on another page:

1755		£	s.	d.
June	Printing 5,000 Proposals in Folio	3	8	0
	24,000 Do in Quarto at 5d.	6	0	0
	250 Folio Titles to Stick up		2	6
	50 Advertisements for Country Papers, with Paper		5	0
	Composing Half a Sheet Brevier for London Magazine	1	4	0
	Printing 38 Sheets No 2,298 at £2 0s. 6d.	76	19	0
	174 Sheets No 1,274 at £1 10s. 6d.	265	7	0
	367 Sheets No 768 at £1 6s.	477	2	0
	For two Red Titles	1	13	0
	For Printing 50 Reams of Blue Covers at 5d.	12	10	0
		£844	10	6

The payments for this account run from 13 September 1755 to 23 February 1759. Strahan received £470 in eight instalments from 'Mr. Bladon' in the course of three years: in March 1758 he was paid £247 8s. 4d. by Longman, Millar and Knapton, and finally the account was closed in 1759 by a payment of £127 2s. 2d. by Longman. Samuel Bladon, a bookseller, was an expert accountant, according to Timperley, and was often called on to settle complicated or disputed accounts.

The 'proposals' mentioned in the ledger may refer to the reprinting of the Plan, as well as to the proposals which were issued for subscription to the Dictionary if published in serial form as 'numbers'. The red titles of course are the title pages for the two volumes, which were printed in two colours, while the 'Folio Titles to Stick up' were the equivalent of showcards for the booksellers' window.

The 1755 account also itemizes the paper usage.

		R	Q
500 Folio Proposals takes up		10 R	Q
24,000 Quarto do		12	
250 Folio Titles			5
38 Sheets 2,298 at 4R 12Q		174	16
174 Sheets 1,274 at 2R 11Q		443	14
367 Sheets 768 at 1R 10 3/4Q		564	5
579		1205	0

These figures as posted in the ledger are presumably the final charges made to the partners, although they do not tally with the figures in the rough book. There the printing charges for the 1755 account are listed as:

Partners In Johnson's Folio Dictionary	£	s.	d.
Printing Do 580 No 2,000 at £1 18s. p. Sheet	1102		
Two Red Titles	1	18	0
Paid for Alterations and Additions in Do	132	11	0
Reprinting of Plan 2½ Sheets No 1500 at £1 5s.	3	2	6
	£1239	11	6

In the rough book the paper usage is given as:

		Reams
Received of Bloss and Johnson		2341
Used for 580 Sheets	2320	
— for the Plan	7½	
— for a Pamphlet of Mr. Johnson's by Order	5	
Spoilt	8½	
	2341	

It will be noted that the final account exceeded the rough book account by £22 19s.; that the number of sheets is stated as 580 in the latter and 579 in the former; and that the cost of the two title pages is reduced in the final account from £1 18s. to £1 13s., possibly by an error in transcription. Finally there is a marked discrepancy between the two accounts in the printing numbers, given as a uniform 2,000 in the rough book (the number printed of the first 70 sheets); the final account shows that it ranged from over 2,000 of 38 sheets down to less than 1,000 in the case of 367 sheets.

What of the actual printing of the book? Updike writes of the Dictionary: 'It was printed by William Strahan in 1755 in a monotonous old style type, in size rather small for the folio double column pages. The title page, in its leaded lines of small spaced capitals, shows a modern tendency toward light effects. In the preface, blank lines between paragraphs also exhibit a new detail of composition, much in favour as the century went on . . . These pages (of text proper) of mild colour and easy air seem old-fashioned to us now, but not antique.'[1] The Dictionary may possibly seem less old-fashioned to us than it did to Updike; it is a pleasure to read a work of reference in which successive entries are clearly delimited without the disfiguring use of bold type. It cannot be claimed that the Dictionary is an example of superlatively good printing, but it is a worthy piece of book-work, handsome if not resplendent.

[1] *Printing Types*, II, 140.

4

The Trade

STRAHAN had no interest in the Dictionary beyond its printing, though there is little doubt that his dealings with all the publishers involved encouraged him to 'buy copies'. In 1771 he told his friend Hall that he owned the copyright or held shares in about 200 books, explaining that:

I quickly saw, that if I confined myself to mere *printing for Booksellers*, I might be able to live, but very little more than live, I therefore soon determined to launch out into other Branches in Connection with my own, in which I have happily succeeded, to the Astonishment of the rest of the Trade here, who never dreamt of going out of the old beaten Track. Thus I have made the Name of *Printer* more respectable than ever it was before, and taught them to emancipate themselves from the Slavery in which the Booksellers held them.[1]

Strahan's ledger of 'Copies Taken' is in the British Museum with his other papers.[2] It runs from 1751 to 1775, and since we have no other records of his share in books it is a possible deduction that he bought no rights before or after these dates. It may be the case, however, that Strahan tried his hand at publishing before he was well established as a printer. In 1778, dining with Edward and Charles Dilly, Johnson mentioned a new translation of the Duke of Ber-

[1] 15 June 1771; *Pennsylvania Magazine of History and Biography*, vol. LX.
[2] Add. MSS. 48805.

wick's memoirs. 'I offered them to Strahan, who sent them back with this answer: "That the first book he had published was the Duke of Berwick's Life, by which he had lost: and he hated the name."' Now the *Life of James Fitz-James, Duke of Berwick* was 'printed for and sold by A. Millar' in 1738, and Millar may have induced the young printer to buy a share in it. Whenever it was that Strahan embarked upon the publishing of books as a side-line to printing them, the middle years of the eighteenth century were a propitious time to do so. The increasingly well-organized book trade was not yet so prosperous that it could find all its own capital and it welcomed the adventurous newcomer.

The structure of the trade today is fairly sharply defined. The writer produces a work which the publisher agrees to issue; as the entrepreneur, the publisher at his own risk buys paper and pays the printer and binder to produce copies of the book. These he sells, some to the export agent or direct to overseas markets, some to the wholesale bookseller for distribution to the retail bookseller, others to the retailer direct; and the retail bookseller completes the process, if all goes well, by selling the copies to the public. Some booksellers also publish; some publishers own, or are owned by, printers; on occasion an author will publish his own works. But these are exceptions to the general rule of one individual or firm fulfilling one and only one of the various functions necessary to transmit the original manuscript or typescript in the shape of a marketable book into the hands of as many of the public as wish to read it.

In the eighteenth century these functions were confused, both because one or two of the steps might be by-passed altogether and because the same man quite often performed different functions when dealing with different books. That all the modern functions existed is shown by Johnson's well-known letter to Dr. Wetherell.[1] He is arguing that the University Press of Oxford would have to give more generous

[1] *Letters*, 473.

discounts to the trade if its books were to be efficiently distributed.

... It is perhaps not considered through how many hands a Book often passes, before it comes into those of the reader, or what part of the profit each hand must retain as a motive for transmitting it to the next. We will call our primary Agent in London Mr. Cadel who receives our books from us, gives them room in his warehouse and issues them on demand. By him they are sold to Mr. Dilly a wholesale Bookseller who sends them into the Country, and the last seller is the Country Bookseller. Here are three profits to be paid between the Printer and the Reader, or in the stile of commerce between the Manufacturer and the Consumer; and if any of these profits is too penuriously distributed the process of commerce is intercepted.

We are now come to the practical question, what is to be done? You will tell me with reason that I have said nothing till I declare how much according to my opinion of the ultimate price ought to be distributed through the whole succession of Sale.

The deduction I am afraid will appear very great. But let it be considered before it is refused. We must allow for profit between thirty and thirty five per cent. between six and seven shillings in the pound, that is for every book which costs the last buyer twenty shillings we must charge Mr. Cadel with something less than fourteen. We must set the copies at fourteen shillings each and superadd what is called the quarterly book or for every hundred books so charged we must deliver an hundred and four.[1]

The profit will stand thus.

Mr. Cadel who runs no hazard and gives no credit will be paid for warehouse room and attendance by a shilling profit on each Book, and his chance of the quarterly Book.

Mr. Dilly who buys the Book for fifteen shillings and who will expect the quarterly book if he takes five and twenty will sell it to his country customer at sixteen and sixpence by which at the hazard of loss and the certainty of long credit, he gains the regular profit of ten per cent. which is expected in the wholesale trade.

The Country Bookseller buying at sixteen and sixpence and commonly trusting a considerable time gains but three and sixpence, otherwise than as he may perhaps take as long credit as he gives.

[1] This form of extra discount no longer obtains save in the case of sales of sheets or books to American publishers when the quarterly book is still exacted.

With less profit than this, and more you see he cannot have, the Country Bookseller cannot live; for his receipts are small, and his debts sometimes bad.

In this imaginary transaction, Cadell is the publisher in the technical sense; Dilly acts as the wholesaler—the modern W. H. Smith and Sons—from whom the retailer can purchase his stock. The London retailer might go to the wholesaler or direct to the publisher. But at the time Johnson wrote, all these roles were interchangeable. Cadell was a bookseller with premises in the Strand and was also a publisher in our sense of the word, in that he bought copyrights and issued books at his own risk. The Dilly brothers were also and perhaps primarily publishers—Boswell was one of their authors. Perhaps the first publisher in the modern idiom was James Dodsley, who succeeded to his famous brother Robert's publishing and bookselling business in Pall Mall; it is recorded that he was the first man to sell only his own publications in his shop.

To be a publisher in the eighteenth century was to be a secondary link in the chain of distribution. 'If the proprietor of a bookshop owns the copyright of a book, seeks out a printer for it and then manages the sale to the public, his role is that of a *bookseller*. If on the other hand the author (or printer) owns the copyright and secures the services of the proprietor of a bookshop in selling a book, then that proprietor is in the role of publisher.'[1] In 1749 Samuel Richardson gave Aaron Hill advice on a projected collected edition of the latter's works, and recommended the services of Andrew Millar. He wrote that, had Hill's poems and pamphlets in the past been 'of Bulk, and fitter for a Bookseller's than a mere Publisher's Management, I should have desired his (Millar's) name to them, preferably to any other Man's that I know'. He added that Millar 'has great business, and is in a Way of promoting the Sale of what he engages in'.[2]

Johnson's calculation allows a discount of between 30 and

---

[1] Sale, op. cit.   [2] Ibid.

35 per cent, including the equivalent of an extra discount through the system of the quarterly book. This of course was on the sale of University Press publications, and Boswell indicates that the proposed discount was liberal. 'I am happy', he says in a note to this letter, 'in giving this full and clear statement to the publick, to vindicate, by the authority of the greatest author of his age, that respectable body of men, the Booksellers of London, from vulgar reflections, as if their profits were exorbitant, when, in truth, Dr. Johnson has here allowed them more than they usually demand.' Cadell as publisher or agent earned a profit of 7 per cent on his outlay plus a possible additional 4 per cent from the quarterly book; Dilly as wholesaler earned 10 per cent plus 4 per cent if he ordered 25 copies at a time from Cadell; and the retailer earned just over 21 per cent. These profits of course are conditional upon the successful sale of the book to the next purchaser; if the retailer buys ten copies and can only sell eight of them, he has made a net loss.

On the other hand the late Mr. Cyprian Blagden quotes evidence from Sion College that 'a popular line like *The Gentleman Instructed* was advertised at 6s., exchanged unbound through the trade at 4s. 9d., sold to the trade by the publisher or wholesalers at 3s. 4d. and sold to the wholesalers at 2s. 10d.'[1] The deduction is that the retail bookseller had a discount of 45 per cent off the advertised selling price while the wholesaler had about 55 per cent.[2] But the bookseller had to pay for the cost of binding the book. Allowing on the generous side a shilling a copy for this, the discount is reduced to 25 per cent. The exchange of books through the trade was a common and convenient way of distributing copies when so many publishers, in one sense, were also booksellers. As we have seen, Strahan accepted books in payment or part-payment of his printing bills.

[1] *The Bookseller*, 11 April 1953.
[2] Strahan told Hall that '5d. for Magazines and Plays is as universal a Charge as a halfpenny for a halfpenny Loaf'; plays usually cost 1s. 6d. sewn, so this represents a discount, on the export trade, of nearly 75 per cent.

Strahan told Hall in Philadelphia (p. 79) that a profit of
5 per cent was too low to justify the export of books to anybody but him, and was horrified when his competitor James
Rivington offered 16 per cent discount on a sale or return
basis—'such terms as Mr. Rivington's were never heard of
till now'. On one occasion Strahan was offered a consignment of books for the American trade at a discount of 10 per
cent or 15 per cent, and although he commented on their
cheapness, he saw nothing unusual in the discount. One can
assume that he worked on a basis of at least 10 per cent; we
know that his orders from Hall were 'firm' and that he only
took back as returns books which he had exported at his own
risk. He expected to give up to twelve months credit. His
rate of profit was affected by the price of binding; for this
reason it was brought down to 2 per cent in the case of one
of Hall's orders.

The price of binding naturally varied greatly with the
materials used. In 1767 Newbery advertised William Dodd's
poems at 4s. 3d. sewed (i.e. the printed sheets folded and
sewn together) or 5s. bound—obviously a thin book and
a cheap binding. In 1775 the same firm issued Ward's *A
Modern System of Natural History* at '4s. elegantly bound, or
1s. bound in the vellum manner', the latter being half-binding
in green paper and green vellum.[1] Binding was the task of
the bookseller to the order of the buyer; Johnson boasted
that he had been 'bred a bookseller and that he could still
bind a book'.

Book prices remained fairly steady until the end of the
century. Plays nearly always cost 1s. 6d., duodecimos about
2s. 6d. a volume, octavos 5s. or 6s., and folios or quartos 10s.
to 12s.; and these were 'sewn' prices. By about 1790, prices
had risen. Boswell's *Life* (1793) was priced at two guineas
for two quarto volumes and the second edition, in three
volumes octavo, cost 8s. a volume. By the early years of the
nineteenth century the high price of books was a common
source of complaint.

[1] Marjorie Plant: *The English Book Trade*, London, 1939.

Such formal organization as existed in the eighteenth-century book trade was still represented by the Stationers' Company, of which Strahan was in due time to become Master. In its earlier days the Company had been a corporation of all those engaged in the trade and had derived its power from the strictly controlled concentration of nearly all printers, binders and wholesale booksellers in London—a concentration welcomed by successive governments. But the trade had grown too fast to be confined within the framework of a guild system, and by the eighteenth century the Company had degenerated into a trading society which still retained a few of its old functions, such as the entering of apprentices before its officers. Its trade derived from the 'English Stock' —a number of privileged publications, the most lucrative then being almanacs, of which the Company had a monopoly.[1] It behoved the young journeyman to become a Freeman if he were ambitious and aspired to the Livery and, later, the higher offices of the Company, since only thus was he eligible for a chance of allotment of shares in the Stock and its very regular dividend of $12\frac{1}{2}$ per cent. The Company's tendency to restrict its activities to its own investments encouraged individuals to organize their trade through private alliances. These were of two kinds.

There was the ad hoc partnership between two or more men to share the capital outlay, the risk of loss and the chance of profit on the publication of a book. Such an arrangement often endured for a long time and over many books. Hence it has often been stated that Strahan and Millar, and later Strahan and Cadell, were in partnership together; this was not the case but they took shares together in so many books that the mistake is easily made.

The other type of trade alliance bore a greater resemblance to a joint-stock company, or at the least to a formal partnership, and clearly derived from the English Stock. The Printing Conger or Old Conger was formed in 1719

---

[1] The monopoly in almanacs was successfully invaded in 1775 by Thomas Carnan.

with seven booksellers as members. A rival group, the New
Conger, came into being in 1738 with ten members, three of
whom had deserted the Old Conger to join it. In 1742 a
tenth share in it was bought for £366 14s. 3d.; by 1745 the
members each held a tenth share in 85 publications.[1] The
New Conger in turn gave way to a larger organization, the
famous Chapter, so called from its meeting in the Chapter
Coffee House. Still another group, archly entitled the Associ-
ated Busy Bees, was formed at the end of the century.

These associations were of course accused of monopoly,
of keeping down the prices paid to authors and of preventing any book published by a non-member from circulating
through the trade. There was sufficient ground for belief in
these charges to lead to the formation in 1736 of the Society
for the Encouragement of Learning, whose object was the
reward of scholarly authorship and the publication of non-
commercial books. The Society began by abusing the booksellers, ran headlong into debt and eventually turned to the
leading bookseller of the day, Andrew Millar, with a request
to act as its agent. Whether or not the episode shows that the
Conger was too powerful to be broken, there is no doubt
that some such combination of traders was essential. The
capital outlay on Johnson's Dictionary for instance was between four and five thousand pounds, far beyond the resources of a single firm.[2] Chapman points out that 'literary
historians have naturally focused their attention on the
famous writers, and nearly all they tell us of publishers is in
relation to their writers' work. But most of the largest under-
takings of the period were not the work of a Johnson or a
Gibbon, but of lesser, often of nameless men', and instances
the *Biographica Britannica* (1747–66), Chambers's *Cyclopaedia Britannica*, or *Dictionary*, as it was commonly called

[1] Septimus Rivington: *The Publishing Family of Rivington*, London, 1919. The
ten members in 1745 were Richard Ware, Aaron Ward, John and Paul Knapton,
Thomas Longman and Co., Richard Hett, James Hodges, Charles Hitch, Stephen
Austen, Henry Pemberton and John Rivington.
[2] Printing cost £1,239 11s. 6d., Johnson was paid £1,575 and the paper cannot
have cost less than £1,500.

(1728), the *Universal History* (1747–66) and the *Harleian Miscellany* (1744–6).[1] The only method of capitalizing such costly ventures was by a combination of shareholders. The system had another advantage in that if enough booksellers took shares in a publication, it was unlikely that a rival work on the same subject would be issued.[2]

The shareholding partnership became unnecessary as publishing firms grew larger in the nineteenth century and as the capital at their disposal increased. Until then it met an important need and also afforded an opportunity to the beginner in the trade, like Strahan, to invest small amounts at a time in different books—the sort of role played now in relation to industrial investment by unit trusts.

In his life of Addison, Johnson reckons the average sale of *The Spectator*, a highly successful periodical, at nearly 1,700; in the 1750s *The World*, in the face of more competition, was usually printed in issues of 2,500. Again, Johnson says that 11,000 copies of Swift's *Conduct of the Allies* were sold in three months; in 1776 a pamphlet with the same sort of appeal, Price's *Observations on the American War*, sold 60,000 copies 'in a few months'. In the 1790s Burke estimated the reading public at some 80,000. These figures are quoted by A. S. Collins,[3] to point the emancipation of the author from the patron, if not from 'Toil, envy, want, the gaol'; they also explain why the book trade flourished in the eighteenth century. 'At present the few poets of England no longer depend on the great for subsistence', wrote Goldsmith; 'they have no other patrons but the public, and the public, collectively considered, is a good and generous master.'

There was an uncomfortable gap between the patron and the new public, and in the gap there existed the miseries of Grub Street. Journalism helped to end them; the reviews and newspapers which appeared in the '40s and '50s offered

---

[1] 'Authors and Bookselling' in *Johnson's England* (ed. Turberville), Oxford, 1952.
[2] See Strahan's comments in connection with Rivington's piratical activities, p. 85.
[3] *The Profession of Letters in Johnson's Day*, London, 1928.

ready money for the quickly turned piece; the writer need no longer go hungry while he completed a full-length work for the booksellers. The latter in turn grew more generous as their sales increased; and the literary market was no longer undercut by authors too genteel to accept payment for their work.

In one way Pope showed the way to the dunces he castigated. He was perhaps content to accept £7 from Lintot for *The Rape of the Lock* in 1712 but he published his translation of the Iliad by subscription direct to the public. Johnson in his *Lives of the Poets* writes:

The greatness of the design, the popularity of the author, and the attention of the literary world, naturally raised such expectations of the future sale, that the booksellers made their offers with great eagerness; but the highest bidder was Bernard Lintot, who became proprietor on condition of supplying at his own expense all the copies which were to be delivered to subscribers or presented to friends, and paying two hundred pounds for every volume.

In fact Lintot's accounts show that he paid £215 for the first three volumes and £210 for subsequent ones. Johnson goes on to relate how Lintot was 'after all his hopes and all his liberality' defrauded of his fair profit by a pirated edition smuggled in from Holland. The subscribers numbered 575 and they undertook to pay six guineas for the set of six volumes. Johnson shows that Pope earned over £5,300 by the Iliad.

If the author were very sure of success, as was Pope, or wanted funds to enable him to complete a work, like Johnson with his Shakespeare, to publish by subscription was a sound method since the subscriber paid half the price in advance and half on publication. It lasted a long time; as late as 1796 Fanny Burney cleared about £3,000 by publishing *Camilla* in this way. But the system was exploited until it broke down. Johnson's Shakespeare is again the evidence of this. It will be remembered that nine years intervened between the issue of the Proposals to subscribers and the appearance of the edition. By then Johnson could not, as was customary, print a list of the subscribers for the two good reasons that he had spent all the money and lost all the names.

The normal reward for an author was the price paid by the bookseller for the outright purchase of the copyright. Writers have never been markedly enthusiastic over their earnings, but in the course of the eighteenth century the scale of payment rose to tempting levels. Millar did a great deal to further this trend by recognizing the stronger bargaining power of his authors when they were once established. He paid Fielding £183 10s. for the copyright of *Joseph Andrews*, £600 plus an additional £100 for *Tom Jones* and £1,000 for *Amelia*. He paid £600 for Dr. Robertson's *History of Scotland*, when the author was new to the public, and is said, with his partner Thomas Cadell, to have 'got six thousand pounds by it'—presumably turnover, not profit; but Robertson was paid very large sums for his later works. Hill states[1] that he had seen a letter dated 27 May 1768 from Robertson to Strahan; 'I do agree to accept from Mr. Millar, Bookseller in Pall Mall, or, in case of his declining it, from yourself, of the sum of £3,400 for the copyright of my *History of Charles V* in three volumes quarto, and of your engagement to pay me £400 more in case of a second edition. The terms of payment to be afterwards settled.' But Strahan told Hall in 1770 that 'the Copy Money was no less than £4,000' for this publication.

The writer need not part with his entire copyright. He could sell the bookseller the right to print only one edition, or could lease his copyright for a fixed period; in such cases a lesser price would be paid of course. In this connection Chapman quotes[2] the negotiations over *Rasselas* (see p. 146) and the arrangement whereby Pope earned £200 from Gilliver for a year's lease of *The Essay on Man*. Again, instead of receiving a lump sum in advance, the author might share the profits with the publisher as did Gibbon.

The modern system of payment by royalty has disadvantages but at least it protects the publisher from heavy loss on

[1] Op. cit.   [2] Op. cit.

the author, unless he is cajoled into paying rash advances against putative royalties, and it ensures for the author a due share of the rewards if the book sells well. The lump sum or profit-sharing systems always risked leaving one party or the other with a grievance in the event of complete failure or unexpected success. Still, on balance it produced a rough justice between the authors as a profession and the booksellers as a trade, however hardly it bore on individuals. At times it seems to have produced rewards almost unreasonably large for the author. 'I have heard lately', wrote Mrs. Carter in 1764, 'that Churchill, within two years, has got £3,500 by his ribald scribbling.' Lackington records in his Memoirs that 'the late Mr. Elliott, bookseller, of Edinburgh, gave Mr. Smellie a thousand pounds for his Philosophy of Natural Beauty when only the heads of the chapters were wrote'. Satirists and philosophers would be glad to accept such rewards even in the debased pound of today.

Against that is the price of £30 paid to Fanny Burney for *Evelina* which at once rocketed to fame. In such instances the publishers' profit was undeservedly high; but first novels are not always successful, and their writers seldom tell us of their pangs when they make more out of the work than the publisher has done. *The Vicar of Wakefield*, be it remembered, went through three editions without recovering its costs. *Humphrey Clinker* was published in three volumes, in a printing of 2,000 copies, by Collins and Johnston in 1770. Smollett was paid £210 for the copyright; printing and paper cost £155 15s. 6d.; nine copies for Stationers' Hall and ten for the author cost £6 1s. 10d.; advertising cost £15 10s. After selling the entire edition at £24 a hundred the publishers only made £46 6s. 4d. each. Of course the book was a success and in the following year there was a second edition which yielded a total profit of £240 12s.; it was presumably a larger edition, and the cost of the copyright had been worked off on the first one.[1]

The collected *Idler* was published in 1761 in two volumes

[1] The account is quoted in Plant, op. cit.

at 5s. sewed or 6s. bound. The paper cost £52 3s., the printing £41 13s. and advertising £20 0s. 6d., a total of £113 16s. 6d. for 1,500 copies. The sets were sold at £16 a hundred bringing in £240. The profit amounted to £123 3s. 6d. of which Johnson was paid two-thirds while Newbery, the publisher, took one-third. The discount, by the way, works out at roughly 35 per cent. Strahan's career will afford many more examples of prices paid to authors, and of the losses that resulted when his judgement was bad.

5

David Hume

DAVID Hume and Strahan were friends for twenty years. For the greater part of that time they were separated by the distance between Edinburgh and London and in consequence their surviving correspondence bulks almost as large as that between Strahan and Hall in Philadelphia. Hume first learnt to value Strahan as a congenial person with whom to do business. He welcomed his opinion on matters of style and asked him to report both favourable and adverse criticisms of his works.[1] He relished Strahan's accounts of political affairs—'I have always said without flattery that you may give instructions to statesmen'—and this despite the fact that the two men did not always agree politically. When Hume was in London or Strahan in Edinburgh, they saw each other frequently.

Their friendship began when Millar became Hume's London publisher, taking over the second volume of *The History of Great Britain*. It is perhaps not surprising that Hume, a nationalist to the heart, should have come to terms with a Scots bookseller in London; the same spirit may account for Millar's choice of Strahan as printer and as the partner with whom he published many of Hume's works.

[1] He would have agreed with Robertson, who wrote to Andrew Strahan on 11 September 1791: 'Pray communicate to me any remarks or criticisms that you can pick up, for hardly any of these are so frivolous but that an Author may profit by them.' Add. MSS. 40886 f. 80.

The earliest of Hume's letters to Strahan is dated 30
November 1756, but in April 1748 the latter had invoiced
Millar for *Hume's Essays*, 11 *Sheets*, *No. 750 at £1 8s. p.
Sheet—£15 8s.*[1] This item was part of an account totalling
£504 18s. 4½d. against which on the contra side Strahan
noted in 1749 *Abated for Prompt Payment £31 0s. 3½d.*

Strahan may have played a part in persuading Millar to
bid for the second volume of the *History*; at least he knew
the details of the original publisher's transactions over the
first volume. Hill quotes[2] a letter in his possession dated
29 January 1754, from Gavin Hamilton in Edinburgh to
'Mr. William Strachan', which begins 'My dear Willie' and
describes 'a bargain that is reckoned very bold by every body
that hears of it, and some think it rash'. He tells Strahan
that:

John Balfour and I have agreed to pay 1200£ sterling of coppy
money, for a single impression of a book, 'tis the history of great
britain composed by David Hume our scots author. I print 2000 and
have right to print no more, the calcul stands thus, to print 3 quarto
volls which it will make, will cost with advertisements and incidents
about 320 per voll: the book will sell at 15/ bound or ten shillings to
Bk. Sellers in sheets, but let us reckon the London coppies only producing 9 shilling, then 2000 coppies will yeald about 920£ sterling
per voll after deducing 320£ for printing and 420£ to the author
which is not payable very soon, there remains of profitt for ourselves
about 200£ per voll, which we are content to putt up with as we are
perswaded that this first impression will be short while in hands . . .

Like too many optimistic forecasts in publishing, this one
was sadly out. After an initial sale in Edinburgh of about
450 copies in five weeks, the book 'stuck', and in the following year Hume wrote to Andrew Millar: 'I think the London booksellers have had a sufficient triumph over him
[Hamilton] when a book, which was much expected and

[1] This must have been the third edition of *Essays Moral and Political* rather than
the first edition of *Philosophical Essays on Human Understanding*, later re-titled
Enquiry concerning Human Understanding, which is listed in the *Gentleman's Magazine* for the same month, April 1748.

[2] Op. cit.

was calculated to be popular, has had so small a sale in his hands. To make the triumph more complete, I wish you would take what remains into your hands, and dispose of it in a few months.'[1]

Hamilton is not the last publisher to have lost an author who was dissatisfied with his sales; he would have been sardonically amused to read in Hume's autobiography that 'Mr. Millar told me, that in a twelvemonth he sold only forty-five copies of it'. However, Millar published the second volume which in Hume's words 'not only rose itself, but helped to buoy up its unfortunate brother', and found it sufficiently profitable to contract with Hume for the third volume for the price of £1,400.

Hume clearly found Strahan agreeable to deal with. In 1757 there had been some suggestion by Millar that an edition of the *Essays and Treatises* should be printed by William Bowyer. Hume wrote to Strahan: 'I hope henceforth he will never think of any but you, whenever any of my writings are concerned.'[2] He asked Strahan's advice on how much he should ask Millar for selling the complete copyright of the first two volumes of the *History*[3] and he asked him to read and comment on a letter he had written to Millar disputing the terms offered for the next volume: 'Your general Character and the Instances, which I have receivd of your Friendship, assure me of your conduct and make me have recourse to you on this Occasion.'

He also found that Strahan was a competent printer. 'I have received the first two Sheets of the Quarto Edition of my philosophical Writings; and am very well satisfy'd with it. Please only to tell the Compositor, that he always employ a Capital after the Colons.' And later, of the same work, he wrote: 'I am so sensible of your great Care in this Edition,

---

[1] Hill, op. cit.

[2] Ibid., 1 February 1757.

[3] 800 guineas. Hill calculates that Hume was actually paid £400 by Hamilton for one edition of the unlucky first volume and £700 by Millar for one edition of the second. If he did get 800 guineas for the copyright, he received a total of £1,940 for what constituted one-third of his *History*.

that I have desird Mr. Millar to give you one of the Copies, which he delivers to me on every Edition, and I beg of you to accept it as a small Testimony of my Regard.'

It was not until the autumn of 1758 that they met, when Hume came to London. 'I shall be sure to see you as soon as I arrive,' he wrote, 'and hope then to commence a personal Acquaintance with you, and to return you thanks for the many Instances, which I have receivd of your Attention and Friendship.' The acquaintance prospered, though it continued to be very largely an epistolary one. Hume returned to Edinburgh, whence in 1761 he recommended to Strahan's friendship James Macpherson whose *Ossian* he was to print; and then went in 1763 to Paris with Lord Hertford's embassy. From Paris he scolded Strahan for not writing: 'I have long expected to hear from you and to learn your Sentiments of English Politics, according to the Promise you made me on parting.'[1]

The traffic was not intended to be one-sided. Hume engaged to tell Strahan—whom he now regarded as a publisher as much as a printer—of interesting new French books.

I have been on the Watch this Winter for any publication, which might answer in an English Translation, and have even fix'd a Correspondence with one of the Licensers of the Press to give me early Intelligence; but there has nothing appeard, which I thought woud answer . . . Are you acquainted with the Merit of Madame Riccoboni's Novels? She is the author of Lady Juliet Catesby, and others which have been very well receivd both in France and England; and are indeed wrote with great Elegance and Decency. She has just now in the Press a Novel, wrote upon English Manners, from which great Success is expected. Woud you think it worthy of being translated?[2]

Before Strahan could give an opinion based upon such scanty information, Hume had sent him the first five sheets. 'The work seems to be very fine ... I have again seen Madame Riccoboni, who tells me that she is now near a Certainty with regard to the Size of her Work. It will be 4 Volumes in twelves of about 240 pages each.' Strahan should have taken fright at the thought of a writer who was doubtful of the extent of her novel even after the first chapters had been printed; instead he agreed to undertake the book in partnership with Thomas Becket, a bookseller who had first met Hume as an apprentice of Millar's.[1] Strahan told Hume on 10 July 1764 that the book, *The History of Miss Jenny*, was almost translated and printed.[2] In December Hume wrote to him, 'I see sometimes Made. Riccoboni, who is extremely surpriz'd, that Mr. Becket answers none of her Letters, sends her none of the Copies which she bespoke, informs her nothing of the Success of her Book, and in short takes no manner of Notice of her. I beseech you make him write, or write yourself for him, if he continues obstinately negligent.'

Strahan replied next month: 'Mme Riccoboni's book does not sell at all. Of course we must be losers'—an opinion endorsed by the author who told Garrick that 'Monsieur Becket s'est ruiné avec Miss Jenny'.[3] Hume took this reflection on his literary judgement philosophically. 'I am sorry, that the last Publication has not been successfull. I only saw the Beginning and judged from the Authors Character. The Beginning is much the best of the Work.'[4] It is not clear how much the book did lose for its publishers. Strahan's ledgers show that in September 1764 he invoiced *Becket and Strahan, History of Miss Jenny*, 2 *vols*, 20 *Sheets*, *No* 1,000 *at* £1 2s.—£22. The bill was not paid until October 1769.

Hume proferred no more advice from Paris—he was perhaps too busy in parrying the first of a stream of requests from Strahan to continue his *History*—but on his return

---

[1] Becket had set up by himself by 1760, when he appears in Strahan's ledger as the publisher of Chippendale's *Cabinet Makers Director*. Strahan charged him £5 14s. for 750 copies of 6 sheets at 19s. each, and £5 5s. for 250 copies of the French edition, 7 sheets at 15s.

[2] Burton: *Letters of Eminent Persons to David Hume*, Edinburgh, 1859.

[3] Letters of 15 May and 31 August 1765: *The Private Correspondence of David Garrick*, London, 1832.

[4] Hill, op. cit.

home he continued to recommend aspiring authors to go to
his friend in London. In 1773 Strahan was once again embarrassed by Hume's assistance. 'I have at length agreed,
but after much difficulty, with Capt. Brydon', he wrote:
'You had raised his expectations so very high, and so much
beyond the real worth of the book, which will hardly make
two 8vo volumes very loosely printed, that he could not be
satisfied with the very utmost the size and nature of the book
would admit of. You spoil all young authors, by leading
them to expect prices only due to veterans in literature and
men of established reputation.'[1]

Becket and Strahan had been involved with Hume in
the course of the latter's famous quarrel with Rousseau. To
clear himself from Rousseau's demented accusations, Hume
decided to publish, in Paris and London, his correspondence
with him. He wrote to Strahan:

The whole will compose a pretty large Pamphlet, which, I fancy,
the Curiosity of the Public will make tolerably saleable. I desire you
to take upon you the printing and publishing of it; and if any Profit
result from it to you, I shall be very happy; reserving the after property and Disposal of the Pamphlet to myself. You will take in what
Bookseller you please; Becket or Caddel or any other: For Mr.
Millar would not think such a Trifle worthy of his Attention.[2]

He was wrong. Millar wrote promptly to tell him that he
'was much hurt yesterday with yours to Mr. Strahan' and
pointed out that 'in the eye of the World where I have so
cordial a friendship, to see others names and not mine looks
as though you were offended'.[3] Hume was contrite. 'Your
Letter gave me a great deal of Uneasiness, by letting me see,
that I had, innocently and undesignedly given you uneasiness', he replied to Millar. To Strahan, in addition to giving
confused instructions about the printing of the pamphlet, he

[1] Burton, op. cit. Patrick Brydon was the author of *A Tour through Sicily and
Malta*. He also happened to be the son-in-law of another of Strahan's authors,
William Robertson.
[2] Hill, op. cit., October 1766.   [3] Burton, op. cit.

admitted 'I am certainly in the wrong, not to have conjoin'd him, if I could have imagin'd, that he would have thought it worthy of his Attention. I wish you may find it worth while; but I fancy 500 Copies will be more than sufficient to gratify the Curiosity of the Public.'[1]

Since Hume had given him a free hand, why did not Strahan go to his old friend Millar, or to Cadell with whom he was later to publish so many books? The answer lies in a letter which Becket wrote to Hume on 11 November 1766.

Sir, The Week before last I recd. from my friend M. Suard of Paris a Letter acquainting me he had for me for publication here four Copies of the *Exposé Succinct* which I have since recd. and advertised.[2]

A Gentleman favoured me with a Copy before I recd. those M. Suard sent me & I immediately advertised a *translation* & gave it to the gentleman who translated M. Rousseau's other pieces for me—he directly set about it, & last Saturday sennight I gave Mr. Strahan Copy to begin printing—He then shewed me your Letter just recd. in which you very obligingly mentioned my Name. As I had got the Original & advertised a *translation* he thought me every way in-titled to it, (for it is a rule in the trade, whoever advertises a translation first has the exclusive right) but he thought it best to shew Mr. Millar, who was then in town, your Letter—& who I find, *then*, gave up the point.

. . . What a pity it is that Mr. Millar should at this time of day give himself so much uneasiness, or reflect on Mr. Strahan about this affair—which I find he has done, & most unfriendly—for to my knowledge Mr. S. has acted in the most open manner possible—having communicated the Contents of your Letter to him on the receipt of it.[3]

The partners thought that Hume had been too modest in

---

[1] Hill, op. cit.

[2] *Exposé succinct de la Contestacion qui s'est élevée entre M. Hume et M. Rousseau, avec les pièces justificatives*—the French version of Hume's pamphlet. Suard was in demand as a translator. Hume wrote to Robertson in connection with the latter's *Charles V*, 'I got yesterday from Strahan about thirty sheets of your History to be sent over to Suard, and last night and this morning have run over them with great avidity'. Stewart: *Life . . . of William Robertson*, 1802.

[3] Royal Society of Edinburgh, calendar III, 41.

assessing the potential sale at 500 copies. Strahan's ledger for
November 1766 has the entry:

	£	s.	d.
Becket and Strahan. *Controversy between Hume and*			
Rousseau 6½ Sheets. No 750 at 17s.	5	10	6
Extra corrections in do		9	6
	6	0	0

Poor Strahan's troubles over this pamphlet were not yet
done. As well as leading to a quarrel with his original bene-
factor, Millar, it led to ill-feeling with the author, despite or
perhaps because of the 'extra corrections'. Hume was irri-
tated by Strahan's failure to reply to his letters and accused
him of not conveying his instructions to the translator.
Strahan's reply to these angry complaints has not survived,
but he must have satisfied Hume, who was writing to him in
a few months as cheerfully as ever. It is not clear whether
his relations with Millar were permanently soured by this
episode; in this same year, 1766, Thomas Cadell opened
a printing account with Strahan and in 1768 Millar's last
account was settled by 'Mr. Cadell, one of his Executors'.

From a publisher's point of view Hume was an exaspera-
ting author. Millar, Strahan and Cadell in turn implored him
to continue his very successful *History*, but instead, with what
seems good sense to posterity though it did not to his contemporaries, he concentrated upon revising his *Essays*. As
far as the *History* was concerned he corrected and re-
corrected the existing volumes. Such striving after perfection
did not reconcile his publishers to the lack of a new best-
seller from him. Hume himself told Strahan, 'I believe this is
the historical Age and this the historical Nation:[1] I know no
less than eight Histories upon the Stocks in this Country;
all of which have different degrees of Merit, from the life of
Christ, the most sublime of the whole, as I presume from the
Subject, to Dr. Robertson's American History, which lies in
the other extremity.' Strahan needed no reminding about

---

[1] Hill, op. cit. Hume means Scotland.

the historical age. Millar had published Robertson's *History of Scotland* and he was himself to publish the same writer's *History of America* and *History of Charles V*; he was to have a share in Smollett's, Macpherson's, Dalrymple's and Henry's Histories; and to crown all was to print and to publish with Cadell *The Decline and Fall*. It must have been doubly galling to have no new historical work from Hume.

The process of producing new editions was not entirely smooth running, as is indicated in this letter of Strahan's in reply to a complaint from Hume. He wrote from Glasgow, where he was on holiday with his wife, on 27 July 1768; Hume was at that time in London.

Dear Sir, I have this moment received your Note of July 12th which vexes me more than I am able to express. I had committed the immediate Care of correcting your History to one of whose Diligence and Accuracy I was well assured from many Years Experience, it being impossible for my Son, who is extremely careful, as he has the Superintendency of the whole business during my absence, to read all the Proofs himself.—This Person, I find, has been somewhat indisposed of late, which may have prevented him, for a little time, from revising some of the Sheets. I am certain this must have been the Case, and that all Cause for Complaint has long since ceased. I have, however, written, with the utmost Earnestness, about this Matter to my Son by this night's Post, that you may have immediate Redress. I hope the Errors already overlooked are neither numerous, nor such as materially affect the Sense. But however that may be, you may depend upon it every Reparation in my Power shall be made by reprinting, at my own Expence, whatever you shall think necessary. . . .

I hope you are now fairly begun to what I find every body here, as well as elsewhere, so much longs for; and most heartily do I wish you Health and Spirits to prosecute it, to your own Satisfaction, and to the further Extension (if that can be) of the Universal Reputation you have already acquired.[1]

No sooner had Hume completed a revision of the *Essays* than he returned once again to the *History*. He wrote to Strahan from Edinburgh on 25 March 1771:

I long much for an Opportunity of bringing my History to the same

[1] R.S. of Edinburgh, calendar VII, 59.

degree of Accuracy. Since I was settled here, I have, from time to time, given Attention to that Object; though the Distance and Uncertainty of the new Edition threw a Damp on my Industry: But I shall now apply seriously to the Task; and you may expect the Copy about August. I beseech you do not make this Edition too numerous like the last. I have heard you frequently say, that no Bookseller woud find Profit in making an Edition which woud take more than three Years in selling. Look back, therefore, and learn from Mr. Millar's Books what has been the Sale for the last six Years; and if you make the usual Allowance for a Diminution during the ensuing three, from the Number of Copies already sold, I am persuaded you will find 1500, a number large enough, if not too large . . .[1]

I have found by Experience that nothing excites an Author's Attention so much as receiving the Proofs from the Press, as the Sheets are gradually thrown off . . . the last four Volumes you may throw off at your Leizure: But the Sheets of the first four, I shoud wish to receive by the Post five times a week. They will make about 250 Sheets and might be finish'd in thirty weeks.[2]

Strahan did not demur at the prospect of a new edition of the *History* as far as it went, but he still wanted a continuation of it to offer to the public and was willing to pay any price for it, as he told Hume in reply.

The proofs of the first four volumes shall be regularly transmitted to you as you desire . . . The impression is to be 1500 and no more, which is of all others the most proper number; nor is it the interest of the proprietors to print more at a time . . . If you write another volume, which the best judges of writing are daily enquiring after, you may demand what you please for it . . . I heartily wish you would seriously think of setting about it. It is the only thing wanting to fill up the measure of your glory as the Great Historian and Philosopher of the Eighteenth Century . . . I am afraid, too, that when you are universally known to have given up all thoughts of this yourself, we shall be pestered with *continuations* from some of our hackney writers . . .

Hume was unmoved by the suggestion that he could

---

[1] Hume of course had sold the copyright and had no financial interest in the number of copies sold. A small edition would bring nearer the opportunity for yet another revision.

[2] Hill, op. cit.

demand what he pleased for a new volume, although his interest in the earnings of rival historians was a lively one. In 1771 Strahan was a partner in the publication of Sir John Dalrymple's *Memoirs of Great Britain and Ireland*. Hume wrote to him on 11 March:

> But what shall we say to Sir John Dalrymple's new History, of which, I see, you are one of the publishers? He has writ down that he has been offerd 2000 pounds for the Property of it: I hope you are not the Purchasers; tho' indeed I know not but you might be a gainer by it: The ranting, bouncing Style of the Performance may perhaps take with the Multitude . . . But really I doubt much of his Veracity in his Account of the Offer: I shoud be much obliged to you for your Information on that Head.

Strahan replied in May: 'The offer of £750 to Sir J. D. turns out to have been more than the real value of it, as the sale of it seems to be already over here. Not above 1000 are yet sold, which was the number first printed, 220 of which arrived here after the second edition was finished. So that will probably stick on hand for a great while to come . . .'[1]

Strahan was not soured by experiences like this, and continued to be a liberal paymaster to his authors. Boswell notes in his journal, in 1778:

> In the forenoon I called on Dr. Blair at his country house between Edinburgh and Leith, and, at Mr. Charles Dilly's desire, made him an offer of £300 for a second volume of his sermons. The Doctor said Strahan had behaved so handsomely to him that he could not but give him the first offer, but he would let me know before a bargain was concluded, that Messieurs Dilly might treat either with himself or with Strahan.[2]

Strahan gave Blair 100 guineas for his first volume of sermons, and another £100 after its great success. He matched

---

[1] Ibid.

[2] *Boswell Papers*, Isham Collection, 1928, vol. 13. Hugh Blair was minister of the High Church of Edinburgh and Regius Professor of Rhetoric; and a close friend of Hume. Boswell noted (ibid., 18 September 1777) that Johnson said Strahan 'had no opinion of the sermons till he got an opinion from HIM much in their praise'. The first volume reached its nineteenth edition by 1794.

Dilly's offer by paying Blair £300 for the second volume, and paid him £600 each for the third and fourth volumes; over £1,700 in all.

The composition of the new edition of Hume's *History* was put in hand in the late summer of 1771. Hume made elaborate plans with Strahan for the flow of proofs between London and Scotland; they included complicated arrangements for having the packets franked to save postage—Strahan, not yet a Member of Parliament, could not himself frank letters. A new fount of type was ordered which Hume approved. 'I like the Paper and Type very much, only I think this Size of Type woud have suited better a Duodecimo than a large Octavo: However it will do very well.' The reason for this care perhaps lies in a comment made by Hume in the previous year with reference to the 1763 edition in eight volumes 8vo: 'I suppose', he told Strahan, 'you will not find one book in the English language of that size and price so ill printed.' Hume must have forgotten the appearance of the first edition of his first volume, printed for Hamilton and Balfour in Edinburgh. It is a shocking piece of bad workmanship.

Strahan himself kept an eye on the work, although it proved impossible to meet the author's request for proofs of a complete sheet by every post. His help was on some occasions at least positive. 'I thank you for your Corrections, which are very judicious; and you see that I follow them for the greatest part', wrote Hume; and later, 'Your remarks are always very judicious and just; and I am much obliged to you'. His most flattering thanks are found in a letter of 22 February 1772:

As we are drawing near a Conclusion, I cannot forbear giving you many and hearty thanks, both for your submitting to so troublesome a Method of printing and for the many useful Corrections you have sent me. I suppose, since the days of Aldus, Reuchlin, and Stevens there have been no Printers who coud have been useful to their Authors in this particular. I shall scarcely ever think of correcting any more; tho' I own that the receiving of the Sheets regularly by post has been an Amusement and Occupation to me, which I shall have a Difficulty to supply. I fancy I must take to some kind of Composition in its place.[1]

Strahan, while appreciative of Hume's praise, was not slow to seize this chance to urge a continuation of the *History* when he replied on 27 February.

The approbation of those whose praise is real fame is, in the very nature of the thing, extremely desireable. Judge then how very acceptable your last kind letter was to me; in which you acknowledge my small merits in a very generous and goodnatured way, and much above what they have any title to . . . The reading a sheet of your *History* every day with care and precision, though I at first imposed it on myself as a task, soon became a most agreeable amusement . . .

You say the correcting the sheets has been an amusement to yourself, and an occupation which you will now find a difficulty to supply. This I can easily believe. And here let me make one observation, which I dare say has frequently occurred to yourself, because it is founded on experience and a knowledge of the human mind.—To render life tolerable, and to make it glide away with some degree of satisfaction, it is necessary that a small part at least of almost every day be employed in some species of *real* or *imaginary business*. To pass our whole time in amusement and dissipation leaves a depression upon the spirits infinitely less bearable than perhaps the hardest labour. The sentence of, *In the sweat of thy face shalt thou eat bread*, pronounced against Adam after his fall, as a punishment, is an apparent mistake, which I am not scholar enough to rectify, but which I hope will not escape future commentators.—My application of this doctrine you will easily guess, which is no other than to add this to the other motives I have formerly taken the liberty to urge, to persuade you to the continuation of your *History*; in which, if you will make some progress, however trifling, every day, I will venture to say you will find your *immediate account* in it, in point of ease and cheerfulness and general flow of spirits. Fame which in some sense may be considered as a *future reward*, I will not mention. The various and complicated miseries to which mankind are subjected, the loss of those who are deservedly dear to us, the precariousness of our own existence; in

[1] Hill, op. cit. Reuchlin was a fifteenth-century classical and Hebrew grammarian, not a printer. By Stevens Hume meant the great Robert Estienne, or Stephanus as he latinized his name.

short the contemplation of every thing around us, demands a constant diversion of our attention to some object or other. I have generally, if not always found happiness to dwell not with men of much leisure and retirement but with those who had a *little less* time than they had employment for . . .[1]

Johnson would have approved the ring of truth in these determinedly realistic sentences, so unlike the sentiments one might expect from a successful man of business. But Strahan's character played as great a part in his success as his commercial acumen; and it is tempting to trace at least an element of his friendship with Johnson in a shared acceptance of the harsh nature of earthly life.

Hume was not moved into action by Strahan's attempt to present the writing of another volume as an agreeable way of filling up time; he felt that he had already been bitten once. Millar had been driven to the expedient of lying to Hume about the rate of sale of the 1763 edition—he had in fact vastly overprinted and the edition was not sold off ten years later. His object in the deception was not of course to cheat the author of his due; Hume had been handsomely paid in advance; but to induce him to continue the work. Hume discovered the trick after Cadell, who had been a party to it, had succeeded Millar; and he was also inclined to blame Strahan:

I find that your great Reluctance to write me on a certain Subject proceeds from your Unwillingness to retract every thing that you have been telling me these seven Years: But your Silence tells me the Truth more strongly than any thing you can say. Besides, I know not why you shoud have a Reluctance to retract. What you told me was for a good End, in order to excite my Industry, which might be of Advantage both to myself and to the Proprietors of the former Volumes . . . I am fully determined never to continue my History.[2]

Strahan went on pressing the point unavailingly, and in 1773 wrote to Hume: 'After what you now tell me I altogether despair of seeing a continuation of your History from yourself; but I have some notion it may be done by

[1] Hill, op. cit.   [2] Ibid., 22 May 1770.

some other hand; perhaps Sr. John Dalrymple or Mr. Macpherson.'[1] Hume did not even rise to this fly, beyond re-
marking that he would like to be consulted before any steps
were taken, and reverted to his favourite preoccupation, a
new edition—impeded as he felt by the remaining copies of
the 1763 one. He went too far, in his impatience, in a letter
of 15 March 1773:

> You and Mr. Cadel had so much lost all faith with me, that indeed
> I thought it was impossible for you any longer to deceive me: Yet
> when you mention'd a new Edition, I own I was so simple as to
> believe, that all the old one was nearly sold off. This woud have been
> very blameable in you, if you had proposd any other End than that of
> seducing me into the continuing of my work, which you thought, and
> probably with Reason, woud have been for my own Advantage in
> more respects than one. But however the Consequence is, that I am
> now at a Loss and shall ever remain so, what I am to think and believe;
> And many Questions, interesting to me, which I wishd to ask you,
> woud, I find, be entirely vain and fruitless; and therefore I shall for-
> bear them, since I can give no manner of credit to the Answers.[2]

Strahan's reply was immediate and decisive. He was not
so awed by Hume's eminence, or so mollified by years of
friendship, as to swallow charges of this nature.

> After having been most unfeignedly attached to you ever since I
> had the pleasure of your acquaintance; after having done every thing
> in my power to oblige you; after having given the most careful atten-
> tion to your works when under my press, for which I received your
> repeated acknowledgements; and after having behaved to you in the
> most open, candid and ingenuous manner upon every occasion since
> I became a proprietor in your works; I did not, I could not expect to be
> told by you, after all, that I was a lying scoundrel, who had constantly
> deceived you, to whom you could give no manner of credit.
> Such, it seems, is your deliberate opinion both of Mr. Cadell and
> myself. Produce, I call upon you, and have a right so to do, one single
> instance to support the heavy charge you bring against us; concealing
> from you, at the desire of the late Mr. Millar, the number of the 8vo
> edition of your History alone excepted; which we did purely at his

request, having then no interest, nor the least shadow of interest, to deceive you in that or any other particular.

I own I am quite astonished at the style of your last letter, which is such as should be directed to one of the most worthless of the human race, and to such only.

Do not imagine, however, that I mean to enter into a laboured defence of myself. Far from it. I have nothing to apologize for; nothing have I said or done respecting you, that I now wish unsaid or undone . . . True it is (and this does not depend on my veracity or else I would not have mentioned it) that I have said and done every thing in my power to persuade (or, if you prefer, to *seduce*) you to continue your History, from a full conviction, as you express it in your last, *that it would have been for your own advantage in more respects than one.*—Your answer was constantly in the negative; of late, that *such an absurd and extravagant idea never entered your head*; and *that you had thrown your pen aside for ever.*—Whether I did well in thus repeatedly obtruding my advice upon you, and you in as repeatedly rejecting it, time alone can discover. I know I meant well; that to me is a great cause of satisfaction.—And now I cease to trouble you on this head for ever . . .

Some time or other you will perhaps discover with certainty, whether I am or not

Your faithfull and Obedt Servt
W. S.[1]

Hume apologized at once, and handsomely:

There is no man of whom I entertain a better [opinion], nor whose Friendship I desire more to preserve, nor indeed any one to whom I have owd more essential Obligations . . . Sick People and Children are often to be deceivd for their Good; and I only suspected you of thinking that peevish Authors, such as I confess I am, are in the same Predicament . . . I entreat the Continuance or rather the Renewal of your Friendship.

The entreaty succeeded, for although there appears to have been a gap of several months in their correspondence, by January 1774 Hume was sufficiently confident of Stra-

---

[1] Quoted by Hill from a draft or copy kept by Strahan; it seems that Hume did not care to preserve the original he received. Strahan was always quick to resent any slight upon his character; see Noorthouck's valedictory verses, p. 209.

han's goodwill to 'beg his Vote and Interest in the India House' for a friend; and shortly afterwards he appointed Strahan his literary executor—a position that was to lead the printer into difficulties.

6

David Hall and America

ONE of Strahan's fellow-apprentices in Edinburgh was David
Hall, indentured on 16 April 1729 to Mosman and Brown.[1]
He followed or accompanied Strahan to London and worked
with him for some years. He was anxious to get on in the
world, and to help him Strahan wrote on 17 January 1743
to a Philadelphia lawyer-cum-bookseller, James Read, whom
he had met in London three or four years earlier.

Since you mention printing, pray do you think there is Encouragement for another Printer with you? There is one who was my Fellow-
prentice, and who has worked with me some Years (his Name is
Hall, you have seen him at my house to be sure, for he lodges with
me) whom I have a great Inclination to serve. He understands his
Business exceedingly well, is honest, sober and Industrious to the last
Degree. Do you think you and he could make anything of it in Partnership? Or could you point out any Way to serve him in your
Country, if you do not care to meddle with it yourself? He has no
fortune, but I have so good an Opinion of him (founded upon the experience of a Dozen Years of close Intimacy) that I would cheerfully
assist him as far as my small Fortune would allow me; . . . this is to
endeavour to place a deserving young Man in a way of Business that
will probably soon turn out better than working Journey-work. . . .[2]

Read showed the letter to his next-door neighbour and

[1] His father was James Hall of Westfield. Boog-Watson, ed.: *Registers of Edinburgh
Apprentices, 1701–1775*, Scottish Record Society, 1929.
[2] American Philosophical Society, Misc. MSS. Collection.

relation by marriage, Benjamin Franklin. This occasioned the first letter in a correspondence and a consequent friendship that was to last, with few interruptions, until the end of Strahan's life.

Philadelphia, July 10 43

Sir, Mr. Read has communicated to me part of a Letter from you, recommending a young Man whom you would be glad to see in better Business than that of a Journey-man Printer. I have already three Printing-Houses in three different Colonies, and propose to set up a fourth if I can meet with a proper Person to manage it, having all Materials ready for that purpose. If the young Man will venture over hither, that I may see and be acquainted with him, we can treat about the Affair, and I make no doubt but he will think my Proposals reasonable; If we should not agree, I promise him however a Twelve Months Good Work, and to defray his Passage back if he enclines to return to England.

I am, Sir, your humble Servant unknown

B. Franklin[1]

As his letter indicates, Franklin was already a man with a considerable business; more, he was by this time well on the road which led him to pre-eminence in Pennsylvania and to unsurpassed fame in America and Europe. He was of course a printer, and a shopkeeper who sold not only books and stationery but all the miscellanea of a provincial store, from lampblack to barrelled mackerel. Since 1729 he had been publishing the liveliest newspaper in the colony, *The Pennsylvania Gazette*, and for some ten years had been writing and publishing his famous almanac, *Poor Richard*. He had begun to play a part in local affairs as clerk of the Pennsylvania Assembly and also as postmaster, admittedly in the one case to secure some official printing and in the other to facilitate the distribution of his newspaper. As a private citizen he had been a prime mover in the founding of the Union Fire Company and of the Library Company, and in this same year he issued a circular throughout the colonies

[1] *The Papers of Benjamin Franklin*, II, Yale, 1960.

proposing the formation of the American Philosophical Society.

His offer was too good an opportunity to miss, and David Hall did decide to 'venture over hither'. On 4 July 1744 Franklin was able to write to Strahan reporting Hall's arrival in Philadelphia and stating his belief that they would come to terms. Hall probably lodged in the rather crowded Franklin house, which was also the shop and printing office, in Market Street. The household consisted of Franklin and his wife Deborah, his illegitimate son William, now thirteen or fourteen, and his mother-in-law; a son of the marriage had died in infancy, but there was a baby in the house, their daughter Sally. In addition it accommodated at various times apprentices and journeymen like Hall.

Franklin went on to say in the same letter:

I am much obligd to you for your Care and Pains in procuring me the Founding-Tools;[1] tho' I think, with you, that the Workmen have not been at all bashful in making their Bills. . . . I have long wanted a Friend in London whose Judgment I could depend on, to send me from time to time such new Pamphlets as are worth reading on any Subject (Religious Controversy excepted) for there is no depending on Titles and Advertisements. This Favour I take the Freedom to beg of you, and shall lodge Money in your Hands for that purpose.

It was this request of Franklin's, coupled of course with the presence of his close friend Hall in Philadelphia, that led Strahan into the American trade, which in time formed a useful proportion of his business. It was not altogether a one-way traffic, for as early as 1744 Franklin shipped him 300 copies of James Logan's translation of Cicero's *Cato Major*, better known perhaps as the dialogue *de Senectute*, which he had just printed in Philadelphia. It is sad to relate that this early example of the export of American books was a financial disaster.[2] The transaction was referred to in letters exchanged between the two men during the War

---

[1] The matrices and moulds, and possibly punches, necessary for type founding.
[2] In 1953 a copy was bought at Hodgson's for £150 by Messrs. Maggs.

of American Independence. Franklin wrote on 4 December 1781 from Passy:

> I formerly sent you from Philadelphia part of an edition of Tully on Old Age, to be sold in London; and you put the books, if I remember right, into the hands of Mr. Becket for that purpose. Probably he may have some of them still in his warehouse, as I never had an account of their being sold. I shall be much obliged by your procuring and sending me one of them.[1]

Strahan replied:

> I remember perfectly well receiving from you some copies of Tully on Old Age printed in Philadelphia, but have totally forgot what became of them. Becket, into whose hands I think they were put, can recollect nothing of them. He became a Bankrupt some time ago, so that had any remained unsold, they must have appeared in the general Sale of his Stock.—However, in my Enquiry among the Trade, I found on Sale an Edition of the Book, seemingly printed from yours, which I send you; and this, I hope, will answer your present Purpose.[2]

This was not the only import of American works through Strahan's agency. In 1762 Franklin wrote to him from Philadelphia: 'Mr. Hall sends you I believe, for sale, some Poetic Pieces of our young Geniuses;—it would encourage them greatly if their Performance could obtain any favourable Reception in England;—I wish therefore you would take the proper steps to get them recommended to the Notice of the Publick as far at least as you may find they deserve. I know that no one can do this better than yourself.'

David Hall's decision to go to America in 1743 proved a successful one for himself and for Franklin, who described his new employee as 'obliging, discreet, industrious and honest' and took him into partnership in 1748. Clearly Hall had misgivings to begin with, answered by Strahan in the first to survive of the dozens of letters he sent him. Some of these letters have been printed in the journals of historical

---

[1] Smyth: *The Writings of Benjamin Franklin*, New York, 1905–7. Unless otherwise stated, Franklin's letters are quoted from this source.

[2] 27 May 1782. The letter is in the possession of Miss S. Madeline Hodge, Princeton, N.J.

societies, but the greater part of the originals, including that of this letter, have not been published; they are in the Library of the American Philosophical Society in Philadelphia (abbreviated in the notes following to APS).

London, March 9 1745

Dear Davie,

As I have an Opportunity, I now sit down to tell you all about it. I have been of late so busy, that it is with Difficulty I can find time to recollect myself to write so particularly as I could wish; but my Peggy and Geo. Reid in theirs have saved me a good deal of writing—

Since I wrote last, which was Sepr. 10, I have received yours of Sepr. 13 and Novr. 2 by which I am glad to find you are well and in good Spirits. I hope *your* Scheme will succeed to your Wishes, and that it will enable you to keep your Appointment with me. But if things should not answer, in reasonable time, *remember what I say to you*, I advise you by all means to return to Old England; for I don't doubt but I can do something for you at any time that will make it worth your while, in a Way perhaps you don't think of.—You know 'tis good to have something to look home to at all Events.—I have been very busy lately. 13 at Case, and 2 Press and a half is no bad Business, and I have a very good prospect of being fully employed all this Summer. I am now beginning to print a little for myself, as there are sometimes Prizes to be had in that Way. The first thing I tried was a Pamphlet, which I shall clear a Dozen pounds by, and I am now doing a Small 120 which I hope will sell. I find always some new friend or another start up every Day, so that I shall be as universally known (and I hope employed too) by and by, as any other of the Employment. The only thing that gives me most uneasiness is the Longwindedness of the Booksellers, who keep me pretty bare of Money; but I am hopeful I shall conquer that at some time or other, and be a great Man, as the Saying is, by the time you return, be it as soon as it will. Mr. Richardson, whom I mentioned in my last, has turned out a good Friend, of which I leave you to judge, when I tell you, that the Work I have done within these Eight Months by his Recommendation, comes to upwards of £300. The Patent which I mentioned in my last to be in Quest of, I have been obliged to drop for the present, by Reason of the late Change in the Ministry.[1]—So much for my own Affairs.

[1] After Walpole's fall in 1742 a stop-gap ministry was formed by the Earl of Wilmington; this in turn had been succeeded in 1743 by that of Henry Pelham.

I have sent the Fount of English by this Ship, which I hope will arrive in time, so as not to hinder your making a speedy Beginning. As to your Terms with Mr. F I again tell you I think they are very fair. But at all Events it is your Part to trust to his Generosity; and I dare say he will deal honourably by you.

I have, as you'll see by the annexed List of what is contained in the Box No. 3 (No. 1 and 2 containing the Fount of English) that I have sent your nine Night Shirts, for the making of which, and a Nail of Cambrick, I paid Pole £1 1s. and a Hatt which cost 10/6. So that now you owe me as follows:

	£	s.	d.
By a Note of Hand	21	0	0
For making Six Ruffled Shirts	1	5	0
For making Nine Night Shirts, & Cambrick	1	1	0
For a Hatt		10	6
	£23	16	6

The Money you left me to insure for you did not quite answer (the Premium rose so fast after you went away) but the Overplus I make you a Present of, as I think your Voyage has cost you dear enough already. You can't imagine how pleased I was, that supposing you had been nabbed by the French, I should have had a good hundred Pounds to remitt to you.

Mr. Franklin sent me Bills to the Value of £20 13s. but he made no mention of applying any part of it to paying your Freight. The Fount of English, with the other things I sent him by you, &c, will come to near double the sum. But as to that, never trouble your Head about it. If he pays it, good. If not, I desire not to be repaid till you can well spare it. So far from that, if you should in your new Settlement, find a little more Money will be of use to you, you may at all times command from me what I can possibly spare.—I have also sent you 100 Pens and the London Magazine for Jany and Feby last, and shall send you the following as they come out.

I hope your jaundice is left you, and that dear Davie is quite well. Never fear the French, notwithstanding the Negligence of your Governors. I hope we shall give them so much Employment in Europe that they won't find time to trouble you. The Scheme for your Coffee-house I think a very good one. Your Business to be sure is as much as in you lies, to cultivate a good Correspondence with all the honest and creditable People you can.

Your Brother Willie I have not heard of a great while;—John, I hear, is as usual.

I now think I have said every thing I can think of at present. I would write oftener, but I am generally so busy, and have such a Variety of things upon my Mind, that I have seldom time to sit down to write: besides, the Ships that sail your Way generally sail all at once about the same time; so that I have not often an Opportunity; but I shall write as frequently as I can, as I expect you will. Remember me in the kindest manner to Mr. Franklin and his Spouse, (and tell little Miss her Husband is this Day five Years old, and a brave thriving Fellow) and to Mr. Read and his Mother. Every body sends their Service. I long impatiently to hear of your Success. Remember your Appointment. There is one Year gone already.

I am ever, Dear Davie,

Your very affectionate friend & humble Sert.

Will: Strahan

Are you like to get married yet? Surely the Girls are (some of them at least) tolerable.

Strahan, it will be noted, was already trying to ensure a flow of regular work by acquiring a share in patent printing; I do not know which particular patent he was pursuing at this time, but it may well have been that for Law Printing in which he secured a share in some years' time. One or two other points in the letter call for comment. The French threat to the colonies arose from the War of Austrian Succession, or King George's War. The 'little Miss' was Franklin's daughter, Sally, then eighteen months old, and 'her Husband' was young William Strahan. Their fathers' joke about their marriage died a hard death; as we shall see, it was seriously considered in 1760 and might well have taken place if Deborah Franklin, the girl's mother, had not been invincibly opposed to crossing the Atlantic. Finally, one at least of the girls was tolerable, for on 7 January 1748 David Hall married Mary Leacock of Philadelphia; her sister Susanna was the wife of James Read.

Strahan sent further reassurances to Hall about his prospects with Franklin in a letter written on 22 June 1745:

I hope every thing will turn out for the best. I am glad to find

WILLIAM STRAHAN
*From the painting by Sir Joshua Reynolds
in the National Portrait Gallery*

THE

HISTORY

OF

GREAT BRITAIN,

FROM

The Accession of JAMES I.

TO

The REVOLUTION in 1688.

By DAVID HUME, Esq.

VOL. VIII.

A NEW EDITION, Corrected.

LONDON:

Printed for T. CADELL, (Successor to A. MILLAR) in the Strand.
MDCCLXX.

Mr. F writes in the handsomest Manner of you, and is perfectly pleased with your Conduct and Behaviour. You will, I dare say, have all the Reason in the World to like him; for he seems to me, by his Manner of writing to have a very good Heart, as well as to be a Man of Honour and Good Sense. Give yourself no manner of Uneasiness about me; let every thing come of himself; and when I can be of any further Use to you, command me. I am sorry the War is like to do you so much Hurt in America, but things are not much better in Europe, the French having the best of it every where this Campaign; however, 'tis to be hoped Affairs will soon take a better Turn.[1] I am glad you keep your Health so well in so inconstant a Climate. No doubt you will find Temperance and Sobriety of great Service to you in that Respect.

Business with me continues much the same. I keep two Presses constantly, which, if properly employed, will answer my purpose well enough. All my Family are well. Bill is a fine Boy, and Rachie, who remains in Scotland, a fine Girl. George is at Chigwell, and looks as if he would be a very honest Fellow; and I have another upon the Stocks; so that I believe I must send some of them to America to help to people some Colony there. . . .[2]

The friendship between Franklin and Strahan prospered because the two men were of service to each other. While they were still only friends by letter it was their business that bound them together; many years of mutual trust laid a sound foundation for the true friendship that sprang up when they eventually met. For Franklin, Strahan was a helpful London correspondent; in that capacity he was not only a wholesaler of books and a supplier of ink and printers' materials, but also a general merchant and a banker. When he could supply a journeyman printer like Hall, and political news as well, he was worth cultivating. From Strahan's point of view, Franklin and then Hall provided the means of extending his trade with America. There was of course no question of printing for the colonies; houses like that of

[1] Strahan could not know that the French fortress of Louisburg had just surrendered to the colonial volunteers; he was thinking of the allied defeat at Fontenoy a month before.

[2] APS. The child 'upon the Stocks' was Samuel, b. 15 September 1745, d. 21 April 1747.

Franklin himself in Philadelphia could undertake all the job-bing and general printing that was required. But, although books were printed in America—witness *Cato Major*—the greater part of the books distributed in the colonies were imported from Britain where the larger market and the more highly organized book trade offered lower costs than could a colonial press. Strahan often supplied Hall with an assort-ment of 'light reading' but his invoices show that America wanted above all books for use rather than entertainment: Bibles, educational works, law books and manuals of instruc-tion on every subject from astronomy and navigation to medicine. Strahan, as he told Hall, was determined not to remain a 'mere printer', and he easily added export book-selling to his other lines.

It is hard to visualize the difficulties of such a trade in the eighteenth century. Depending on the season of the year, and whether the Atlantic were free of privateers and warring navies, an order from Philadelphia might take up to three months to reach Strahan in London. The books wanted might not all be available; should the order be filled with other, similar, titles or left incomplete? The books them-selves crossed the ocean equally slowly, with a letter and an advice note; a copy letter would follow by a later ship. Pay-ment was slow, and usually by bills of exchange which might not be accepted in London; the exporter had to reckon on giving very long credit. Strahan had a great deal of trouble over payment with some of his American customers, but never with Franklin or with Hall.

Franklin's conduct shone the more brightly in contrast with that of his relation by marriage, James Read, Strahan's first business correspondent in Philadelphia. Read must have seemed at first the ideal customer; there is an air of stability about a bookseller who is also a lawyer. Strahan had liked him when he met him in London, and had no hesitation in sending several small parcels of books. In 1745 he dis-patched a consignment worth £132 3s. 1d. The story of Strahan's attempts over the next forty years to obtain a settlement of this debt is told by J. Benett Nolan in *Printer Strahan's Book Account* (Reading, Pa., 1939). In 1745, however, so far was Read's credit from being questioned that Strahan asked him to collect the debts of others. On 22 June he wrote to Hall:

> You mention Mr. Whitefield. Pray get J. Read to speak to him as you propose, when he comes to Philadelphia. He owes me above £150 which is a great deal of money to lie dead in one hand. . . . I wish J. Read all the Happiness in the World, and I esteem him most sincerely in every Account. You are very happy in being so near him, and I am delighted you find him so honest, so worthy and so friendly.[1]

But Read's own debt remained unpaid. His subsequent bookbuying in London was, prudently, not carried out through Strahan. Read explained his system in a letter to Hall:

> I got the books in Reading [Pennsylvania] less than four months from the time I wrote for them. I pay Dr. Bass in London 112% advance on the sterling pound so that for Dean Bolton's letters (beautifully printed, well bound in calf, lettered) which cost five shillings sterling, I pay ten shillings seven pence Pennsylvania money, whereas at a bookseller's shop in Philadelphia I would have paid twelve shillings sixpence at least for the same book, unlettered.[2]

By 1748 Franklin had taken the place of the still stubbornly defaulting Read as Strahan's adviser on American trade. A letter of 19 October in that year from Franklin shows the footing upon which their relationship then stood.

Dear Sir,

I receiv'd your favour of April 25, with the Maps &c.—I am glad the Polybius did not come, and hope you will not have sent it when this reaches your Hands; it was intended for my Son, who was then in the Army, and seemed bent on a military Life; but as Peace cuts off his Prospect of Advancemt. in that Way, he will apply himself to other Business.[3] Enclos'd I send you his Certificate from the Governor of New York, by which he is entitled to £98 16s. 4d. Sterling,

[1] APS. George Whitefield, the Methodist preacher, was then in Pennsylvania.
[2] Nolan, op. cit.
[3] The Treaty of Aix-la-Chapelle had been signed.

DAVID HALL AND AMERICA

being his pay; with a Letter of Attorney impowering you to receive it; I know not what the Deduction will be at the Pay Office; but desire you will give my Acct. Credit for the net Proceeds. I am in daily Expectation of a Bill from Virginia of 50£ which I shall remit you towards the Balance, & Mr. Hall will acct. with you for those Things you have sent me, that are put in his Invoice. Our Accts. agree, except that I have chargd you £1 9s. 7d. for the Ainsworth & James Read, the 6/7 being the Proportion of Charges on that Book and the Bill on Geo Rigge my Acct. called £15 7s. 11d. yours £15 7s. 1d.; which is but a small Variation; I know not but yours may be right.

I have lately sent a Printing house to Antigua, by a very sober[1] honest & diligent young Man, who has already (as I am informed by divers Hands) gain'd the Friendship of the principal People, and is like to get into good Business. This will open another Market for your Books if you think fit to use it; for I am persuaded, that if you shall send him a Parcel with any Quantity of Stationery he may write to you for, he will make you good and punctual Returns. His name is Thomas Smith; he is the only Printer on that Island:—had worked with me here and at my Printing-house in N York, 3 or 4 Years, and always behaved extremely well.

Mr. Tho' Osborne Bookseller of London is endeavouring to open a Correspondence in the Plantations for the Sale of his Books: he has accordingly sent several Parcels, 1 to Mr. Parker of N.York, 1 to Mr. Read here, & one to Mr. Parks in Virginia. I have seen the Invoices to Parker & Read; and observe the Books to be very high charged, so that I believe they will not sell. I recommended Parker to you for Books, but he tells me he has wrote you several Letters, & in two of them sent a Guinea to purchase some small Things, but never receiv'd any Answer. Perhaps the Guineas made the Letters miscarry. He is a very honest, punctual Man, and will be in the Way of selling a great many Books:—I think you might find your Acct. in writing to him. Mr. Read having left off bookselling Osborne has wrote me, & desir'd me to take those Books into my Hands, proposing a Correspondence, &c. but I have declin'd it in a Letter per this Ship.— My spouse will write to Mrs. Strahan, to whom my best Respects. By this time twelvemonth, if nothing extraordinary happen to prevent

---

[1] Unfortunately he was not. He died in 1752, and Franklin replaced him by his nephew Benjamin Mecom. He reassured Mecom's parents about the salubrity of the island: 'My late partner there enjoyed perfect health for four years, till he grew careless and got to sitting up in taverns.'

it, I hope to have the Pleasure of seeing you both in London; being,
with great Esteem and Affection, Dr. Sir,

Your obliged Friend & Servt

B. Franklin

By this time Strahan had despaired of getting any payment from Read, and asked Franklin to accept his power
of attorney to recover the debt. To Read himself he wrote
angrily:

> I am really greatly surprized at your Manner of writing, and equally
> at the Difficulties you therein hint at. I was in good hopes your Affairs
> were in a most flourishing Condition from your former Accounts of
> the many Offices you were possessed of. Sure there must be some Mis-
> conduct on your side, else things must be better with you than you
> describe them to be . . . I have by Mr. Wallace sent a Power of Attor-
> ney to Mr. Franklin to receive from you what is due to me. . . I do
> assure you it is no small Inconvenience to me to be out of so much
> money so long.[1]

Franklin was not a very active prosecutor of his London
friend's cause; he told Strahan candidly 'if the debt were to
me, I could not sue him', but this was probably owing to
their relationship. After Franklin's failure Strahan engaged
Hall's services, although he was Read's brother-in-law, and
then those of a Captain Stirling, who was engaged in the
Atlantic trade. This led to fresh disaster, for Stirling not only
got nothing out of Read but himself went bankrupt, owing
Strahan £300. By 1755 Strahan was reduced to writing to
Read directly, but all he received were promises. In 1769 a
Philadelphia lawyer, John Morris, was enlisted but proved
no more successful than the other agents had been. In 1771
Franklin introduced Strahan to Samuel Wharton, the London agent for the Ohio Company, whose brother Thomas
was a Philadelphia merchant. Thomas Wharton agreed to
collect the debt, now twenty-five years old, and in a few
months had secured the payment of £60. Strahan pressed for
the balance, and Wharton managed to secure a bond. But
revolution was in the air, and Wharton realized there was no

---

[1] Nolan, op. cit., 1 December 1748.

prospect of enforcing a settlement; indeed he was himself imprisoned as a suspected loyalist. Finally Read himself re-opened the correspondence in 1785, though without making any mention of payment; he was in any case too late since Strahan had died that summer, leaving it to his son Andrew to write off the balance as a bad debt.

If Franklin failed to recover the Read debt, he made up for it in other ways, as a letter to Strahan dated 18 April 1754 shows:

By Capt. Gibbon I receiv'd a Copy of yours pr the Myrtylla, but she's not yet arrived. I am glad to hear the Bills I sent you for 100£ Sterlg. are accepted, and the Goods were to be ship't soon for Connecticut . . .

I am glad you have sent again the Things that were ship't in Davis. As to that Loss, give yourself no Concern about it. It is mine, and but a Trifle. I do not know or regard what the Custom of Merchants may be in such Cases; but when I reflect how much Trouble I have given you from time to time in my little Affairs, that you never charged me Commissions and have frequently been in advance for me; were the Loss much greater, to be sure I should not suffer it to fall on you.

Benja. Mecom writes me that he has remitted you Thirty Pounds Sterlg. which I am pleas'd to hear. And am glad you have not sent him the great Parcel of Books, &c. which you mention he has wrote for. He is a young lad, quite unacquainted with the World, and I fear would be much embarrassed if he went suddenly into Dealings too deep for his Stock. The People of those Islands might buy his Books, but I know they are very dull Pay, and he would find it impracticable to collect the money when it ought to be sent you. Pray keep him within Bounds, let him have good salable Sortments, but small, and not suffer him to be more than Fifty Pounds in your Debt, if so much. It is best for him to proceed gradually, and deal more as his Stock and Experience increases. I am thankful to you for prudently delaying to send what he so indiscretely wrote for, till you had advis'd me of it. Our Compliments to Mrs. Strahan and your Children . . .

Please to send me the Philosophical Transactions from the End of Martin's Abridgement 1744 to the present time. I suppose they are not abridg'd: Send them large as they came out. Also Dampier's Voyages, 4 vols. 8vo.

Strahan was undoubtedly thinking of his unfortunate

losses through customers like Read and, later, Parker and Mecom when he told Hall in 1770 how much he valued his punctuality in settling his accounts—'I believe there is hardly such another Correspondent, anywhere, with regard to that Particular'.[1] Fifteen years earlier he had told Hall, 'You have no Reason to make the least Apology for my being a little while in Advance for you on his [a bookseller's] account, as you are so very punctual in your Payments to me'.[2] The payments were sometimes considerable. Strahan refers in a letter of 15 July 1761 to an order just dispatched to Hall to the value of £1,727 8s. 4d;[3] in June 1763 Hall's account was debited with £3,449, with a balance of £2,103.

For his part Strahan proved a very diligent and obliging agent for Hall, who appears to have made few complaints about the service he received, considering the volume of goods shipped by Strahan to Philadelphia over the years. To fulfil the orders, Strahan had not only to supply books in which he had a share of the copyright but to run to earth other publishers' titles, sometimes scarce or out of print; he had to supply paper and paper-making moulds, type and ink; he had to transact a great deal of banking business, and to procure various odd items which Hall wanted.

These last are a curious miscellany. 'The Coffee-pot, Tea Pot and Server I have sent in the James and Mary . . . came to £31 3s.'[4] A consignment of cheap watches was unsaleable, though this was not Hall's fault—Strahan had sent them out in a misguided attempt to help the watchmaker. Spectacles were sent on several occasions, some 'of a cheaper Sort', others 'best Stone Spectacle Glasses, for 60 years, 1½ inch Diameter' which cost 15s. each. In 1756 he wrote to Hall:

The black Lead Pencils are of different kinds and Prices; you may choose which kind I shall send for the future. The Penknives are cheap too; but if you want better, I shall send others next time.—The Pocket Books you'll find a very good Sortment; and I hope every

---

[1] *Penna. Mag.*, 7 November 1770. [2] APS, 3 March 1755.
[3] Ibid. [4] *Penna. Mag.*, 4 February 1763.

thing will please; for I assure you I have spared no Pains in getting what I thought was fittest for you.[1]

There are naturally frequent references to printing materials ordered by Hall—moulds for paper, 'weak ink' by the barrel, type and printers' flowers. Paper was of course an important item, though it is not clear what sorts of paper Hall could buy of local manufacture and what had to be imported from England. At least there was competition between the various London paper merchants.

. . . inclosed you have Job Johnson's [the stationer] Account discharged, to whom you see I have paid £105 6s. 8d., for which you'll credit my Acct. I said nothing to him about leaving him, lest, if the Cargo now sent does not turn out as it ought to do, and at least as reasonable as he used to send you, it may be thought for your interest to return to him again. For I have bargained with the Stationer from whom I had this Paper, that if any Article of it is charged higher than you have paid before for it, that they shall deduct it at clearance. This I am sure they will stick to, and therefore I should be glad you would examine every particular of it, and let me forthwith know how it answers, that at least you may be no Sufferer, if you are no Gainer, by the Exchange.[2]

The financial side was mainly a matter of getting Hall's bills accepted. A typical opening to his letters to Hall—since it was of first importance to both men to know what had arrived safely—is: 'Dear Davie, I wrote you by the Mercury in Novr. last and sent you to the Amount of £194 16s. 5d. since which I have received yours of Decr. 21 inclosing Eight Bills, value £398 6s. which with £32 13s. the value of the Books returned by Captain Stirling, makes £430 19s. for which I have given you Credit . . .'[3]

Occasionally there was difficulty; on 22 May 1769 he had to return to Hall a bill for £200 which had been protested for non-payment. Apart from this necessary accountancy, Hall sometimes asked him to undertake other transactions. In 1768 Strahan sold 2,000 Spanish dollars for him for £458 17s. 9d. net. Possibly the buying of lottery tickets

---

[1] APS, 11 September 1756.
[2] APS, ibid.   [3] APS, 3 March 1755.

should be included in this category of activities. Strahan often bought tickets for Hall and his friends, but only once do they seem to have been lucky. Strahan reported on 24 March 1759:

Your Ticketts in the Lottery, viz. No 26,801 and 26,802, the first yours the last Mr. Stewart's are both come up Prizes of £20, which sold for £17 11s. each, the Amount of which, being £35 2s. I have also given you Credit for. The three following Numbers I had for myself, one of which came up also a Prize of £20, and the other two Blanks; by which I lost between £8 and £9 and yet three Prizes out of five Ticketts is not very common. I hope, however, our Luck will be better next. Money is very scarce here just now, occasioned by the great Export of it to the Continent, and the great Demand for Supplies to the Government, so that the Stocks have fallen 8 p Cent within these six Months, and are still falling every Day, as you will see by the Papers; it was lucky, therefore, I did not purchase any Stock for you about that time, for you must have been thereby a considerable Loser.[1]

The insurance of his cargoes to Hall caused Strahan some trouble. On one occasion he overlooked it and more than £60 worth of uninsured books were lost in the *Britannia*. He told Hall at once[2] that he would stand the loss since the lack of cover was his fault. Even then, he did not insure as a matter of course; this must have been in an endeavour to save Hall's pocket, for he always charged him for the cost of insurance when applicable, as well as that of packing and freight. In 1765 he wrote as a postscript to a letter to Hall: 'Since writing my Letter, I have thought better of it, and as it is the Winter Season, I have insured £25 on Sparks and £30 on Egdon, the Charge of which is £1 12s. which I have put to your Debit.'[3] This represents a premium rate of about 2½ per cent. In contrast the rate in 1758 had been 15 guineas per cent; on £220 worth of books shipped in the *Speedwell* on 8 June that year, Strahan charged 'Insurance

---

[1] APS. This was the critical period of the Seven Years War.

[2] APS, 12 November 1753.

[3] Letter dated 14 December: printed in Catalogue 26 (1954) of the Seven Gables Bookshop, N.Y. The names are those of ships' captains.

of £220 at 15 Gs p Ct and Policy—£34 7s. 6d.' in addition to £5 16s. 6d. for 'Freight, Primage, &c.'[1]

An added complication lay in getting the drawbacks due to Hall on insurance premiums.

I have never yet been able to get the Returns on former Insurances settled. Mr. Seton has of late taken to drinking in a beastly Manner, which will be the Ruin of his Family, one of the finest you ever saw, six charming Girls and two Boys; so that I have been at last obliged to leave him, and employ another much against my Inclination; however, as soon as I can get former Returns settled you shall know and be credited for them.[2]

Some months later it was still not possible to report any progress:

The Drawbacks on the Insurances I am endeavouring to get settled, of which I doubt not I shall be able to give a full Account in my next. I find it a very difficult Task; for Mr. Seton, whose proper Business it is, has now rendered himself quite useless by drinking.—The last Parcel by Paton was insured by another Broker, so we shall be quite regular for the future; and as for what is past I will not rest a Moment till they are adjusted.—You'll find by our Accounts that the last, and I believe the only Return that ever was made you was in July, 1749, £8 10s. being 5 p Ct. on £170 sent by Mesnard in April 1748. This was during the last War, and I believe there are some others about that time.[3]

Hall always wanted the latest newspapers and periodicals to be sent by each ship, which entailed arranging for a final delivery on board when the vessel had worked its way down Channel. 'I have some time ago agreed with a Person at Portsmouth to send you out the latest Papers, which I fancy you will find come pretty regularly; but lest they do not, I am determined to take a trip there myself to fix it beyond a Possibility of Mistake for the future, of which you shall hear in my next.'[4] The arrangements often broke down, which is hardly surprising in view of the irregularity of the sailings;

[1] APS.   [2] APS, 24 March 1759.
[3] APS, 17 July 1759.   [4] APS, Strahan to Hall, 10 August 1762.

'Those Newspapers and Magazines are a constant Plague to us both', Strahan exclaimed.[1]

Discounts and prices are perennial difficulties in the export trade, and Strahan was to have his full share of trouble over them. Apart from the discount allowed, the price of books fluctuated with the availability of copies and the style of binding; there was no Net Book Agreement and although new publications were commonly advertised at a certain price, standard works were charged by the bookseller at the price that the market would bear. Many of Strahan's letters to Hall bear upon this point.

I could only get 20 Telemachus, no more being left, and those very dear, for they cost the whole Money I charge for them. All the Glasgow Classicks that could be got I have sent, and as neatly bound as can be.[2] I hope they will please your Friend, for I took some pains about them. I have also sent you six of all the Numbers yet published of the Dictionary I mentioned to you,[3] which I hope you will find no Difficulty in disposing of. I shall send you also six of the first Volume bound in two Parts (being too thick for one) which I believe will be the most eligible way for you, as Binding is dear in America. Let me know by your next if you think you shall want more, or if I have sent too many, for if they stick on hand, I shall think myself obliged to take them back again: And yet after all, I hardly imagine this will be the Case, for it sells extremely well here; but it is a very chargeable Work, requiring £4,000 and upwards to pay Expences, and we print but 5,000; so that our Dependance is on a second Edition, which we are in great hopes of, as we sell above 3,000 already.[4]

On 3 March of the following year Strahan noted ruefully 'I see you have returned the Dictionary in Numbers. I had sent you some more by the last Parcel, which please return also.' He speaks again of high prices:

Herewith comes all you have ordered in these Letters, amounting to £185 16s. 7d., priced as low as possible, and lettered as you desire.

[1] *Penna. Mag.*, 13 February 1768.

[2] The editions of the classics printed by Robert and Andrew Foulis at the Glasgow University Press. By this date they had produced over 30 titles.

[3] *The New Universal Dictionary*, see p. 103.

[4] APS, 9 May 1754.

The Law Books are all the best Editions; and tho' some of them may seem dear, such as Lord Coke's Reports, Crooke's Do. and Coke on Littleton, which are greatly advanced lately, yet you may depend on it, I paid ready money for them within a very Trifle of what I charge you; so that nobody can afford them cheaper. The two Trunks which contain Mr. Franklin's Review of Pennsylvania are not charged to you, nor the Proportion of the Freights of them . . . He and his Son are in good Health; and I still think him one of the most agreeable of Men, and spend many a happy Hour with him.[1]

The 'lettering' was not always as Hall had desired, and some years later Strahan agreed that 'the Mistakes of the Binders are really provoking, but there is no guarding against them always. They are often prodigiously hurried and Blunders will then often be made.'[2] The cost of binding fluctuated: 'In particular, Leather has of late risen to double what it used to sell for, so that the Binders have been forced to raise their prices twopence each Octavo and Twelves Volume . . . It falls very hard upon the Country Booksellers here, who can not easily raise their prices to Gentlemen, tho' they talk of endeavouring it, viz. a 5s. Book to 5s. 6d. etc.'[3]

Although Hall usually wanted his books sent bound and not in sheets, he ordered from Strahan on at least one occasion 'top and bottom cases' and 'Bookcases' and a consignment of eighteen dozen was shipped to him on 8 June 1758. They ranged in size from Large, through Demy and Foolscap to Pott, and in quality from 'Morocco, gilt' to 'Black, plain'.[4]

The trade with America was affected sometimes by the lack of an operative copyright agreement. Strahan pointed out the results of this to Hall:

I don't wonder Hamilton and Balfour charge what they send you cheap; for both printing and binding are cheap in Scotland, and they pay no Copy Money for what they print. Before I directed him to send Books to you, they sent me up a List, priced very cheap indeed, and

---

[1] APS, 17 July 1759. The Franklins were then in London. For the 'Review of Pennsylvania', see p. 106.

[2] *Penna. Mag.*, 7 April 1765. [3] APS, 21 June 1760. [4] APS.

an Offer of a Considerable Discount, 10 or 15 p Ct. if I would take them myself, and send them to you; but I told them that as you made punctual Remittances, the Profit ought to be yours, and that I would not have a sixpence of it.—And in truth, as far as this Stock goes, they can, for the Reasons above assigned, sell on much better Terms than you can have them from London.[1]

Again, if a book were sufficiently popular, Strahan might lose his market because of an American edition. He told Hall, 'I am sorry Charles Vth is printing with you as the Copy Money which was no less than £4,000, has not yet been repaid from the Sale. However, I am determined to print it in 8vo next Summer, in 4 Six Shilling Volumes which I hope few People will grudge to pay for it; and I will take Care that it be done elegantly and correctly.'[2]

On 30 December 1768 Strahan acknowledged the receipt of a book which Hall had returned as too expensive, and continued, 'Every Law Book I send you, except those I am concerned in,[3] I buy with Ready Money, and upon my Word, upon an Average, I have not 5 p Ct. by them. You may easily judge therefore that they are not worth sending; nor would I to any person but yourself, under the full Price marked in Worral's Catalogue. The Profit allowed on Law Books was always trifling'.[4]

A year later he explained to Hall that he had charged Coke's Dictionary 6d. higher than usual:

It is nearly out of print, will not be reprinted for Years, if at all, and cost me the very Money I charge them to you . . . others are charged somewhat higher on account of the increased price of Binding, which still continues so high, that by one third of what I have lately sent you I do not get 2 p Ct.—This is the Reason also why I have bound a few of your Books in Sheep, otherwise I must actually have lost by them. But as you tell me, they will not answer in that way with you, I will send no more in that Manner.[5]

---

[1] APS, 17 July 1759.   [2] *Penna. Mag.*, 8 December 1770.

[3] Strahan had acquired a share in the Law Patent in 1761.

[4] The catalogue was John Worrall's *Bibliotheca Legum or A List of all the Common and Statute Law Books of this Realm &c to 1749.*

[5] *Penna. Mag.*, 11 January 1770.

It was not only law books on which the profits were trifling. In the same letter Strahan refers to the Bible trade, in which his interest was increasingly engaged since he was about to become King's Printer.

What you say about the Bible, I fear, is too true, and that no considerable Sale can be expected with you, as you deal only in the cheapest Sort, which are here hardly worth printing . . . Upon this Branch of the Business I have indeed little Dependance. The chief Profit lies in Acts of Parliament, Proclamations etc. etc. of which I shall now, in a very little time, know more, as the Patent takes place in a few Days.

Hall must have commented on this, for Strahan reverted to the topic a few months later:

What you say in regard to the sale of bibles and prayer books with you, and the low prices of those which have any considerable vent in America, I suspected to be the case. However when I have got anything ready for the market that I imagine may suit you, I will send you a few (and, as you desire, only a few) for a trial. The truth is, as the two Universities here have the privilege of printing bibles etc. as well as the King's Printer, and as they now more than ever avail themselves of that privilege, I have little dependance upon that branch of the Patent. The Acts of Parliament, speeches, addresses, and other public papers, which nobody else can meddle with, are what I chiefly rely on, and are profitable articles being punctually paid for by the government. And yet I shall certainly attempt several schemes in the Bible way, as I have as good a chance for a sale here as the Universities; but still three shops instead of one, make a vast difference in a species of business, where the prices are so low, and the profit depends solely upon the large consumption.[1]

Strahan may have suffered from the competition of the two Universities in his sale of Bibles, but he suffered far more in his general American trade from the unscrupulous activities of a fellow-publisher. For six years his letters to Hall are full of references to James Rivington's undercutting, and the progress of the price war may be traced in the gradations of Strahan's tone from surprise and indignation to

[1] *Booghers Repository*, April 1883: 7 April 1770. For the profits of the Patent, see p. 127.

angry expostulation. The first observations are calmly objective.

What you tell me from Mr. Hunter about the Rivingtons surprised me. I am sure they cannot serve him on these Terms without being considerable Losers. But upon Enquiry I find it was only an Artifice of one of the Brothers (*James*) to wrest him from his old Correspondent Mr. Birt, which has had the desired Effect; but I much question whether Mr. Hunter will not soon have Reason to be tired of it, for *John* Rivington tells me he cannot nor will not send him a general Order upon these Terms, but only such a Sortment as he had before, which are mostly heavy Books, and many of them unlikely to find a Market in America. This is truly the Case, and I have no doubt but Mr. Hunter, who I am told is a very sensible Man and a good Judge of Books, will soon find how little he will avail himself of so seemingly advantageous a Contract. Sixteen p Ct. deducted from the Gentlemen's Prices brings the Price of most Books under what is given Ready Money, how then can he give a Twelvemonth's Credit, and run the Risque of having part of them returned? But however that may be, I am certainly greatly obliged to you for your friendly Declaration of abiding by me at all Events; and would be vastly glad to accommodate you to your entire Satisfaction. I would therefore have you to send me a List of such Books as stick on Hand with you, which perhaps, on looking into, I may be able to take back again without much Inconvenience: and if I can I will: But such Terms as Mr. Rivington's were never heard of till now. I have seen the Invoice, and there are many waste-paper Books among them, and many are considerably overcharged yet I am certain they cannot nor will not continue to serve him on these Terms.—This a short time will discover.[1]

Strahan knew the Rivington brothers well. His printing account with them had opened in 1749, but from the time of this quarrel he worked only for John Rivington, and even he proved an unsatisfactory customer. By 1759 the account had reached a total of £444 18s. 1d.; the contra note states 'N.B. This Account was settled by Mr. John Rivington Octr. 29, 1783'. James Rivington's next move touched Strahan's pocket directly.

[1] APS, 3 March 1755.

James Rivington the Bookseller, whilst he was to my face pretending the greatest Friendship and Attachment, was at the same time endeavouring to undermine me with the Charles Town Library Society, whom I used to serve with Books and by the Death of my particular Friend Mr. John Sinclair he at last succeeded. When I came to the knowledge of this, I immediately determined both for this Reason and for his general indifferent Character to have nothing further to do with him, and therefore refused even to print a large piece of work for him, (a new History of England in 3 vols 4to by Dr. Smollett).[1]

Even worse was to follow, when Rivington tried to supplant Strahan as Hall's London agent.

I shall now, without further Delay, set about answering the Paragraph in your Friend's Letter.—That Mr. James Rivington, who has taken, and every Day takes, the most low, dirty and unwarrantable Methods to supplant his Neighbours (his own Brother not excepted) should endeavour, by all the Arts in his Power, to undermine me with you, is not in the least surprising.—His Enmity to me, and your known good Character as to Punctuality, which I have never made a Secret of, must be strong Incentives with him to wish for your Custom.—The Paragraph is most certainly dictated by him; for I am certain there is not one of the Trade, except himself, who would have dared to assert that I charged you 10 or 20 p Ct. more than other Booksellers charged. I appeal to all my Invoices from the Beginning of our Dealings to the present Time. Compare them with those of any others who deal to America, and see if there be any Truth in the Assertion.—But true it is, that the last Packett, and some other Vessels that have arrived from America lately, have brought heavy Complaints of the same Nature from several Booksellers there to their Correspondents: and by these Accounts it appears plainly that for these two Years past he has exported (mostly on his own Risque) near as many Books as all the rest of the Trade put together; that *some* of these Books he has charged at a less Price than they must have cost him in Ready Money here; and that in all his Letters he professes to deal on much lower Terms than any other ever did. This Conduct of his, tho' looked for by most People who know him, has given a general Alarm, and will determine the Trade, I believe, to take such Measures as will render it impossible for him to undersell them, and rather to sell

[1] APS, 11 September 1756.

A N

I N Q U I R Y

INTO THE

Nature and Caufes

OF THE

WEALTH OF NATIONS.

By ADAM SMITH, LL. D. and F. R. S.
Formerly Profeffor of Moral Philofophy in the Univerfity of GLASGOW.

IN TWO VOLUMES.
VOL. I.

L O N D O N:
PRINTED FOR W. STRAHAN; AND T. CADELL, IN THE STRAND.
MDCCLXXVI.

THE

HISTORY

OF THE

DECLINE AND FALL

OF THE

ROMAN EMPIRE.

By EDWARD GIBBON, Esq;

VOLUME THE FIRST.

Jam provideo animo, velut qui, proximis littori vadis inducti, mare pedibus ingredi-
untur, quicquid progredior, in vaftiorem me altitudinem, ac velut profundum invehi ; et
crefcere pene opus, quod prima quæque perficiendo minui videbatur.

LONDON:

PRINTED FOR W. STRAHAN; AND T. CADELL, IN THE STRAND.
MDCCLXXVI.

for no Profit at all than he should gain his Ends. In this I shall strictly follow their Example, tho' it would have been ungenerous in me to have begun the Practice. For the future, therefore, I desire you would compare my Invoices, not only with those of other Booksellers, but even with his; and if you find I, upon the whole, charge higher than he, I will forfeit all Pretensions to your Friendship forever. I say *upon the whole*, because it is his Custom to charge a few Articles much under the common Price, which he throws out as a Bait, in order to make it believed that the rest are charged in Proportion. In those he sends on his own Risque there are also a great Number of old Trash, little better than Waste paper, which are finely bound and lettered, that can never sell any where. I dare say some of the Parcel he sent you are of that Kind.

But you will naturally ask how he comes to be enabled to undersell every body else without ruining himself?—I will tell you how.— About a year ago, under Pretence of want of Money, he made a Sale of all his Copies, some of which I, among others, purchased. His real Drift we could not then dive into, but it since appears, that he is determined to pirate every good Book in the Trade. He has already printed a good many. These *Modern Travels* are a Transcript of a few of the best Books in that way, and are printed by him, tho' he does not choose to put his Name to the Title. The great Success he has met with in Smollet's History has made him slacken his Career a little, lest his Brothers should make Reprisals upon him while it is publishing in Numbers and interrupt the Sale. But as soon as that is over, it is agreed he will stick at nothing.—As to the Assertion, *that you can have Books directly from the Booksellers as cheap as I have them*, it is absolutely false. The Booksellers always consider me as one of them, I buy upon as good Terms as any other Person whatever, and am myself possest of the Property of more Copies than most of the Booksellers in London can boast of; for all the Money I could spare I have for several Years laid out in that Way. Mr. R. has few or no Copies; and without he pirates those of other People, cannot serve any body on even so good Terms as his Brethren.

What I here advance in regard to him, is known to the whole Trade; you may therefore make any Use of this Letter you see proper, and make it as public as you please . . . But as it would be most ingrateful in me to suffer you to be a Loser by your Attachment and Friendship, so you may depend upon it, that rather than that should be the Case, I will serve you without a Farthing Profit, or even with some Loss.

The Booksellers are about contriving some Plan, by which they will make a Difference in the Price of those Books that are sold to go abroad, and those for Home Consumption, in order to save the Trade to America from falling into the Hands of a Man who will stick at nothing to accomplish his Designs. This is a Circumstance much in my Favour, and will enable me, I hope, to supply you, for the future, to your entire Satisfaction.

Mr. Hunter (whom I see often with Mr. Franklin) tells me, that among the Books he formerly had of Rivington, on which he had 16 p Ct. Discount, with liberty to return what he did not sell, as you may remember you wrote to me, there were a great many extreme dull Books, which bore no Price here; so that reckoning them at the full Price, the Abatement was not near so great as at first sight appeared.—Your Orders, however, have never consisted of any such dull Books: and yet, very often, I am told, Books of that kind may be sold in America—Did you ever think it adviseable to order a Cargo consisting partly of such as these, I could afford you that or a larger Discount, and venture also to take back what you could not sell in a reasonable time.—But enough of this Subject at present. Our future Dealings shall shew how much I am disposed to remove all just Causes of Complaint.—You may shew this Letter to any Person you think proper. And if Mr. Dunlop proposes to deal in the Book-way, you may assure him I can and will serve him as cheap as any body whatever. I have indeed a pretty Assortment of Copies, and a large Stock of Books, which is continually increasing; and having now generally some Ready Money by me, I am really in a Capacity of dealing in Books to more Advantage than nine of ten of the Booksellers in London.[1]

For all his indignation at Rivington's prices, Strahan felt obliged to match them in order to maintain his connection with Hall, as a subsequent letter shows:

I have perused the Comparison between Mr. Rivington's Prices and mine, which are indeed considerable and may very justly alarm you: But it does not at all surprize me, who know how he comes by the Books. There is not a Copy hardly that is good for any thing which he has not pirated, or is not now pirating in some part of Britain. He went to Scotland last Summer, and set all the Presses agoing there with English Books. Dyche's Dictionary is now printing for

[1] APS, 11 July 1758.

him at Aberdeen, which is the sole Property of Mrs. Ware, a Widow
with seven Children—Bailey's Dictionary at Edinburgh by Hamilton
and Balfour, in which his own Brother has a large Share—[   ]'s
Meditations, the Property of which he sold about two Years ago, he is
printing somewhere in the Country—Ruddiman's Rudiments he has
lately printed here in London, the Property of old Thomas Ruddiman's Widow, who is now prosecuting him for it, as are also the Company of Stationers for printing their Psalters, & the Proprietors of
Watts's Works for printing his Psalms and Hymns. It is also lately
discovered that he has printed Clark's Introduction, Ruddiman's
Cordery, Bailey's Exercises and Pope's Works, for all which, and for
every thing else that may afterwards be discovered, as soon as Evidence
can be procured of his selling them, separate Prosecutions will be
commenced against him, so that it is not unlikely he will in the End
lose as much by this dirty and scandalous Dealing as he once thought
to get by it. . . .[1] His scheme was a pretty extensive one, viz. to undersell every body, in order to get a large Country Trade, and then to
print every saleable Book; but he has already fairly run himself aground
by going too precipitantly to work, and must have been at a full Stop,
even if he had not been called to account by those he has injured. The
Scots Booksellers, by the same Methods, can undersell any body here,
and as far as their Stock goes, their Books must come vastly cheap.[2] But
to trouble you no more on this Subject, I shall only add that tho' I
am certain he has charged many Articles *cheaper*, and many more
as cheap as he could buy them himself for *Ready Money* (but those
he pirates come sufficiently cheap to him) I will accommodate my
Prices to his, be what they will; for I would rather, with all my Heart,
lose £100 a Year than he should gain his Ends; and surely if I was to
lose Money, there is no Man on Earth I would so soon choose to give
it to than yourself, and I beg you will use no Ceremony in telling me
when I seem to deviate in the least from this Resolution. Mr. R will be
sending you a Parcel every now and then, whether you order them
or not, so that you will have frequent Opportunities of comparing his

[1] I do not know to what *Meditations* Strahan refers. Amongst the other titles are:
Thomas Dyche, *A New General English Dictionary*, 3rd ed. 1740, or possibly his
The Spelling Dictionary, 3rd ed. 1731; Nathan Bailey, *Dictionary*, 1731 and many
eds., and also his *English and Latin Exercises*; Thomas Ruddiman, *Rudiments of the
Latin Tongue*, 1714 and many eds.; John Clarke, *An Introduction to the Making of
Latin*, 1740 and many eds. Clarke was also the compiler of *A Select Century of
Cordery's Colloquies*; I do not know of an edition of Corderius by Ruddiman.
[2] See p. 78.

Prices with mine—I shall take your Hint in regard to Mr. Dunlop and am grateful to you for giving it me; as well as for your honest, candid and friendly Behaviour to me in all our Transactions, which I shall never forget, nor ever think I can sufficiently acknowledge.[1]

Strahan was as good as his word and although his refusal to be undersold by Rivington must have been expensive, he kept his account with Hall. Later in that year he wrote to Hall, 'The Plays and Magazines I have charged at $4\frac{1}{2}d$. agreeable to Mr. Rivington; tho' they cost me exactly the same in Ready Money. Nay, there are many Articles charged *cheaper* than they cost, rather than be outdone by him—$5d$. for Magazines and Plays is as universal a Charge as a halfpenny for a halfpenny Loaf.'[2]

This unprofitable trading continued for another twelve-month; but then with what triumph Strahan reported his rival's downfall: 'This is to acquaint you that Mr. James Rivington broke last week for £20,000, or rather £30,000 . . . Several Booksellers are great sufferers, many Printers very deep, and four or five Bookbinders quite ruined . . . Riv. will hardly pay 10s. in the pound.'[3] Justice, one feels, has won the day and the principles of sound business have been vindicated. Rivington disappears from the scene with a final reference, in one of Strahan's letters in 1761, to his departure for New York with a cargo of books collected on the credit of Mrs. Rivington's annuity of £300 a year. His subsequent career was eventful. After failing in business in Boston he set up as a bookseller in New York, starting in 1773 *Rivington's New York Gazeteer*, a pro-government journal that brought him into trouble with the colonists, who twice mobbed his establishment in 1777. He returned to England, purchased a new press and, on going back to America, was appointed King's Printer for New York; he then began to publish *Rivington's New York Loyal Gazette*. About 1781 he was said to have turned spy and to have

[1] APS, 24 March 1759. [2] APS, 17 December 1759.
[3] APS, 7 December 1760. It is hard to make out from the manuscript whether the doubtful payment will be 10d. or 10s. in the pound.

furnished Washington with important information. He remained in New York after it was evacuated by British troops, changing the title of his paper to *Rivington's New York Gazette and Universal Advertiser*. This came to a stop in 1783, and James Rivington passed the remainder of his life in comparative poverty.[1]

The library business in America was important to Strahan. I do not know whether he recovered the account of the 'Charles Town Library Society' after Rivington's bankruptcy, but ten years later he was energetically exporting books to the Union Library in Philadelphia. It is curious that Hall, as the city's principal importer of books, apparently showed no desire to supply the library himself. Strahan wrote, for instance, to the Secretary:

> I am favoured with yours of the 3rd February, on behalf of the Union Library Company of Philadelphia, inclosing a Bill of Exchange for £64 12s. 1d. which is accepted and when paid shall be placed to the Credit of the Society, and an Order for some Books, which are herewith sent amounting to £41 13s. agreeable to the inclosed Invoice. I hope you will find them all right; and that I shall be favoured with the Continuance of the Society's Order. I shall always charge them as low as possible, and use my best Endeavours to procure the Editions they write for. Several of the present Order are now out of print; but if I can afterwards pick up any of them, they shall be sent by next Opportunity. There is in the Trunk a small Paper Parcel directed to Mr. David Hall which you will please order to be delivered to him, as soon as it arrives . . .[2]

Strahan never gave up hope of seeing his old friend again. He refers in several letters to a compact between them that Hall should cross the Atlantic for a visit once he had settled himself in Philadelphia; but the success of his establishment there, and no doubt his wife's indifferent health, made it impossible. Strahan never admitted the impossibility—after all, had not Franklin made the journey?—forgetting that Franklin was able to come to England because in Hall

---

[1] I owe the information on his career in New York to Mr Gerald Rivington.
[2] Haverford College Library, 14 May 1767.

he had a partner to run the business. In 1756, for example, he tried to tempt Hall once again:

Thus, my dear Davie, have I imparted to you all my Joys; and have a peculiar Pleasure in so doing, as I know your honest Heart will rejoice with me, and feel an Accession of happiness yourself in being informed of that of your old Friend. How pleased should I be to have you here, to see every thing, to talk over old Stories, to enumerate past Difficulties now happily surmounted, and to communicate to each other that mutual Satisfaction which an early Friendship can alone inspire. I have forebore to mention this great while, because you forbid me, but pray tell me, may I never expect to have the Pleasure of seeing you in Britain? Shall we never travel to Scotland together, and view the many Changes that have happened in Auld Reekie since you left it? Lord, how it would strike you, were you just now at the Cross! Take my Word for it, such a Jaunt would give you more Joy than you can easily conceive. I am sure there would not be two happier Souls in the Country. But I will now forbear, and say nothing further on this Subject till you inform me you have some Prospect of putting this agreeable Scheme in Execution.[1]

The passing years and Hall's continued inability to abandon his business for a period of months did not deter Strahan. He wrote in 1762:

And now you mention a Meeting, which I have so long wished for, I am very sorry you mortify me so far as to say there are small Hopes of its taking place. I still think it may. True, it will be both inconvenient and expensive to you; and what then? Have we not both more than ever we had reason to hope for? And may we not, without Censure from others, or Self Reflection, take upon us to spend a small part of it in indulging our own Inclinations, especially in a Way so very natural, and so extremely excusable, as seeing our native Country and our old Friends once at least before we must, in the Course of Nature, leave all? Let this have its due weight with you. You may get your Business managed for you by another for a few Months; not so well, I would allow, as you may yourself, but tolerably; and lay your Account with sacrificing something to the procuring so much Pleasure as a Voyage to Britain must certainly give you. On your Arrival I will lay all Business aside, and devote my whole time to the travelling

[1] APS, 17 September 1759.

with you from one End of the Island to the other, and indulging ourselves to whatever Amusements we like best.—I know we shall be
happy— Nor would I have you look on it as an impracticable Scheme.
I have several times made Excursions, which tho' necessarily attended
with some Inconvenience never with so great as to deter me from
repeating the Experiment whenever my Inclination prompted me to
take a little Relaxation. Come then, I conjure you, next Spring, and
let us *personally* renew old Friendship. You will be surprised to find
me so much the very same Person you left me; as young, as blyth, and
as frolicksome as ever, tho' very near being a Grandfather.[1]

In 1766 Hall became sole proprietor of the business,
which had been paying Franklin around £500 a year; but
even in this new capacity he felt unable to leave Philadelphia.

Strahan's extensive export trade to America, as well as his
friendships with Franklin and Hall, led him to follow with
the utmost interest the relations between the home country
and the colonies. His politics are examined elsewhere; it is
enough here to remark that his desire to maintain his market
possibly induced him to make light of the gathering clouds.
In his view trade and not principles were in question, and
he found it hard to foresee a real storm until it had broken.
At least he could realize that the political situation added
another and final barrier to the prospect of Hall's coming
back to Britain for a holiday.

Hall warned Strahan of the probable effects of the duties
levied by the home Government, and indeed had cause to
feel them himself, since he stopped publication of *The Pennsylvania Gazette* for a short time in fear of incurring penal-
ties under the Stamp Act.[2] Hall's letter book is in the possession of the Salem County Historical Society; it records
various letters to Strahan in 1770 about the increasing difficulties of trade. On 18 June for example he wrote:

On Tuesday last, there was a general Meeting of the Merchants,

[1] APS, 10 August 1762. His elder daughter Rachel was about to have her first child.

[2] He had not been able to obtain the stamps. Strahan wrote to him on 14 December 1765 that he had been ill-advised: 'You could not possibly run any Risque in
printing it as usual, when no Stamps could be got; and I dare say you have begun
again before now.'

and others, at the State-house here, to consider what was to be done with respect to the Importation of Goods from Great Britain on the partial Repeal of the Revenue Act, when it was Unanimously agreed, that the Non-Importation Agreement as entered into by the Merchants on the Tenth of March, 1769, should be strictly adhered to, without the least variation until the Duty on Tea, as well as on the other Articles included in that Law, should be taken off.

In the Papers by this Vessel, you will see the Resolves of Boston and New York relating to the Rhode Islanders, for basely breaking thro' their Non-Importation Agreement; also the Conduct of the New Yorkers to Captain Spier who lately brought in a large Quantity of Goods from Glasgow contrary to their Agreement. And you will find, that as fast as Goods may be sent from England contrary to the Inclination of the People on the Continent in general as fast will they be sent back again, the Americans being resolved, (except for a few mercenary Wretches, whose Number is so small that it is not worth mentioning) closely to stick to their Non-Importation Agreement, be the Consequences what they will . . .

It is quite clear from this on what side Hall's sympathies lay; even so, this letter concludes with a list of books to be sent 'by the first Vessel for this Port'. Strahan was inclined to dismiss these warnings. He pointed out to Hall that New York merchants had been buying woollen goods heavily, and still believed that 'the Matter now in Dispute between us a mere Bagatelle'.[1] Earlier he had observed to Hall that:

. . . exports from this country to America in general are not at all, or but very little diminished; at least not so far as to be any where, or among any species of manufacturers, sensibly felt . . . It seems, and indeed the thing speaks for itself, that tho' the exports to Boston, New York, and Philadelphia have been considerably diminished during this contest, those to Rhode Island, Quebec and other places, have proportionately increased, and that the goods there imported find their way to the other provinces by the back settlements, or by some means or other. Of the truth and practicality of this, you are a better judge than I can be.[2]

Hall continued to order books and Strahan to supply them, although in Hall's letter book during 1770 and 1771

[1] *Penna. Mag.*, 24 August 1770.   [2] *Booghers Repository*, 7 April 1770.

there may be detected, says Dr. Whitfield J. Bell, Jr., 'a note of mounting impatience and even asperity at the delays and inaccuracies in filling his orders'. This should probably be attributed to Strahan's new responsibilities as King's Printer rather than to any interruption of the channels of trade.

David Hall died at the age of 58 on 17 December 1772, before he could find himself divided by war from his old friend in London. Strahan wrote to the son, his namesake William Strahan Hall, to condole with him on the death of his father, whose character and abilities he praised with all the warmth at his command. But politics soon began to master trade: in the last of the letters to his Philadelphia correspondents, written to young William on 5 July 1775, Strahan speaks sadly of 'our present Quarrel, of which at present I see no End. I am particularly sorry that Blood has begun to be shed . . . In any Shape, every Step leads to our mutual Destruction.'[1] Within a few months, young Hall was to find himself busy printing the paper money issued by Congress; and the long series of entries on the Hall account in Strahan's ledgers ends on 11 June 1776 with a balance due of £363 10s. 11d.

[1] *Penna. Mag.*

7

Family Life

STRAHAN often refers to his wife and children in his letters
to Hall, usually in the course of a paragraph or two of personal news after business and the politics of the day have
been dealt with. Hall knew Margaret Strahan as well as her
husband before he emigrated to Philadelphia, and Strahan
sometimes speaks of her as 'your Mother' when writing to
him. Strahan's desire to persuade Hall to come home for a
holiday was doubtless another reason for seasoning his letters
with news of his family and of common friends. In 1753, for
instance, he reports on his children's well-being:

My family are all in perfect health; the two youngest Children,
Andrew and Peggy are at nurse at Chigwell; Rachie at a Boarding-
school at Bromley in Kent; and Billy and George at Brompton, a mile
beyond Hyde Park, with their Uncle, Mr. Elphinston, who has just
opened an Academy there. He is extremely well qualified for that
Employment, and as he is one who makes a Conscience in doing his
Duty, which I already experience, I have no doubt but he will succeed well. Billy is now near 14 but as he is in such good hands, I
intend not to take him home for a Year or two yet. George is also a
very fine Fellow; and all of them very promising. Inclosed you have a
Line from Mr. Elphinston; and I know if it lies in your Power to
recommend him you will do it; especially when I tell you that if he
was noways related to me, his Merit in his Profession, and his extreme
Assiduity, would induce me to prefer him to every body else I ever

knew. You would be surprized to see the Improvement my little Rogues have made in the little while they have yet been with him.[1]

Rachel was probably sent to boarding school on the recommendation of Johnson. Mrs. Thrale records a conversation with him in which he had said:

Boarding Schools are made to relieve Parents from that Anxiety which only torments them: A Man and his Wife cannot agree which Child to fondle, nor how to fondle them; so they put them to School, & remove the Cause of Contention—Strahan & his Lady added he are a good proof of all this; the little Girl pokes her head, the Mother reproves her the Father says My dear don't mind your Mama but do your own Way—Mrs. Strahan complains to me on't: Madam says I your Husband is right enough: he is with you two hours in the Day only; & then you torment him by making the Girl cry—Is not ten hours sufficient for you to tutor her? put her to School however, & have done; tis better she were away than you should quarrel.[2]

James Elphinston, Margaret Strahan's brother, had settled in London that year to establish his academy. He moved it in time from Brompton to Kensington. The school had a mixed reputation. Franklin sent his illegitimate grandson there, presumably at Strahan's suggestion, and in 1773 Johnson sent a boy to him.[3] But in 1772 Johnson had remarked of Elphinston to Boswell that 'He has a great deal of good about him; but he is also very defective in some respects. . . . I would not put a boy to him whom I intended for a man of learning. But for the sons of citizens, who are to learn a little, get good morals, and then go to trade, he may do very well.'[4]

Elphinston's qualifications consisted in his having been a tutor in two households and in his publication of the Edinburgh edition of *The Rambler*. Despite the flattering terms in which Strahan wrote of him to Hall, the brothers-in-law fell out on a number of occasions. As well as the quarrel mentioned in the next letter, there was a disagreement over Elphinston's proposal in 1776 to translate Martial.

[1] APS, 1 November. [2] Balderston: *Thraliana*, Oxford, 1942, I, 178.
[3] *Letters*, 304. [4] *Life*, II, 171.

Both Garrick and Johnson had advised him against the scheme but he persisted in enlisting subscribers. Strahan, said Johnson, 'sent him a subscription of fifty pounds, and said he would send him fifty more, if he would not publish'. 'GARRICK: "What! eh! is Strahan a good judge of an epigram? Is he not rather an *obtuse* man, eh?" JOHNSON: "Why, Sir, he may not be a judge of an epigram: but you see he is a judge of what is not an epigram." '[1]

A theory of Elphinston's led to a much later disagreement with Strahan. This was his wildly conceived system of rationalized spelling, eventually published as *Propriety ascertained in her Picture*. It was obviously repugnant to a printer but secured, according to a rather unlikely note in his obituary in *The Gentleman's Magazine*, the backing of Franklin as 'his great, if not his only supporter'. Boswell described Elphinston as 'a worthy hospitable man; but has an affectation, a pedantry, and an anxiety to please that makes him in some measure disagreeable. He had a foolish laugh too, a made giggle.'[2] Nichols records his old-fashioned dress, crowned with a bag-wig and a cocked hat, and set off by an amber-headed cane. In the company of ladies, when 'bosoms were at all exposed, he would fidget from place to place, look askance, with a slight convulsion of his left eye . . . and say, "Oh yes, indeed! it is very pretty, but it betrays more fashion than modesty".'[3] He was as renowned for his habit of correcting other persons' pronunciation as for his crank spelling.

To return to his early days as a schoolmaster, his nephew Billy Strahan did not spend long in his care. Only six months after his praises of Elphinston's ability Strahan wrote to Hall:

I hope you are all well, and Billy [young William Hall] in a thriving way, as all my young Folks are. My Billy was bound to myself last Month, and seems to take with the Business bravely. I did not purpose to take him home so soon, but a Difference happening between Mr. Elphinston and me, in which he used me extremely ill, and which

---

[1] *Life*, III, 258.   [2] *Boswell Papers*, 9, 4 April 1772.
[3] *Literary Anecdotes*, III, 30.

is absolutely irreconcileable, and breaks off all Connexion with his family and mine, I thought it needless to put him to any other School. As for George, I have sent him to Kew from whence he was taken to come to his Uncle.[1]

The difference was not soon composed. Strahan was still in an unforgiving mood a year later.

My Family are at present in a good deal of Distress, Andrew, Peg, and young Davie, beside a Maidservant, being all at present down in the Small Pox; but, thank God, they are every one like to do well, and then it will be a good Job over; tho' in the mean time my Wife is prodigiously fatigued. However, the Hopes of seeing them all speedily restored to health keeps up her Spirits, and makes her undergo the Toil with Alacrity. They are all very full, but I hope they won't be marked, being a very good Kind. Your Namesake is really a charming little Rogue, and Peg has long been the Favourite of everybody. All the rest are bravely. Bill will make a good Printer, and what is better, an honest Man. George continues at School, as does Rachie . . .

The Difference between Mr. Elphinston and me can never be made up, as you shall see by a Letter or two which shall be sent to you as soon as Billy has Leisure to transcribe them. Luckily his Sister was witness to his Behaviour, and is as sensible of Weakness and Folly, and of his ill usage of me, as I can be; so we are both of a Mind in that Respect, and she is so well convinced of his Obstinacy, that she desires as little to see him as I do.[2]

The change of school had no ill-effects on the children, in their father's estimation. He told Hall on 11 September 1756:

Rachie comes home from Boarding school at Christmas, and is almost marriageable; and a charming Girl. George, a fine blunt, good-natured, honest Fellow. Andrew, a very decent little Rogue; and Peg, the favourite of everybody. Poor thing, she has now ill of a fever, but is not thought to be in danger. My Wife has been long out of Order with a Cholicy Disorder, which has not yet left her. But every thing else goes extremely well with me. I have generally more Business than any of my Brethren here; and am now so very well established, and I thank God, in such general Esteem, that nothing can now do me any Prejudice in my Trade; and if Bill follow the Path which I have

[1] APS, 9 May 1754. [2] APS, 3 March 1755.

95

chalked out to him, it will in all probability fix the Happiness of my Family upon a firm and lasting Foundation.[1]

Margaret Strahan never recovered her full health after the birth and early death of her son David. Strahan had told Hall in May 1754 that he had been 'greatly indisposed with a most severe cold ... My Wife was also in the same Condition ... What made it the more severe with her, was her happening to be breeding at the time, of which I hope to give you a good Acct. by and bye.' In November he told Hall that his printing house was very busy, adding 'I have observed for a long time that I am always hurried when my Wife lies in. She was safely delivered of a very fine Boy on the 20th of last Month, whom I have named after you, *David*. They are both doing very well.'[2] As we have just seen, the infant had smallpox with the other children in March 1755; on the 13th of that month he died. Margaret had lost two other children in infancy, Samuel and Anne; indeed to rear five children out of eight was fortunate by the standards of the century. Perhaps it was her illness during this last pregnancy, or the fatigue of nursing her family through the smallpox, that weakened her health. Strahan's letters thereafter are filled with references to her illnesses, in particular a form of gout and a 'bilious, cholicy disorder'. Although he can sometimes report to Hall that she 'is tolerably well', she was more often 'ill', 'far from well', even 'dangerously ill'.

Strahan's sympathy for David Hall in the loss of several of his children sprang from a fellow-feeling:

We were much concerned to hear of the Death of your little Boy, and most sincerely sympathise with you and Mrs. Hall on your repeated Losses of this Kind, because we know, that of all others you will feel them most. I hope Billy will be preserved to you, and that all your Misfortunes of this Nature are now at an End ... On these Occasions I cannot say any thing better than what is commonly said by the good old People of Scotland, I hope these Dispensations will be sanctified to you. For surely one may, without the Imputation of Enthusiasm, fairly conclude that such Events, however grievous, or

[1] APS.   [2] APS, 9 November 1754.

detrimental to our interests in our present View of things they seem
to be, are upon the whole kindly intended; and it is obvious, that they
have a direct Tendency to loosen our Attachment for the Things of
this Life, to raise our Minds to aspire after more durable Felicity than
our present State can afford us, and in the mean while teach us to
acquiesce with some Degree of Patience under all our Losses, Afflic-
tions, and Disappointments.[1]

Strahan himself seems to have enjoyed good health.
Admittedly he told Hall in 1758 that he had been advised
to take up riding for the good of his constitution, but six
months later he broke the tendon in his right leg and we
hear no more of the riding. Despite his own good health and
his wife's apparent frailty, she was to outlive him, if only
by a month. His specific for all disorders was a jaunt. His
devotion to London did not extend to its air. He was constantly dispatching his wife to Bath, sometimes to Salisbury
and even to Scotland under his own escort, when his sons
were old enough to keep an eye on the business. Once at
least he left her in London to look after the younger children
while he made a trip to Scotland; he wrote to Hall:

I am very glad you have all got well over the Measles: and hope
next to hear of your poor Wife's being in a fair Way of Recovery; for
I am sensible that if she does not get the better of her Ailments, your
Loss will not be repairable. Next Week I intend to set out for Scotland, along with my Daughter Rachel, who has been for some time in
a bad State of Health. This I do partly to try whether so long a
Journey will do her some Service; and partly to see my old Mother
for the last time, as she is now in a declining Way; but chiefly to take
some Care of a young Family of Six Children, who have now nobody
to look to for Support but myself. These are my poor Sister's, who died
in Childbed last Month. Her Husband is an absolute Fool, and can do
nothing for his Family; so that the whole Burden will lie on me, and I
cannot nor will not see them want. Poor Creature, her Death is the
less to be regretted, as she had no Prospect of seeing an End to the
Difficulties in which she has been for a long time involved.[2]

Rachel was then seventeen. Strahan's sister, Helen, a year

[1] APS, 1 November 1753.   [2] APS, 17 July 1759.

younger than himself, had married in 1742 William Gordon, a dyer. By the time Strahan came to draw up his will, only four of these Gordon children had survived: William and George, and Ann and Isabella. There is a glimpse of two of the children in a letter Strahan wrote to Sir Alexander Dick, in Edinburgh: 'The Account you give me of my Niece [presumably Isabella, for Ann had married one Nesbitt] is most agreeable. We are much obliged to you for the Notice you take of her, and for the Employment your Lady gives her. I hope she will continue to do well. Her Brother George is now with me, and promises to make a good Boy and a good Printer.'[1]

How Strahan settled the children at the time of his sister's death is not clear, but he did make some arrangements. In October 1759 he reported the success of his trip to Hall:

Last Friday I returned from Scotland, after a very pleasant Excursion of near ten Weeks, and had the finest Weather ever known in this Country. I found all my Friends in pretty tolerable Plight; only my Sister's Family of Children were in a very poor Condition, but I have disposed of them in the best Manner I was able, which cost much Trouble as well as Expence. I have been in the Highlands also, where if you remember I went 22 years ago to see Mrs. Wishart, and as the Air of that Place seemed to agree with Rachel, I have left her behind me till next Summer, by which time I hope she will be restored to a confirmed State of Health.[2]

In the following June he gave Hall a budget of news on the whole family. 'My Wife is returned from Bath greatly recovered; Rachel is still in Scotland pretty well; Billy is Director-General above Stairs; and George is still with him, tho' I think of making a Bookseller of him soon. Andrew and Peggy are still at Boarding School, all in good health.'[3] He explained his plans for the boys more fully a year later in a letter written from Bromley, where he had gone on a jaunt with Franklin.

[1] 12 May 1770. The letter is in the possession of Mrs. Dick-Cunyngham of Prestonfield.
[2] APS.   [3] APS, 21 June 1760.

As to the Printing-house, my Son Billy so effectually takes the Care of that off my Hands, that I am not in it twice in a month . . . My Son George is now commenced Bookseller, having put him to one Mr. Durham in the Strand (formerly Partner to Mr. Wilson, and one whom I brought up from Edinr. when I was there in the year 1749) to serve the rest of his Apprenticeship. I am at present Partner with Mr. Durham myself tho' it is carried out in his name only; and at the Expiration of George's time I intend to resign my interest in the Shop to him, which I hope will do very well. Billy as I told you makes a most compleat Printer . . . my Son Andrew who is now between 11 and 12 I purpose to make a Stationer of, so that they will all have a Connection with one another, and yet not interfere. This is my Scheme; how it will answer I shall be better able to tell you some years hence, if we live so long.[1]

Like so many neat schemes devised by parents, it did not answer at all. Billy was to leave his father in order to set up as a printer on his own, George jibbed at any connection with the trade, and Andrew alone was left to carry on the business.

[1] APS, 15 July 1761.

8

The Franklins: Warburton

IT was after the two printers had been corresponding for fourteen years that Franklin held out to Strahan serious hopes of a meeting. His earlier plans of coming to London in 1749 or 1750 had come to nothing, but he had a clearer prospect when he wrote to Strahan in 1757.

> I shall not fail on every occasion to recommend you to my friends in the book account. I wish I could give you any hopes of soon receiving your debt of J. Read. Mr. Hall, no doubt, writes you more fully concerning him. It gives me great pleasure to hear so good an account of our son Billy.[1] In return, let me tell you that our daughter Sally is indeed a very good girl, affectionate, dutiful, and industrious, has one of the best hearts, and though not a wit, is, for one of her years, by no means deficient in understanding. She already takes off part of her mother's family cares. This must give you and Mrs. Strahan pleasure. So that account is partly balanced.
>
> Our Assembly talk of sending me to England speedily. Then look out sharp, and if a fat old fellow should come to your printing-house and request a little smouting depend upon it 'tis your affectionate friend and humble servant . . .[2]

Franklin with his son and two servants reached London on 26 July 1757. He must have sent word at once to Strahan

---

[1] Strahan's eldest boy, then seventeen. The project of a marriage between him and Sally Franklin was being half-seriously considered.

[2] The Huntington Library, HM 22614: 31 January 1757. 'Smouting' was casual jobbing work.

who called upon him on the 27th where he was staying at
Mill Hill. Any qualms he may have felt at meeting in the
flesh one who had proved so delightful a friend on paper
were immediately dispelled. Franklin being the man he was,
Strahan was captivated at once. He wrote to Mrs. Franklin
in Philadelphia, 'For my own part, I never saw a man who
was, in every respect, so perfectly agreeable to me. Some
are amiable in one view, some in another, he in all.' He took
to young William Franklin also—'one of the prettiest young
gentlemen I ever knew from America'—though this compliment may have been less pleasing to Deborah Franklin than
Strahan supposed; there is some evidence that she was
jealous of her bastard stepson. The visitors found lodgings
in Craven Street, whence the intercourse with New Street
was constant.

Franklin of course was no stranger to London or to its
printing houses. In 1724 he had crossed the Atlantic, deluded by false promises of help and credit in stocking a
bookshop, and found himself in London almost friendless
and with only a few pounds in his pocket. He was fortunate
in being master of a craft and promptly found work as a
journeyman, first at Palmer's office[1] and then at Watts's. His
Memoirs include a well-known description of how the work
was carried on at Watts's; conditions in the trade had not
altered much 33 years later when he visited Strahan's new
printing house.

As has been noted, Strahan had moved from Wine Office
Court to 10 Little New Street in 1748, but within a few years
he once again found himself cramped for space and had to
enlarge his premises. The printing of Johnson's Dictionary
had helped to establish him in the forefront of the London
trade while at the same time it put him in touch with the
leading booksellers. It is a token of his ability that in less
than fifteen years from his arrival in London he should
have felt the need to expand and should have been able to

[1] In Bartholomew Close, and now restored to its original function as the Lady
Chapel of St. Bartholomew-the-Great.

finance the expansion. In 1753 he told Hall about his new building:

In a former Letter I gave you a particular Description of my House, which you may remember is a pretty large one; and yet, as I hinted last Year, it is really become too small for me. For this twelvemonth past I have employed seven Presses; and if I had had Room, could have kept two or three more. I have therefore taken a Lease (of 61 Years) of Six Old Houses, belonging to the Goldsmith's Company, which lay contiguous to mine, for which I pay Six Pounds a Year. These I have pulled down, and am erecting an additional Building of 40 feet square, two Stories high, which will cost me about £500. A large Sum! but it will render my Habitation exceeding commodious, for I shall have room for 4 more Presses, and Compositors in proportion, with Ware-house-Room, etc, and a pretty piece of Ground to add to my Garden besides. In short, when it is finished, which will be about Christmas, my House and Garden will stand upon a Spot of Ground near 90 feet square, and be beyond Dispute the largest and best Printing-house in Britain; and I have, and am likely to have, as much Business as I can possibly do; so that you see how bravely Matters go with me. It is true, the precipitate Increase of my Business, with the dilatory pay of the Booksellers, this extraordinary Expence, with some other acciden-tal Losses (some of them heavy ones) have hitherto kept me bare of Money; but I daresay I shall get the better of that too, if I live a few Years; and am, and have long been, as I have the greatest Reason to be, not only content, but thankful in the highest Degree.[1]

A few months later Strahan could report that 'My new house is compleatly finished, and I have at present Nine Presses going, which, you know, will do a great deal of Work. I have now the most complete, large and com-modious House that can be.'[2] This was too good to last, and business fell off. In August he wrote to Hall:

The printing Trade has been slacker here this Summer than I have known of it a long while. However having two or three Books of large Numbers, I have made a Shift to keep 6 or 7 Presses going all this Time; but I assure you there is not that Profit in proportion attending the carrying on a great Stroke of Business, which requires a vast deal of extraordinary Expence, as accrues from a snug Trade managed all

---

[1] APS, 1 November.   [2] APS, 2 February 1754.

under one's own Eye with Oeconomy and Frugality: So that tho' I am doing exceedingly well, you must not expect to hear of my growing rich in a hurry.

These are the doubts of a man who wonders if he has stretched his resources too far. Strahan now began to wish that his sons could come to his help in the management of the printing house, and he pushed on Billy, the eldest, as fast as he could. But at least his financial worries were soon over; as he reported to Hall on 9 November 1754, 'I am at present very busy, having no less than Nine Presses going wh. is indeed a great deal of Business, and Composition in proportion, so that I now pay near £40 a Week in Wages. It is impossible this can last for any Time . . .'[1]

What was keeping the presses going? Johnson's Dictionary had almost finished printing in 1754, but it was succeeded in Strahan's office by the *New Universal Dictionary*. In August 1755 he charged the partners in its publication £1,239 7s., of which he was paid £470 for work in hand from May 1754 to August 1755; the balance was not cleared until 24 June 1761. The printer was one of the partners, and an enthusiastic one. 'It will be an exceedingly good thing,' he told Hall, 'and cannot fail, I think, of doing greatly in America.'[2] He asked Hall to advertise it, not only in the *Pennsylvania Gazette* but also in other papers, explaining that 'I not only print it, but am interested in its Success. I need say no more. I hope that when the thing is seen, it will speak for itself.'

Strahan was not content to rely on the necessarily chance nature of book work to keep his plant occupied. As early as May 1749 he had started to print the *Monthly Review* for Ralph Griffiths.[3] He had begun to initiate book work for his presses by buying 'copies', and in 1757 he extended his interests by printing the *London Chronicle or Universal Evening Post*. The first issue appeared on 1 January that

[1] APS.   [2] APS, 2 February 1754.
[3] The circulation was 1,000 copies, dropping to 500 in December, January and February.

year with an Introduction by Johnson, procured by Dodsley for a fee of one guinea. The editor was one Spens who insisted on inserting 'personal Invective of the most infamous and scurrilous kind', according to an angry letter which Dodsley sent to Strahan. The printer would not, or could not, control the editor, and Dodsley abandoned his share in the venture. Strahan may have been one of the partners from the paper's inception or he may have bought Dodsley's holding; he certainly owned a one-ninth share at the time of his death. The tone of the *London Chronicle* cannot have been as bad as Dodsley made out, or perhaps it sobered with time; it was the only newspaper which Johnson took in regularly.

The periodical must have proved profitable, for in the following year Strahan added to his output the *Grand Magazine*, of which 5,000 copies a month were printed. Here again he was part-proprietor as well as printer. He wrote to Hall on 22 February 1758: 'You will find also 25 of the Grand Magazine (or return) in which I am half concerned. There are some clever hands employed in it; and therefore I dare say it will succeed. I beg you to promote it all you can, as it is of consequence to me that we should sell a good Number, else much will be lost by it. For what I send you I shall charge only the Ready-Money Price.'[1] He went on in the same letter to tell Hall that he could not, as requested, arrange to send him a compositor to Philadelphia, adding that he could use ten more himself but could not find good ones 'in the press of work to be had'. William Strahan was thus a man of some standing in the London trade when he and Franklin met. His thriving business enabled him to be both hospitable and helpful to his American friend.

In 1759 Franklin and Strahan were in Scotland, the former making his first visit, accompanied by his son William. The Franklins missed Strahan in Edinburgh—he had travelled north in August, a month before them—but Benjamin immediately sent him a note to tell him of their arrival. The visitors were much entertained and met most of

[1] APS. The 25 copies were invoiced to Hall at 9*s.*

Strahan's Edinburgh friends—Adam Smith, Sir Alexander
Dick, Hugh Blair, Dr. Robertson and of course David
Hume.[1] Father and son were made Guild Brethren of Edinburgh, a gesture that may have been prompted by Strahan
who, as *William Strachan, printer in London,* had been admitted a Burgess and Guild Brother *gratis, by Act of Council,*
on 20 September 1749. Strahan reported the Franklins' success in a letter to Hall, written after his return to London:

> On my return [from the Highlands] to Edinr. I found Messrs.
> Franklin, who were most cordially entertained there, and presented
> with the Freedom of the City, along with Lord Lyttelton (who was
> also there at the same time) in the most genteel Manner imaginable:
> I am sure they will never forget their Reception, or cease to think
> highly of the Conversation of our Countrymen. When I left Edinr.
> which was only on the 25th of September, they were gone to Inverary,
> from whence they talked of returning in about ten Days; but I
> suppose it will be a Month or six Weeks before they return hither, as
> they propose to stop at several Places by the Way.[2]

Among the places at which they stopped was Glasgow,
where they visited Alexander Wilson's type-foundry, the
source of much of Strahan's type. It was a visit with a purpose, since Franklin had been commissioned by Hall to
buy new type for the *Gazette* in Philadelphia. He had in-
spected Baskerville's foundry on his way north; but in the
end he bought neither Wilson's nor Baskerville's types, but
Caslon's. Strahan's pride in Scottish hospitality was justi-
fied: Franklin enjoyed enormously his holiday in Scotland,
saying that it had been 'six weeks of the *densest* happiness I
have met with in any part of my life'.

It was in this year that Strahan began to undertake the
printing of Franklin's skilful propaganda directed against
the Pennsylvania proprietors. His ledgers show the entries
Enquiry concerning the Indians, 11¾ *Sheets, No* 1000 *at £*1 3*s.*
—£13 16*s.* and the charge for printing 29½ sheets of *An*

[1] 'Jupiter' Carlyle records in his *Autobiography* a dinner party at Robertson's
house where the guests included the two Franklins, Hume and Adam Smith.

[2] APS, 6 October 1759.

Historical Review of the Constitution and Government of Penn-sylvania. Probably Franklin found Strahan's newspaper more useful than his book-printing plant; at least he made considerable use of the *London Chronicle* as a sounding-board for his opinions on American affairs.

A pleasing picture of Strahan's family and circumstances is drawn in a well-known letter written by Franklin to his wife in 1760. The old proposal for a marriage between Sarah Franklin and young William Strahan had been revived in earnest.

My dear Child: I receiv'd the Enclos'd some time since from Mr. Strahan. I afterwards spent an Evening in Conversation with him on the Subject. He was very urgent with me to stay in England, and prevail with you to remove hither with Sally. He propos'd several advantageous Schemes to me which appeared reasonably founded. His Family is a very agreeable one: Mrs. Strahan a sensible and good woman, the Children of admirable Characters, and particularly the young Man, who is sober, ingenious, and industrious, and a desirable Person. In Point of Circumstances there can be no Objection, Mr. Strahan being in such a Way as to lay up a Thousand Pounds every Year from the Profits of his Business, after maintaining his Family and paying all Charges. I gave him, however, two reasons why I could not think of removing hither: One, my affection to Pensilvania, and long-established Friendships and other Connections there. The other, your invincible aversion to crossing the Seas. And without removing hither, I could not think of parting with my Daughter to such a Distance. I thank'd him for the regard shown us in the Proposal; but gave him no Expectation that I should forward the Letters. So you are at liberty to answer or not, as you think proper . . .[1]

Strahan cannot have been surprised that Mrs. Franklin would not face the Atlantic crossing. He had written in the course of a letter to Hall, 'I have received Mrs. Franklin's Letter, to whom I beg you will give my sincere Respects, and tell her I am sorry she dreads the Sea so much that she cannot prevail on herself to come to this fine place, even tho' her Husband is before her. There are many Ladies here that

[1] Van Doren: *Benjamin Franklin's Autobiographical Writings*, London, 1945.

would make no Objection to sailing twice as far after him, but there is no overcoming Prejudices of that kind.'[1] Strahan appears to have accepted the refusal with equanimity—young William's feelings are not recorded, nor does it seem that they were considered—and seven years later Sally Franklin married Richard Bache.

Franklin's resolution against settling in England was a little weaker by 1762 when he did in fact return to Pennsylvania. From Portsmouth where his ship lay waiting for a wind he wrote to Strahan, who had continued to urge him to stay:

I cannot, I assure you, quit even this disagreeable Place without Regret, as it carries me still farther from those I love, and from the Opportunities of hearing of their Welfare. The Attraction of Reason is at present for the other Side of the Water, but that of Inclination will be for this Side. You know which usually prevails. I shall probably make but this one Vibration and settle here for ever.—Nothing will prevent it, if I can, as I hope, prevail on Mrs. F to accompany me; especially if we have a Peace. I will not tell you, that to be near & with you and yours, is any Part of my Inducement: It would look like a Compliment extorted from me by your pretences to Insignificancy . . . I trust, however, that we shall once more see each other and be happy again together . . .[2]

Strahan had written at length to Hall on the occasion of Franklin's departure for home.

This will be brought you by our worthy Friend Dr. Franklin, whose Face you should never again have seen on your Side the Water, had I been able to persuade him to stay, or had my *Power* been in any Measure equal to my *Inclination*. From the Acquaintance I have had of him, and the Intimacy with which he has been pleased to honour me for these five Years past, I have conceived, as you may easily imagine, the most cordial Esteem and Affection for him. . . . As for myself, I never found a Person in my whole Life more thoroughly to my Mind. As far as my Knowledge or Experience, or Sentiments of every kind, could reach his more enlarged Capacity and Conceptions, they exactly corresponded with his; or if I accidentally differed from

[1] APS, 11 July 1758.　　　[2] Pierpont Morgan Library: 23 August 1762.

him on any Particular, he quickly and with great Facility and Good-nature poured in such Light upon the Subject, as immediately convinced me I was wrong. . . . . There is something in his leaving us even more cruel than a Separation by Death; it is like an *untimely Death*, where we part with a Friend to meet no more with *a whole Heart*, as we say in Scotland.—But I will still indulge myself in the Hope, however distant, that he may soon find it is his Interest and Inclination to return to Britain, where he can be of great Use to his native Country. . . .[1]

William Franklin had not travelled home with his father. In August he had been appointed 'Royal Governor of New Jersey in North America', and had promptly made a fashionable marriage. Before the young Governor and his bride could sail for America, arrangements had to be made for a bastard son born to him by some unknown woman in 1760. The boy, William Temple Franklin, who was eventually to be accepted by his grandfather, was left in Strahan's care. There is no suggestion that he took the child into his own household, but he was at least entrusted with a will which made provision for him. In a few years' time the boy was sent to Elphinston's school at Kensington.

From Philadelphia Franklin wrote to tell Strahan of a pleasant voyage and safe arrival:

My dear Love to Mrs. Strahan, and bid her be well for all our sakes, Remember me affectionately to Rachey and my little Wife [Peggy], & to your promising Sons my young Friends Billy, George & Andrew, —God bless you & let me find you well & happy when I come again to England, happy England! My respects to Mr. Johnson; I hope he has got the Armonica in order before this time, & that Rachey plays daily with more and more Boldness & Grace, to the absolute charming of all her Acquaintances.[2]

In two years at farthest I hope to settle all my Affairs in such a

[1] APS, 10 August 1762.
[2] Rachel Strahan had married in 1761 Andrew Johnston, a Yeoman of the Society of Apothecaries; they lived in Bread Street. The Armonica, or later Harmonica, was a musical instrument perfected and mechanized by Franklin. It consisted of a revolving set of graded glass hemispheres, played by the fingers.

manner, as that I may then conveniently remove to England—provided we can persuade the good Woman to cross the Seas.

Franklin wrote often to his *Dear Straney*, to congratulate him in 1763 'on the glorious Peace you have made', to condole with him on bad debts owed him by Parker and Mecom, to ask if he 'can find room for four Messages in The Chronicle (but perhaps 'tis too much to ask)', and to respond to Strahan's solicitations to return to London. The flow of political news was welcomed: 'Blessings on your Heart for the Feast of Politicks you gave me in your last. I could by no other Means have obtained so clear a View of the present State of your publick affairs as by your Letter. Most of your Observations appear to me extremely judicious, strikingly clear & true.'[1]

In September 1764 Franklin told Strahan of the storm that had burst upon him with the publication of his *Narrative of the Late Massacres in Lancaster County*.

At present I am as much the Butt of Party Rage & Malice, express'd in Pamphlets and Prints, and have as many pelted at my Head in proportion, as if I had the Misfortune of being your Prime Minister . . . Mrs. Franklin and Sally join me in every good Wish for you and Mrs. Strahan & your Valuable Set of Children.—God bless 'em all, and my Peggy as mickle as any two of them. I want to hear Rachey upon the Armonica;—but her Attention is probably withdrawn from that, by her new Play thing, the Baby, which furnishes more agreeable Music.[2]

In other letters he asks Strahan for books which had been ordered from Becket and not delivered—*Debates of the House of Commons*, Ferguson's *Atronomical Tables*, Hooper's *Concise Account of the Rise of the Society of Arts*—and for two of Ryland's prints of Lord Bute. From the Governor's Mansion in Burlington, New Jersey, William Franklin also asked Strahan for pictures:

[1] 19 December 1763. In the following year he again commended Strahan's reports. 'Your political Letters are Oracles here. I beeseech you to continue them.'

[2] On 20 October 1762 Strahan had told Hall 'my Daughter Rachel was last Sunday safely delivered of a fine Girl; so that I am now a Grandfather!'

I wish the King and Queen's pictures were finished, as there is no Picture of either of them (except the Prints) yet sent to N. America. Please to tell Mr. Myers (if it is possible that he has not yet finish'd the Miniatures) that Mrs. Franklin would be glad to have them made a little fatter, as I have increas'd considerably in Flesh since I left London; but Care must be taken not to alter the Likeness.[1]

William Franklin made use of Strahan's help in a number of ways; he thanks him for advice on how to conciliate the people of his province, asks him to print articles and declarations in the *London Chronicle*, engages him to buy yellow damask window curtains, a quart tankard, Ruffhead's *Statutes*; but makes no mention of the care of his son.

By the end of 1764 Benjamin Franklin was back in his old rooms at Craven Street, acting as agent for the Pennsylvania Assembly and expecting to transact his business— a plea that the State should be removed from Penn ownership and made a Crown Colony—in a few months. Instead he found himself in the midst of the troubles arising from the Stamp Act and, as a consequence of the publication of his examination in the Commons, the hero of its repeal. In addition to his agency for Pennsylvania, he was appointed agent for Georgia, New Jersey and Massachusetts, and his position as unofficial agent-general for all the colonies prevented his returning home until the war he had worked so hard to avert became inevitable in 1775.

The intimacy with Strahan and his family was of course resumed. Franklin was one of the close friends whom Strahan told at once of the sudden death of his daughter Rachel, at the age of 23, on 24 November 1765. Franklin's response was immediate.

Oh! my dear Friend!—I never was more surpris'd than on reading your Note. I grieve for you, for Mrs. Strahan, for Mr. Johnston, for the little ones, and your whole Family.—The Loss is indeed a great

---

[1] 18 December 1763. The letter is printed in a supplement to Stan V. Henkels's Sales Catalogue no. 943, 1905, offering for sale the collection of Governor Samuel W. Pennypacker. It contains a number of letters to Strahan from Benjamin and William Franklin.

one! She was everything that one could wish, in every Relation.—I do not offer you the common Topics of Consolation. I know by Experience how little they avail; that the natural Affections must have their Course; and that the best Remedy of Grief is Time.— Mrs. Stevenson joins her Tears with mine.—God comfort you all. Yours most affectionately.

B. Franklin[1]

The Strahans felt their loss severely; Margaret Strahan, never robust, appears to have been really ill for a year or more after the death of her elder daughter. In May 1766 Strahan thanked Hall for his sympathy

on the Loss of my sweet Girl, which, as it is truly irretrievable, we shall not soon or easily get the better of. The little Infants are the most charming engaging Creatures you ever saw; and tho' infinitely agreeable, put us continually in mind of their Mother, whom they alas! will never know the value of . . . My son in law Mr. Johnston is pretty well, but will not soon forget his beloved Partner, who made him unspeakably happy.[2]

Some years later in the course of a business letter to Hall, Strahan remarked that 'Fordyce's Sermons to Young Women sell much here. They are really well written. The Character of Isabella (Vol. 2nd, page 289) was taken from my poor Rachel, with whom he was intimately acquainted; from whence you may see what Reason I and all that were con- cerned in her have to regret her Loss.'[3] Fordyce's descrip- tion is a charming one:

Her mind was very early accomplished; it was that of a woman, when she was yet but a child. It shone in her face with a generous warmth, and at the same time a calm intelligence, seldom seen in a countenance so young; it produced in her whole deportment a mix- ture of softness and dignity, which she alone did not perceive . . . She was never pert. Her diffidence kept her frequently silent: when she spoke, it was sweet simplicity and smiling respect. Her voice was melody

---

[1] *Atlantic Monthly*, LXI, 36 (1888). Mrs. Stevenson was Franklin's landlady in Craven Street.

[2] *Penna. Mag.*   [3] Ibid.

itself, without that frivolous whine which is often occasioned by dis-
sembling, and often by affectation.[1]

Andrew Johnston kept up the connection with the Strahan
family after Rachel's death. As late as 1773 Beattie, in a
reference to dining with him, calls him 'son-in-law to Mr.
Strahan', adding 'much company; Dr. and Mrs. Hawkesworth, Dr. and Mrs. Grant, Miss Kinnaird etc.' From the
company as well as from the spelling of his name, one may
safely surmise that Johnston was a Scot.

There are a number of references to Franklin, both personal and political, in Strahan's letters to Hall during the
period of this long residence in London. From these it is
clear that, without its affecting their regard for one another,
their views on the American problem steadily diverged,
inasmuch as Strahan, while sympathetic to the colonists'
case, never believed that a rupture was inevitable. On 14
December 1765 he wrote to Hall:

I saw Dr. Franklin yesterday, and found him under deep Concern
for the present distracted State of America. No Father can be under
more Anxiety for his Children. I don't know what People with you
think of him, but I can assure you, from my own Knowledge, that
some of those in Power, to whom he is known, and admit and even
admire his natural Sagacity, and his Knowledge of American Affairs,
think him too partial to his own Country; and yet his Enemies, I am
told, look upon him as a Betrayer of its Interests.—This is truly provoking, and is enough to cool the Zeal of the warmest Patriot—But
if I know anything of his Disposition, he is not to be diverted by any
Insult or Injury done himself, from following the Dictates of his
Conscience, which as he possesses an Understanding enlightened in no
common Degree, I dare say will always prompt him to advise such
Measures (as far as he is consulted) as most directly tend to heal the
Divisions, secure the Liberty, and restore the Happiness, Commerce,
and Tranquillity of America.[2]

---

[1] *Sermons to Young Women,* 4th ed., 1767. They continued to be popular for
many years; it was Fordyce's Sermons which Mr. Collins chose to read aloud to
the Bennetts after dinner at Longbourn, and which so signally failed to capture
Lydia's interest.

[2] Cat. 26, Seven Gables Bookshop.

A month later, he gave Hall an impression of Franklin's ceaseless activities:

It hath not fallen in my Way, to be acquainted with the Agents for the other Colonies, and therefore I cannot pretend to say what Part they act on this Occasion, or how industrious they are in the Service of their several Constituents. But the Assiduity of our Friend Dr. Franklin is really astonishing. He is forever with one member of Parliament or another (most of whom by the bye seem to have been deplorably ignorant with regard to the Nature and Consequence of the Colonies) endeavouring to impress them; first, with the Importance of the present Dispute; then to state the Case clearly and fully, stripping it of every thing foreign to the main Point; and lastly, to answer objections arising either from a total Ignorance, a partial Knowledge, or a wrong Conception of the matter. To enforce this repeatedly, and with Propriety, in the manner he has done these last two months, I assure you is no easy Task. By this means, however, when the Parlt. re-assembles, many members will go into the House properly instructed, and be able to speak in the Debates with Precision and Propriety, which the Well-wishers of the Colonies have hitherto been unable to do.—This is the most necessary and essential Service he could perform on this Occasion; and so effectually hath he done this, and I will venture to say, he hath thrown so much true Light upon the Subject, that if the Legislature doth not now give you ample Redress, it is not for want of the fullest and most distinct Information in respect to the real Merits of the Case. All this while, too, he hath been throwing out Hints in the Public Papers, and giving answers to such Letters as have appeared in them, that required or deserved an answer.—In this manner is he now employed, with very little Intermission, Night and Day.[1]

Admittedly these letters were written with an eye to their publication by Hall, but there is no reason to think that Strahan was insincere in his attempts to buttress Franklin's then rather shaky position in Pennsylvania. Another move in the same direction is his report to Hall on Franklin's famous examination in the House of Commons and his subsequent suggestion that it should be published in

[1] *Proceedings*, New Jersey Historical Society, 11 January 1766.

Philadelphia as a pamphlet.[1] When Strahan's views on the American Revolution are considered, it will be as well to remember his sympathy for the colonists in the '60s, even if a good part of it can be ascribed to a personal affection for Franklin.

In 1769 he told Hall 'I spent the Evening yesterday with Dr. Franklin at Sir John Pringle's, where were the Duke of Rochefoucault, a very agreeable French Nobleman of the first Rank, David Hume etc. The Dr. is in perfect Health.'[2] By the following year he did not see eye to eye with his friend; '[Dr. Franklin] and I differ widely in our American Politics, which I am heartily sorry for, as I esteem him highly. But tho' we *differ* we do not *disagree*, and must ever be good Friends, as I trust we aim at both the same end, tho' we differ in the Means.'

The divergence did not prevent Strahan's taking an active part with Franklin in the affairs of the Grand Ohio Company. This had grown into a major scheme of colonial development from small beginnings as a grant of land to compensate some traders for losses incurred in the Indian wars. One of the merchants concerned, Samuel Wharton, came to London in 1769 with a letter of introduction to Strahan from Governor William Franklin; his object was to push on the confirmation of the grant. Benjamin Franklin gave Wharton advice and help, and eventually a company was formed with a list of shareholders which included Wharton, Franklin and Strahan. The company applied for twenty million acres, from which the promoters hoped to make a fortune. There were aggravating delays on the part of the Government, and Strahan had to get the wheels moving with the help of Hume. Lord Hertford, on whose embassy in Paris Hume had served, was now Lord Chamberlain and thought to be in the King's confidence. Strahan asked Hume for a letter of introduction, and then secured

---

[1] *Penna. Mag.*, 10 May 1766.

[2] Ibid., 5 January. Pringle is chiefly remembered for his work as physician to the army; he was President of the Royal Society from 1772–8.

Hertford's interest by inducing him to become a shareholder. He reported progress to Hume on 1 March 1771:

I was favoured with yours, inclosing your very generous Letter to Lord Hertford, which I delivered to his Lordp.—He received me very politely; and I found no Difficulty in impressing him with a just Notion of the Importance of the Subject I wanted to talk to him about. He was as fond of it, or rather more so, than I was, and for his own Sake will do what lies in his Power to forward it.—The Project is no less than the forming a new Government upon the Ohio. The Country is by much the best and mildest in all our Portion of America, and being situated at no great Distance from any of our Colonies, will, when once settled, fill very fast from the overflowing of them all. The Land Carriage is by no means so great an Obstacle as you seem to imagine,[1] it being already, by means of other Rivers in different parts of the Country, so much shortened as to be considerably lower already than it is in the internal Provinces of England.—The *Policy*, however, of such a Settlement respecting the Mother Country, is not yet decided; and the Affair is still under Consideration . . . Lord Hertford is very fond of the Idea of having a large Tract of Country in America, and is otherwise very attentive to the Improvement of his Fortune, having, I am well assured, profited greatly by the late increase of the Price of Stocks.[2]

Strahan's optimism was still in full flower in June when he wrote to Samuel Wharton's brother Thomas in Philadelphia—in another attempt, incidentally, to recover Read's debt.

The Ohio Business would have been finally completed before this time, agreeable to what I wrote you, had not our domestic Squabbles with the Lord Mayor, etc, wh. engaged the Attention of Parliament, and of course the whole Time of the Ministers, stept in to prevent it.

---

[1] Hume had written to Strahan (Hill, op. cit.): 'I cannot easily imagine how an Estate on the Ohio can ever turn to great Account. The Navigation down to Mississippi is indeed expeditious and safe, except at the Mouth; but the return is commonly so slow, by the violence of the Current, that the Communication of that Country with the rest of the World, will always be under great Obstacles, and be carry'd on under considerable Disadvantages.'

[2] Royal Society of Edinburgh.

At present it waits only for the Meeting of the next Cabinet Council, which cannot be many Days distant, to give the *Fiat*.[1]

Franklin himself was not so sanguine; he had more direct experience than Strahan of the workings of government. William Franklin told Strahan of a letter from his father which 'mentions the Ohio Affair being in a prosperous Way, but directs me not to say anything about it, as Things happen *between the Cup & Lip*'.[2] Although the grant eventually received the approval of the Privy Council, the storm of independence broke before anything had been accomplished except the suggestion of various names for the putative colony—Indiana, Pittsylvania and finally Vandalia. The Grand Ohio Company was for Strahan another American bad debt.

In his account of the *Negotiations to Prevent the War*, Franklin states that when he came to England in 1757, his attempts to meet Pitt were unsuccessful. 'I was therefore obliged to content myself with a kind of non-apparent and unacknowledged communication through Mr. Potter and Mr. Wood, his secretaries.' It was through this Thomas Potter that Strahan was introduced to Ralph Allen, the remarkable postmaster and leading citizen of Bath; and in turn it was through Allen that Strahan made the aquaintance of William Warburton. Potter was rumoured to be Mrs. Warburton's lover—almost an hierarchic scandal, since he was the son of the Archbishop of Canterbury and Warburton was the Bishop of Gloucester.

Strahan soon became a fairly regular visitor to Priory Park, Allen's famous house outside Bath, and to Claverton, another of his houses. Here Warburton's son lived in the tutorship of the local rector; to this boy Strahan took

---

[1] Haverford College Library, 5 June 1771. Brass Crosby, the Lord Mayor, had been committed to the Tower in March for defiance of the House of Commons. He had refused to accept the legality of the Commons' demand that the printer of the *London Evening Post* should attend at the bar of the House for the offence of reporting parliamentary debates.

[2] Henkels Catalogue, 21 June 1771.

a liking, or perhaps—as his father's publisher—feigned a liking. Margaret Strahan was a frequent visitor to Bath for the sake of her health,[1] a fact which no doubt occasioned many of Strahan's visits. Allen kept a number of Strahan's letters, most of which are excellent political reports on the protracted debates in the Commons on the Wilkes affair, and necessarily cover much of the same ground as the letters written at the same time to Hall in Philadelphia. Others are personal, and Strahan's aquaintance with Warburton is referred to in several of them. He wrote for instance to Allen on 25 October 1763:

Sir, I have sent by the machine which sets out tomorrow, the Reading Glass you did me the Honour to desire me to procure for you. It cost £1 4s. If it does not suit your eye, or is not otherwise precisely what you want, I can change it for another. Along with it I sent the History Books I promised Master Warburton, which, tho' of very small Value, have afforded much Entertainment to the Good People of England for some Centuries past. As they contain great Variety, and many of them deal in the Wonderful, it is likely some of them may attract his Attention and allure him to read a little more than he might otherwise incline . . .[2]

Strahan sometimes strikes a toadying note in his letters to Allen, quite foreign to all his other correspondence. This may have been due to Allen's possible usefulness to Margaret Strahan when she was in Bath, or perhaps to Strahan's nose for a good book. This seems to be indicated by a letter to Allen written in the following year.

From the most feeling Sense of your excellent and uncommon Character, which hath inspired me with a Veneration that gives me inexpressible Pleasure, and which I shall ever glory to avow, I am extremely solicitous for the Increase and Preservation of your honest

---

[1] From Bath she wrote to Anna Williams in 1782. Johnson was shown her letter and wrote to Margaret Strahan: 'Let me once more entreat you to stay till your health is not only obtained but confirmed. Your fortune is such as that no moderate expence deserves your care, and you have a husband who, I believe does not regard it. Stay therefore till you are quite well.' *Letters*, 759.

[2] Peach: *The Life and Times of Ralph Allen*, London, 1895.

Fame. With this view I have often observed to the Bishop of Gloucester how very desirous I was that the Influences of your Virtues might
be perpetuated beyond the Period (long as I hope that will be) of your
own Life, and that you could be prevailed with to put such Materials
into his Lordship's Hands, as might serve to illustrate many Parts of
your Conduct, which from your singular Delicacy and Modesty you
have ever been most careful to conceal . . . I past two very agreeable
Hours last night with the Bishop, whom I found in good Health and
Spirits.

This lavish buttering was to no purpose, and the proposed
biography was never written. It was a sensible publishing
project, since Allen was almost a legendary figure in his
lifetime, and Warburton was a popular writer; and it is a pity
that nothing came of it. Allen had no desire to become the
hero of a 'rags to riches' success story; his humble beginnings
were among the things he had 'ever been most careful to
conceal'.

Strahan was proud of his intimacy with Warburton.
Johnson once laughed at him over this in the course of a
conversation in Aberdeen. Boswell says:

Dr. Gerard told us that an eminent printer was very intimate with
Warburton.—JOHNSON. 'Why sir, he has printed some of his works,
and perhaps bought the property of some of them. The intimacy is
such as one of the professors here may have with one of the carpenters
who is repairing the college.' 'But, (said Gerard) I saw a letter from
him to this printer, in which he says, that the one half of the clergy
of the Church of Scotland are fanaticks, and the other half infidels'. . . .
[Johnson] told me, when we were by ourselves, that he thought it
very wrong in the printer, to shew Warburton's letter, as it was raising
a body of enemies against him. He thought it foolish in Warburton to
write so to the printer; and added, 'Sir, the worst way of being intimate,
is by scribbling'.[1]

Strahan certainly showed at least one of Warburton's
letters to Hume. The two men detested each other's opinions, but on this particular occasion the Bishop did not dis-

1 *Life*, V, 92.

play his customary antipathy to the philosopher. Hume wrote to Strahan after seeing the letter:

I return you Warburton's Letter, which diverted me. He and all his gang, the most scurrillous, arrogant, and impudent Fellows in the world, have been abusing me in their usual Style these twenty Years, and here at last he pretends to speak well of me. It is the only thing from them, that coud ever give me any mortification. We have all heard of the several Schools of Painters and their peculiar manners. It is petulance, and Insolence and abuse, that distinguish the Warbur-tonian School, even above all other Parsons and Theologians. Johnson is abusive in Company, but falls much short of them in his writings.[1]

Strahan took this point up, insisting that the Bishop was not as black as Hume had made him out:

What his reasons may be I know not, but I have heard much of his launching out in your praise for some time past, sometimes indeed in my hearing, and with much more seeming cordiality and heartiness than I ever heard him bestow on any other writer . . . As a com-panion he is certainly one of the most tractable men I ever saw. So far from being insolent or overbearing, you can hardly get him to contra-dict you in anything.

This phrase Strahan repeated two years later to James Beattie, Hume's philosophical opponent, when he showed him 'a large parcel of Bp. Warburton's letters' and told him 'that Bp. Warburton is in conversation a most entertaining and agreeable companion and so perfectly modest and well-bred, that you can hardly get him to contradict you'.[2]

The exchange with Hume epitomizes a remarkable faculty in Strahan—one perhaps that has to be developed by any successful publisher—of remaining on the friendliest terms with a number of eminent men who dislike one an-other heartily. Warburton and Hume, Hume and Beattie, Hume and Johnson; Johnson and Franklin and Adam Smith and James Macpherson—there were some pretty antipathies amongst them, yet Strahan seems to have felt no difficulty in

---

[1] Hill, op. cit., 25 June 1771.
[2] Walker: *James Beattie's London Diary, 1733*, Aberdeen, 1946.

preventing his feeling for two men being clouded by a knowledge of their dislike for each other. His friendships on the
whole ring true and do not appear to have been mere business
civilities. The ability to be more or less all things to all men
may be an estimable trait or simply the mark of an un-
thinking complaisance with the present company; Strahan,
I believe, may be credited with a genuine aptitude for
friendship.

However it did not blind him to his friends' likes and
dislikes, and he generally succeeded in keeping the quarrel-
some ones apart. The disastrous exception was when he
asked Adam Smith and Johnson to spend the evening with
him (see page 163) but his tact avoided similar occasions;
the meeting of Johnson and Macpherson took place before
they quarrelled over *Ossian*, and Johnson wrote the famous
letter defying 'the menaces of a Ruffian'.[1] He introduced
Franklin, for instance, to Hume with the happiest results,
but wisely made no attempt to bring Franklin and Johnson
together. He himself suffered cheerfully a stream of letters
of introduction from Scotland and did not hesitate to pass
on fairly casual acquaintances.[2] But with his friends, in that
age of passionate resentments, he learnt to be more cautious.

[1] Johnson told Boswell that it was at Strahan's house he made his remark about
Sheridan's pension, and that Macpherson, who was present, repeated it to Sheridan.
Boswell Papers, 11.

[2] He wrote to Hall, for example, on 26 June 1770 to recommend a Mr. Samuel
Gale 'who has taken an invincible Inclination to visit North America'.

9

King's Printer

ALTHOUGH still technically his father's apprentice, young Billy Strahan was promoted to management in 1756. The vacancy he filled occurred as a result of Strahan's quarrel with James Rivington, when he had refused to print for him 'a new History of England in 3 vols. 4to by Dr. Smollet'. He told Hall:

This when Mr. Hamilton [Strahan's manager] saw, he thought it a good Opportunity to begin for himself, as he found Rivington was willing to give it him. And he is accordingly set up. He had saved about £300 in my Service; for I gave him 30 Shillings a Week, and allowed him to keep always three or four Apprentices; so that one way another his Place was worth above £200 a Year, which most People think he was a Fool to quitt. However, as it happens, it is most agreeable to me, for I have thereby a good Opportunity of bringing Billy forward in the Business, who now supplies his place extremely well and vastly beyond my Expectation, or what could reasonably be hoped for from one of his Years. In short, this Event has given me much Pleasure and Satisfaction. 'Tis true, he has but lately begun to officiate as Paymaster and Overseer; and therefore I will not be too sanguine; but upon my Word Appearances are greatly in his Favour; and I leave you to judge what a Father must feel upon such an Occasion. God grant that the same Joy may be awaiting you, when my Namesake is come to his length.[1]

[1] APS, 11 September 1756.

Billy was only sixteen at that time but proved himself worthy of his father's hopes. In 1758 Strahan called him a 'fine, sensible, industrious, noble-spirited Boy, and takes a vast deal of Trouble off my Hands', and a year later he wrote to Hall 'Business is as brisk with me as ever, having always my full Share of what is going on; and my Son Billy turns out a clever Fellow. He has managed every thing in the Printing-house, and paid the Men (between £40 and £50 a Week) for above two Years past.'[1]

Amongst 'what was going on' was Dr. William Robertson's *History of Scotland*, published on 1 February 1759, in which Strahan was a partner with Millar. The former wrote to Robertson on the 28th of the month to tell him 'I don't remember to have heard any book so universally approved by the best judges, for what are sold yet, have been only to such. The people in the country know nothing of it, unless from the advertisements; and a *History of Scotland* is no very enticing title.' Strahan and Robertson maintained a friendship and a correspondence 'which continued twenty years,' says Dugald Stewart, 'and which Dr. Robertson always mentioned with much pleasure, and with the strongest testimonies to the worth, the liberality, and the discernment of his friend'.[2]

With Billy taking some of the responsibility, Strahan could think once more of increasing his business. He was an established book and periodical printer with the advantage of also being the publisher, in whole or in part, of much of what he printed. He was a bookseller on a considerable scale, both as a partner in Durham's shop in the Strand and as an exporter of books to America; and in this side of his business, as he explained to Hall (p. 83), he had the advantage of being a share-owner in many copyrights. He had been apprenticed to the King's Printers in Scotland and it

[1] APS, 24 March 1759. This represents close on 50 employees. In 1762 Strahan told Hall that there were then 'over 60 men working under Billy'.
[2] Stewart: *Life . . . of William Robertson*, 1802. For Strahan's liberality to Robertson, see p. 40.

was natural that when he wanted to expand his trade still further he should turn to the field of patent printing. In 1762, in partnership with Henry Woodfall, he bought the patent for Law Printing from its then proprietors, the relicts of two famous printers, Samuel Richardson's widow and Bernard Lintot's grand-daughter. The Law Patent had twenty-seven years to run when Strahan became its part-owner.[1] The previous patent, owned by Edward Sayer, had expired in 1749; the renewal, for 40 years, was wholly owned by Henry Lintot, Bernard's son, and in turn by his daughter Catherine from whom Richardson bought his half share in 1760, shortly before his death. The privileges governed by the patent were ill-defined. From the printing of 'all manner of law books which any way relate to the common or statute law of our realm of England' the exclusive right to print statutes had been subtracted, and by Strahan's time the law printer could only be sure of sole rights in common-law books.

The competition for printing patents was intense. Richardson had been since 1753 one of the printers to the House of Commons. He wrote angrily to Mrs. Chapone in 1758, presumably in connection with his parliamentary printing and possibly with reference to Strahan:

A false and perfidious Scotchman [has been] pretending Friendship to me for Years, confessing all the time Obligation to me; constantly visiting me, tho' he had made secretly near a Year before he was detected, Offers of Circumvention and Underpricing, to one of my Friends in a principal Branch of my Business; Himself a prospered Man; a Friend he had never known, but for my Hospitality to him the Invader . . . This Man has already done me great Mischief; obliging me to lower Prices not too high for the Service; and goes on propagating the Mischief . . .[2]

If this were Strahan, he acted ungratefully since he had acknowledged to Hall his indebtedness to Richardson for putting work in his way in his early days in London; and if

[1] His share of the purchase money was £1,250; APS, 6 October 1761.
[2] Quoted by Sale, op. cit.

the 'principal Branch' were the House of Commons print-ing, the attempt failed. Richardson kept the contract, which went on his death to John Hughs.

The law printing patent could not content Strahan and in the next few years his ambition reached for a richer prize.

I am now busy about coming to an agreement with the King's Printer, whose Patent commences next January come twelvemonth, about which I wrote you some Years ago, and to which I refer. As the time is fast approaching, every thing must be got in readiness to set to work at that time.

This is an Affair of Consequence, which at this time a'day I should hardly think of imbarking in, but that I have Sons in the Business to succeed me. The Gentleman, however, with whom I am to be con-nected, as well as every Circumstance attending it, is extremely agree-able. And you know it is the most reputable part of our Trade in Britain, which is some Allurement to invite one to be concerned in it.[1]

This agreeable person was Charles Eyre, a Wiltshire gentleman who had inherited the reversion of the patent as King's Printer from his father; its purchase had cost the latter £10,000. The Eyre rights to the patent came into effect in 1770, and Charles prudently looked round, well in advance of the date, for a printer to undertake the actual work. There seems to be no record of how he and Strahan first came together but as early as 1766 Strahan wrote to thank him 'for the preference you give me in this affair, an obligation which I shall endeavour to return by carrying on the business (when once we are set a-going) to your entire satisfaction'.[2] Strahan paid Eyre £5,000 for a third share in the patent, and it was agreed that in addition to his share of the profits he was to receive £300 a year as manager of the business.

The office of King's Printer in one form or another is almost as old as the art of printing in England; its origin is probably to be found in an attempt to prevent piracy by securing 'a royal grant of the sole right to print and sell a

---

[1] *Penna Mag.*, Strahan to Hall, 12 June 1767.
[2] Austen-Leigh: *The Story of a Printing House.*

particular book for a given number of years, within which it was expected that the whole impression could be disposed of'.[1] It was a short step to the protection of whole classes of books, and for an extended period. A man with such a royal grant might be called a King's Printer; thus in 1663 Thomas Roycroft was King's Printer in Oriental Languages. But the title was more usually appropriated, even in the early days, to the 'official' side, the printing of State publications.[2] It was in this sense that John Cawood became Queen's Printer on Mary's accession, after Richard Grafton had been dismissed for having printed the proclamation of Lady Jane Grey. Cawood's appointment was to print all 'statute books, acts, proclamations, injunctions, and other volumes and things' in English, with a further right to succeed to Reginald Wolfe's grant of the right to print and sell books in Latin, Greek and Hebrew. He managed to keep his appointment when Elizabeth succeeded to the throne, but at the cost of being conjoined in 1560 with Richard Jugge. Jugge was already a patent holder, having been granted in 1550 a licence to print the New Testament in English and in 1556 a seven-year grant of printing all books of common law.

Christopher Barker purchased the office in 1577, with the additional right of printing Bibles, and in 1589 the Queen granted a new patent to Christopher and Robert Barker for life. The patent in theory remained in the Barker family for 120 years, but the rights passed through various hands by lease, sale and forfeit during the seventeenth century. In 1675 Charles II granted a 30-year property in the patent to Thomas Newcomb and Henry Hills, to run from 1709 when the rights of the last Barkers, Charles and Matthew, came to an end. Newcomb died in 1681 and his and Hills's executors assigned the patent to John Baskett.

---

[1] Blagden, op. cit.

[2] The Bible and Prayer Book were of course very much the concern of the State in the sixteenth century and so tended to be assimilated with the official work. By Strahan's time this privilege had long been shared with the Universities.

Baskett thus acquired the patent for the period from 1709 until 1739 but without the prospect of an automatic renewal, for in 1713 Queen Anne awarded the patent from 1739 to 1769 to two booksellers, Benjamin Tooke and John Barber. It may be noted that as the business of King's Printer became more and more lucrative, the reversion of the patent was granted, and then bought and sold, ever more in advance of the date when it would come into operation.

Baskett naturally wanted to keep the property in the patent and accordingly bought out Tooke and Barber. He afterwards obtained a renewal for another 30 years from George II, partly as compensation for a serious fire which destroyed his printing house. Baskett therefore owned the rights in the patent up to 1799; and it was the reversion of the last 30 years of this period which was sold for £10,000 to Charles Eyre of Clapham, the father of Strahan's eventual partner. The purchase was a sound investment; we have seen that a third share was sold to Strahan for £5,000, and this third in turn was to prove very remunerative for the printer.

The history of the patent was very thoroughly examined in 1831 before a Select Committee of the House of Commons which enquired into the cost of government printing and hence into the activities of the King's Printers in England, Scotland and Ireland.[1] By that date the patent had been twice more renewed. The first occasion was when Eyre and Strahan's period expired in 1799; it was then renewed in favour of John Reeves, George Eyre and Andrew Strahan for another 30 years. Reeves, according to Hansard's *Typographia*, 'became a sort of *lay-brother* of our profession, by means of Mr. Pitt, as a reward for some political services which he had rendered the cause of that statesman.[2] Mr. Reeves embarked pretty largely in his new profession of

[1] *Reports from Committees*, Session 6, December 1831 to 16 August 1832, vol. XVIII.

[2] Reeves was a lawyer who held minor offices under the Crown. No doubt his chief merit in Pitt's eyes was his formation, in 1792, of the *Association for preserving Liberty and Property against Levellers and Republicans*.

Prayer-book and Bible-printing, until his interest in the Patent was purchased by Mr. Strahan.' A new patent was granted on 21 January 1830 to Andrew Strahan, George Eyre and Andrew Spottiswoode, William Strahan's grand-son. It was they who were called upon to give evidence before the Select Committee.

Unfortunately their evidence sheds very little light on the profits of the patent as far back as William Strahan's tenure of office, beyond the information that the sale of bibles then entailed a large loss. It appears that in the period 1800 to 1830 the Treasury and the public departments paid the King's Printer in England a total of £1,114,765 12s. 9d., an average annual turnover on this side of the office of more than £37,000. George Eyre stated that for the last six or seven years the average annual net profit available for dis-tribution to the partners was £6,000 after allowing £6,000 interest on the £124,000 capital employed in the King's Printer's business. In comparison it was said in evidence that the King's Printer in Scotland averaged an annual profit of £10,000; it is not clear whether this was net or gross. Eyre's evidence is muddled and defensive, perhaps because —as he and Andrew Strahan had informed the Treasury in a memorandum—'the duties [of the King's Printer] are of a complicated nature, ill-described by the word "Printer" '. He ventured only slightly into the technicalities of the craft with the observation that 'there are two very beautiful en-gines, and one a very ingenious instrument for printing'.

The Committee left the office untouched, but another Select Committee reported in hostile terms against the whole conception of the patent in 1860, when it fell due for renewal. The Report was not accepted by the House and the patent was duly re-granted, not for a fixed period but 'during her Majesty's will and pleasure'. It has since been renewed only once, in 1901, and the office of Queen's Printer is still exer-cised by the same firm, Messrs. Eyre and Spottiswoode.

When Charles Eyre and William Strahan settled their terms of partnership in 1766 they were untroubled by any encroachment of a Stationery Office upon the privileges of the King's Printer. Still less were they troubled by any nineteenth-century doubts about the propriety of large private profits being made from a monopoly of part of the business of the State; indeed they could have justly argued, if it had ever entered their heads that the subject admitted of argument, that the State was wholly incompetent to provide such services for itself.

The reversion of the patent had been expensive to buy but a great capital outlay was still required for premises and equipment. The new partners decided against taking over Baskett's old press at Printing-House Square in Blackfriars, now the site of *The Times* office. Instead Strahan suggested that 'a much more commodious one might be built even upon the spot of ground near me (including the house that already stands upon it)'. His advice was taken and building began in 1767. 'The building goes on extremely well', Strahan told Eyre on 2 September. 'The timbers for the second storey will be laid in about a week and the whole covered in by the end of next month. It will be an excellent house, every way more commodious than that in Blackfriars.' The building, which cost £1,972 14s. 3d.,[1] stood opposite to his own house and printing office. Strahan always kept the two quite distinct and indeed the separation is preserved today by the direct descendants of the two businesses; Eyre and Spottiswoode the Queen's Printers, and Spottiswoode Ballantyne the private and commercial printing.[2]

In preparation for the extra work which the patent would bring and to free himself from the day-to-day running of the private business, Strahan took Billy into partnership at the end of 1767. The partnership appears on at least one title page. Like most of his contemporaries, Strahan was irregular in putting his name to the books he printed; for every occasion on which his imprint appears, there must be

[1] Austen-Leigh, op. cit. The actual address of the King's Printing House was 8 East Harding Street, Shoe Lane.

[2] For the relationship of the two Spottiswoodes to William Strahan, see p. 211.

ten where his name is listed as part-proprietor or publisher. In 1769, however, Robertson's *History of the Reign of the Emperor Charles V* was published with the imprint:

London: Printed by W. and W. Strahan,
For W. Strahan; T. Cadell, in the Strand, and
J. Balfour, at Edinburgh

In spite of his advance planning, the actual take-over of the patent was a hurried rush. He told Hall on 16 January 1770, 'I am now extremely busy in getting the Materials removed from the King's Printing-House in Blackfriars, where it has been for above a Century, to the New Building lately erected next to my own House for that Purpose. The old Patent expires next Saturday.'[1] The name of the new King's Printer was announced in the *London Gazette* of 21 February. It was an inconvenient time to start work since it was the middle of a Parliamentary session 'which meeting late brings all the Acts to be printed together on the shortest Notice'. George III must have made some enquiries about his new printer, for Strahan went on to tell Hall that the King 'spoke very handsomely of me to a friend of mine, near his Person; in terms indeed, which were I to report to you, would look somewhat savouring of vanity'. He ends this letter with a note: 'I inclose you a Copy of the first Act of this Session. I hope, ere it concludes, I shall print one entirely to your Mind respecting America.'[2]

Strahan was now the leading figure in the trade, but success meant unceasing exertion. He wrote to Hall in August 1770, 'I am and have been for some time extremely busy, having not only my own particular affairs, but the whole concerns of King's Printer and Law Printer upon my hands; by all which you cannot conceive in what constant employment I am kept and what uninterrupted attention they require.'[3] Woodfall, his partner in the Law Patent, had died

[1] *Penna. Mag.*

[2] Ibid. Undated, but must be February or March 1770.

[3] Austen-Leigh: *William Strahan and his Ledgers*, London School of Printing, 1924.

the year before, and of course Eyre took no part in the King's Printer's business, nor was he expected to do so.

To make matters worse Billy decided to set up on his own as a printer, and so his father lost his manager and overseer for the private printing house. It was on the face of it a surprising decision for Billy to take, since he was a partner in the very profitable business; though it must be remembered that Strahan was choleric and possibly a difficult man to work under,[1] and that George, the middle son, had chosen some years earlier to abandon a career in the same trade as his father. In spite of the inconvenience which followed the loss of Billy's services, his father accepted the situation with a good grace. He told Hall on 15 June 1771:

My Eldest Son William is now, you know, settled by himself, and will, I dare say, do very well; tho' the Printing Trade is by no means a very profitable one. It requires great Industry, Oeconomy, Perseverance and Address, to make any great Figure in. However he is very clever, has already a good share of Business, and will in time succeed to some of the more profitable Branches of it, as his Seniors drop off.[2]

Billy did not agree that he had a good share of work. He wrote in October of that year to Thomas Hollis for whom he was printing an edition of Algernon Sidney's works: 'I have better health than for many years past; but too much leisure. The ensuing winter will, I hope, produce many good things; tho' I do not hear of any new works of great merit that are expected.'[3] Billy appears in a much more cheerful light the following year in Boswell's *London Journal*: 'I went with Mr. Spottiswood to young Strahan's printing house upon Snow-Hill, where Hastie's Case was printing. I made several

[1] John Calder had offended Strahan in 1776 by 'an improper degree of turbulence and impatience' over the editorship of Chambers's *Cyclopaedia*. Johnson tried to intercede for him but told Calder 'Mr. Strahan is, as I feared, so angry and so resolute that I could not impress him in your favour, nor have I any hope from him'. *Letters*, 453, 456.

[2] *Penna. Mag.*

[3] *Memoirs of Thomas Hollis*, London, 1780. The anonymous editor is hopelessly confused between the elder and younger William Strahans. Hollis had apparently started to deal with Billy when he was manager of his father's business and 'frequently spoke of him as an ingenious and sensible as well as a skilful artist'.

additions . . . Strahan made us take beef-steaks and Porter and a bottel of Port with him. . . . I waited patiently till past ten o'clock at night, when I got our case.'[1]

Strahan may have called to mind his cheerful assumption that Billy's trade would improve as his seniors dropped off when, ten years later, Billy himself died on 19 April 1781. Strahan's correspondence for this period has not survived; Hall and Hume were dead and the American War had temporarily estranged him from Franklin; and we do not know how he took this heavy blow. Johnson wrote on the 23rd to Margaret Strahan, 'The Grief which I feel for the loss of a very kind friend is sufficient to make me know how much You must suffer by the death of an amiable Son, a man of whom, I think, it may be truly said, that no one knew him who does not lament him. I look upon myself as having a friend, another friend taken from me . . . ' Billy had never married, but had adopted a girl, Margaret, whom Strahan cannot have regarded as a grand-daughter since he makes no mention of her in his will.[2]

In his letter to Hall of 15 June 1771, Strahan went on to explain that since George was in Orders 'and will, I am convinced, make a good Figure in that Walk of Life', only Andrew, then twenty-one, could help him in the business:

My youngest Andrew is the only one now with me, and from whom I receive any Assistance in Business: But his Time is almost totally taken up in the Printing-house, in looking after 7, 8 or 9 Presses which are constantly employed there: For besides the *Chronicle* and *Monthly Review* I have always a pretty large Share of Book-work, in many Articles of which I am myself a Proprietor. I have also one half of the Law Printing-house, which is kept, separately, at some Distance from my own House;[3] and as my Partner in that, Mr. Woodfall died about two Years ago, the whole Care of it lies upon me.

[1] *Boswell Papers*, 9, 11 April 1772. Pleadings and evidence in a case taken to the House of Lords must be printed. Boswell records that the Strahans, father and son, listened to his advocacy in this case.

[2] The child grew up to marry in 1803 Robert Snow; one of the two sons of the marriage, William Snow, later changed his name to Strahan.

[3] In Clare Street.

As doth the Management of the King's Printing-house, my Partner Mr. Eyre not being bred to the Business, and being in the Country. It is true, we have distinct Overseers for both these Branches, to take Care of the Conduct of the Business within Doors. But still the general Management, and the Accounts, of all these Branches, falls to my Share, in which I cannot easily receive much Assistance from anybody.

Strahan goes on to tell Hall of 'the Multiplicity of Concerns I have in the Property of Books (about 200 in Number) which require, every one of them, some Attention, and a separate and distinct account'. He added that, not unnaturally, his time was pretty fully engrossed:

Indeed, it is so much so, that I am casting about how to relieve myself from a Part, at least, of the Labour I have now long sustained, but have not yet been able to fix upon a proper Plan. Sometimes I think of selling all my Property in Copies, and confining my whole Attention to printing. But against this there are great Objections, besides that the State of the Trade here is such, that they are hardly able, after so many large Stocks that have been lately brought to the Market, to purchase mine, and of course the present is a very bad time to bring it to Sale. I must wait a more favourable Season.

So far from the market in literary property picking up, things grew worse. Strahan was not alone in his concern; the whole book trade was shaken when the law of copyright was altered. Until 1710 the sole law concerning copyright was the common law which governed any species of property; its right was perpetual and it was as capable as land of being bought and sold, the title passing with any legitimate transaction. In that year, by what came to be known as Queen Anne's Copyright, it was laid down that the copyright of already published books was secured to their owners for 21 years from 1 April 1710. All books published after that date were protected for 14 years, after which the copyright reverted to the author, if alive, for a further 14 years. The booksellers assumed that their old common law rights were unaffected and continued to traffic in copyrights as though they were perpetual; even so, they made two attempts to have perpetual copyright affirmed by statute when, in 1724 and 1731, the 1710 Act began to take effect and copyrights—including those of Shakespeare and Milton—started to fall free. The House of Lords rejected both bills.

The Seasons was twice the *casus belli*. Andrew Millar had bought it from Thomson in 1729. In 1763, fifteen years after Thomson's death, an edition was published by Robert Taylor. Millar brought an action against him and won his case; the Court of King's Bench found that perpetual copyright still existed in common law despite the Act of 1710. The copyright in *The Seasons*, its value re-affirmed, was purchased by Becket. His property in turn was invaded, this time by Donaldson of Edinburgh, who re-issued the poem in 1771. Becket successfully obtained an injunction against Donaldson in the Court of Chancery, but the latter appealed to the House of Lords which found in his favour in 1774. The doctrine of perpetual copyright was dead and the booksellers thought they faced ruin. In the words of the *Annual Register*, 'near £200,000 worth of what was honestly purchased at public sale, and which was yesterday thought property, is now reduced to nothing'.

In their alarm at the consequences of this decision, the trade petitioned the Commons for relief. Strahan, who was Master of the Stationers Company in 1774, was active in the cause and in enlisting support from his authors for the restoration of the principle of perpetuity. That he attempted to do so shows pretty clearly that he and some at least of the writers he published felt that the question was a matter between rival booksellers, scarcely involving the interests of the author. In the spring of 1774 Strahan had replies from Hume and Johnson which went only some way to providing him with the ammunition he needed. In the event, the Commons passed a Copyright Bill in favour of the booksellers but the Lords threw it out. In the Commons the opposition to the Bill was led, clamorously, by Fox, a fact which—apart from their general political antipathy—cannot have made for cordiality between Fox and Strahan when they were returned in that same year as the members for Malmesbury. Hume wrote to Strahan:

> I have writ you an ostensible Letter on the Subject of Literary Property, which contains my real Sentiments, so far as it goes. However, I shall tell you the truth; I do not forsee any such bad Consequences as you mention from laying the Property open. The Italians and French have more pompous Editions of their Classics since the Expiration of the Privileges than any we have of ours: And at least, every Bookseller, who prints a Book, will endeavour to make it as compleat and correct as he can . . .[1]

Johnson was opposed to perpetual copyright, but equally was indignant at Donaldson's invasion of the rights of the London booksellers: 'He is a fellow who takes advantage of the Law to injure his brethren.' The views he expressed to Strahan were as balanced and sound as all his judgements on a trade he knew so well.

> I will tell you in a few words, what is, in my opinion, the most desirable state of Copyright or Literary Property.
>
> The Author has a natural and peculiar right to the profits of his own work.
>
> But as every Man who claims the protection of Society, must purchase it by resigning some part of his natural right, the author must recede from so much of his claim, as shall be deemed injurious or inconvenient to Society.
>
> It is inconvenient to Society that an useful book should become perpetual and exclusive property.
>
> The Judgement of the Lords was therefore legally and politically right.

Johnson goes on to argue that, although perpetual copyright had correctly been abolished, the term of copyright should be extended beyond the period laid down in the Queen Anne statute to a term of about fifty years, since by that time almost every book needs notes, and such notes 'cannot be written to any useful purpose without the text, and the text will frequently be refused while it is any man's property'.[2]

[1] Hill, op. cit.   [2] *Letters*, 349.

In April Hume wrote to Strahan to suggest that he publish a *Treatise on Taste* by a Dr. Wallace,

which I think a very good Book: I told his Son about four or five
months ago, before the Decision of the House of Peers, that he ought
not to expect above 500 pounds for it . . . I shoud wish to know,
therefore, what you think you coud afford. I imagine this Decision
will not very much alter the Value of Literary Property: For if you
coud, by a tacite convention among yourselves, make a Property of
the Dauphin's Virgil, without a single Line in Virgil's hand, . . . I see
not why you may not keep Possession of all your Books as before.[1]

Strahan indignantly refuted Hume's valuation of the
Treatise on Taste (see page 140) and went on:

The *Delphin Classics* are of that species of books that will never be
pirated, and would indeed never be printed in Britain at all, unless by a
large company of booksellers, faithful to one another, by whose joint
trade an impression may be sold off in a reasonable time, so as to in-
demnify them for the expense, with some little profit.—For such books
we want no protection; nor for the large works, voluminous Diction-
aries, School books, etc, which no interloper will ever meddle with;
but for your light and more saleable productions, of two or three
volumes in 12 mo, the profit on which is sure, and the risk small, the
charge of an impression amounting to a small sum.[2]

The author was more correct than the tradesman in dis-
counting the damage to the value of copyright caused by the
Lords' decision, and he was percipient in pointing to the
reason. The 'tacite convention' was maintained, at least between the London booksellers who observed, said Boswell, an 'honorary copyright, which is still preserved among
them by mutual compact'. It was under such a compact that
what came to be known as Johnson's *Lives of the Poets* was
published.

The first cause of the undertaking, as Dilly told Boswell,
'was owing to the little trifling edition of the Poets, printing
by the Martins, at Edinburgh, and to be sold by Bell, in

[1] Hill, op. cit. See his note on p. 282 for the editions of the classics *In Usu Del-
phini.*

[2] Ibid. Strahan evidently felt that James Rivington's piratical exploits were unlikely to be imitated by others.

London'.[1] After commenting on the small size of type and the inaccuracy of this edition, Dilly comes to the real reason for concern, 'an invasion of what we call our Literary Property'. A meeting of the so-called 'proprietors of copyright in the various Poets' was summoned; it consisted of 'about forty of the most respectable booksellers of London', who resolved to print their own edition and deputed Davies, Strahan and Cadell to 'wait upon Dr. Johnson, to solicit him to undertake the Lives'.[2]

The complications of shared copyrights, as also the workings of the 'tacite convention', are displayed by Nichols in a discussion of a projected uniform edition of Swift's works.

A material obstacle in respect of the then existing [1784] state of Literary Property, as far as it related to Copyright (a right still held sacred by every *respectable* Bookseller) prevented *my* undertaking at that time a regular Edition of Swift. Strange as it may appear, the actual property in the Dean's writings was then vested in no less than FIVE different sets of proprietors, most of whom had purchased their proportionate shares at no inconsiderable price. Of the Twenty-Five Volumes *Five* only were my exclusive property, and an *eighth* share of *Six* others, which had been purchased by Mr. Bowyer and myself; and any proposal for an amalgamation was constantly opposed by some of the other proprietors, particularly Mr. Bathurst, who possessed an exclusive right to *Six* of the Volumes.

All these objections were over-ruled on receiving Mr. Sheridan's Proposals for writing a Life of the Dean, and superintending an Edition of his Works.[3]

Nichols prints a letter from Sheridan to Strahan, stating that he was prepared, in a new edition, to go shares with the proprietors 'though, I am sure, few of them could produce any just title to the several copies, and none now any legal one'. Although Sheridan would not have agreed, the partner-

---

[1] *Life*, III, 110.

[2] Johnson was invited to name his own terms, which he set far too low at 200 guineas. The booksellers later presented him with another 100 guineas; but, says Malone, 'they have probably got five thousand guineas by this work in the course of twenty-five years'.

[3] *Literary History*, V, 394. Sheridan 'was paid £300 for the *Life of Swift* and £300 more for editing the Works in Seventeen Volumes'.

ship system was an efficient way of capitalizing costly under-takings, even if it may subsequently have clogged the channel for later editions. It was a method, as we have seen, which Strahan seized upon as a means of diversifying his activities.

Light on some of the '200 Concerns in Books' which he mentioned to Hall is thrown by one or two assignments of copyright to be found in his papers.[1] Here are two relating to well-known books, Anson's *Voyages* and Cruden's *Concordance*.

Received Decr 3 1767 of Mr. Thos. Lowndes Six Pounds Fifteen Shillings in full for one Twenty Fourth of the Copy Right of Anson's Voyages 4to 8vo and 12mo for which I promise to give him a regular Assignment on Demand

Will: Strahan

Bought at the Queen's Arms Apl 8 1777 Cruden's Concord. one Twenty Sixth £8—Recd May 8 1777 of Mr. Lowndes Eight Pounds being the full Consideration of the above Copy—& I promise a further Assignment on Demand
for Messrs Strahan and Longman
Edwd Johnstone

Some prices are shown in a list of copyrights sold by Strahan's executors after his death; presumably these were odds and ends, the most valuable rights being retained by the estate.

Mr. William Lowndes   London Nov. 22 1785
Bought at the Globe Tavern in Fleet Street the following Shares of Copies viz.

	£	s.	d.
Addison's Evidences one twelfth		10	6
Clarkes Aesop one sixteenth		10	6
Chambards Vocabulary one sixteenth	4	6	6
Francis's Horace 4 vols one twenty fourth		10	6
Maclaurins Algebra one twenty fourth		10	6
Potters Antiquities one twenty fourth		10	6
Sentimental Journey one eighth	6	6	0
	£13	5	0

[1] Add. MSS. 38730, folio 181.

Received Jany 2 1786 of Mr. William Lowndes the sum of Thirteen Pounds five shillings by note of hand which when paid will be in full for the above mentioned Shares of Copies, the property of the late William Strahan Esq., & We promise him a further Assignment if required.

> Andrew Strahan
> Tho. Cadell   Exors.[1]

Thomas Cadell had been in turn Andrew Millar's apprentice, partner and successor. Nichols describes him as a man 'eminently characterized by the rectitude of his judgement, the goodness of his heart, the benevolence of his disposition and the urbanity of his manners'. Strahan was a close friend as well as a business associate of Cadell's for many years. They worked together on many publishing ventures; as he told Adam Smith, 'You rightly consider writing to Mr. Cadell or to me as the same when you write about Business'.[2] An association which led to the publication of works by Hume, Gibbon, Johnson, Adam Smith, Robertson, Blair and Blackstone, to name some of their authors, was a noteworthy one. The benevolence of Cadell's disposition was matched by that of one of his assistants, who deserves to be mentioned in any book dealing with the vagaries of the book trade. This remarkable man, Robert Lawless, once asked Cadell for a reduction in salary 'as the year's account was not so good as the preceding one'.

There is in the Library of Haverford College a cheerful letter written to Cadell by Strahan in the course of a family jaunt. Not even Johnson could have felt more strongly about London.

> Scarborough
> July 25. 1777

Dear Sir,

Here we are after a Journey rather fatiguing than pleasant, the Weather was so indifferent. And to let you into a Secret, a Man that lives in London has no Business to travel so far from it *for pleasure.*

---

[1] Add. MSS. 38730, folio 182b.
[2] R. Soc. of Edinburgh, Calendar VIII, 48, 10 June 1776.

Change of Air is to be sure salutary; but I assure you Travellers pay dearly for it, in Fatigue, Expence, etc. etc.—This Place is pleasant, airy, and affords a noble Prospect of the Ocean, which is nearly at the Bottom of our Window, where I now write, so that we have got excellent Lodgings.—Here I shall stay about a Week, and then, I believe, George and I shall travel northward; I say, *I believe*, for I am not yet absolutely determined. I think, however, I shall; but you shall hear.—Do, drop me a Line, just to tell me that London stands where I left it. . . .

We are all in good Health and Spirits, so that we shall soon forget the Fatigue of our Journey; but this is one of the dearest Places I ever was in. Money goes by wholesale; and he that enters it, ought well to afford it, I assure you. And take this for a general Maxim, founded upon Truth and Experience; that no Man leaves London for any length of Time, without repenting it, or at least wishing himself back again.—In short, we have abundant Reason to be thankful that our Lot is cast in a Place, in every Respect the most desirable, perhaps, on the Face of the Earth.

I hope you dine with Andrew at least three or four times a Week, and help to support his Spirits during our Absence. Tell me whether you intend to meet us here. The Excursion will fatigue you, and also do your Health much good. You will chearfully bear the one to purchase the other, which is the only thing you need care for, as you have every thing else at your Feet. Our whole Company join in best Compliments to Mrs. Cadell, your Sister, and your sweet young ones. Believe me

My dear Sir, Most cordially Yours

Will: Strahan

Walpole has left a disagreeable picture of the two colleagues at work. He wrote to Mason on 15 May 1773:

So much for what we *have* been reading, at present our ears listen and our eyes are expecting East Indian affairs, and Mr. Banks's voyage, for which Dr. Hawkesworth has received *d'avance* one thousand pounds from the voyager, and six thousand from the booksellers, Strahan and Co., who will take due care that we shall read nothing else till they meet with such another pennyworth. Our Scotch Aldus's and Elzevirs keep down every publication they do not partake; and there is a society who contribute to every purchase they make of books, to keep the price at high water mark. Another club of printsellers do the same. Woe be to those who do not deal with, and indeed enrich themselves by, the monopolists!

This was cant, as Walpole must have known at the time. His example was an unfortunate one, for the only person who made a profit from the *Voyages*[1]—to which Walpole refers—was Hawkesworth, and even he did not live long to enjoy his £6,000: it was said at the time that his death had been hastened by mortification at the critics' ridicule of his performance as editor. According to Prior, in his *Life of Malone*, 'Hawkesworth was introduced by Garrick to Lord Sandwich (then First Lord of the Admiralty) who, thinking to put a few hundred pounds into his pocket, appointed him to revise and publish *Cook's Voyages*. He scarcely did anything to the manuscript, yet sold it to Cadell and Strahan for £6,000.' Strahan commented bitterly in a letter to Hume on the error of judgement shown in paying this price:

The prices demanded, and indeed given of late for copies, hath had a most strange effect upon our present Authors, as every one is abundantly apt to compare his own merit with his contemporaries, of which he cannot be supposed to be an impartial judge.—Mr. G. Wallace carries this idea farther, and asserts what to me is the greatest of all paradoxes, viz. 'That *little* will ever be made by any work for which *much* is not given.'—I wish I could not produce so capital an exception to this rule as Hawkesworth's Voyages; the event of which, if it does not cure Authors of their delirium, I am sure will have the proper effect upon booksellers.[2]

[1] *An Account of the Voyages undertaken by order of his present Majesty for making Discoveries in the Southern Hemisphere . . .*, London, 1773, 3 vols., 4to. The first volume contained the voyages of Byron, Wallis and Carteret, the second and third the first voyage of Captain Cook. Cook's Second Voyage was published in 2 vols., 4to, in 1777, his Third Voyage in 3 vols., 4to, in 1784-5.

[2] Hill, op. cit., 9 April 1774. Mr. G. Wallace was not cured of his delirium. He wrote to Strahan some months later: 'I have caused a skilful person to make an accurate computation to assist me in judging the value of the book [his deceased father's *Treatise on Taste*] . . . Probably it will swell to 500 pages, and might be decently sold to gentlemen at a guinea. By the computation each copy cost 3s. 3d. prime, and if sold to the trade at 15s. an impression consisting of 1000 copies would fetch £580 of profit or thereby, of which I am told I ought to get about £400. The deuce is in it, if after Kaims's *Elements* have come to a *fifth* edition, *three* have sold of Ferguson's *Society*, and three of Macpherson's *History*, one shall not sell of this Treatise'. The deuce was in it, and the Treatise remained unpublished.

The *Voyages* are referred to in a letter written by Franklin to Andrew Strahan in 1786, after William Strahan's death.

The Admiralty, in consideration of my having forbid our American cruisers to intercept or molest Capt. Cook in case they should meet him on his Return, made me a Present of his last Voyage, which Lord Howe sent to me in France; but unluckily a Mistake was made in sending a Duplicate of the third Volume instead of the first. When my Grandson went afterward to London, I return'd by him the superfluous 3rd Vol. and he obtained for me the first; and it was sent by Mr. Woodmanson, Stationer, to Rouen for me, together with Cook's second Voyage which my Grandson bought me to compleat my Set of the Voyages of the great Navigator. But they never arriv'd or could be heard of. I would therefore now request of you to find me the second Voyage, together with the first Volume of the last; for which my Son, on your presenting him the Account and showing him this Line, will pay the Charge.[1]

This happened to be a somewhat vexatious request, for the firm had lost the printing of the series. There had been some difficulties over the Second Voyage, of which Dr. Douglas was the editor. To him William Strahan had written on 14 January 1782:

Before I received your Letter of the 12th Mr. Nicol called on Mr. Cadell [who had been appointed publisher of the series by Lord Sandwich in 1781] to inform him that he had seen Sir Joseph Banks, and that *his Friends* (who they are we are still ignorant of; for Nicol told me when he called on me that Sir Joseph had no hand in recommending him) had been pleased to grant that Mr. Cadell's name should be continued, *after his*, as one of the Publishers, but gave Mr. C. to understand at the same time that the sole Management and Profit of the Publication was to vest in him (Nicol).[2]

Strahan goes on to thank Douglas for 'the very friendly and warm part you took to save him [Cadell] from the Disgrace intended him ... this is, in truth, a Continuation only of your friendly Conduct towards us both ... The Cost of Advertising will in future fall on Mr. N.' The printing of

[1] The original is in Fordham University Library.
[2] B.M. Eg. MSS. 2180.

that volume went ahead in the next year. On 31 July Andrew Strahan, as manager of the private side of the printing business, told Douglas 'I now enclose a proof of the first Sheet, and have engaged with a Stationer for the Paper, which will be ready for us when it shall be thought proper to go on briskly'. Douglas evidently thought the pace not brisk enough, for there was another note to him from Andrew in September: 'If Dr. D. thinks the Work should proceed with More Dispatch, he will be pleased to supply the Copy accordingly.' The next letter to Douglas, also from Andrew, marks the end of the firm's connection with the *Voyages*. He wrote on 1 July 1784:

I understand that the second Edition of the Voyage has been given by the Admiralty to their Stationers (Laurence and Winchester) to get printed. This I learnt from Mr. Nicol, who says he declined having any Concern in the Printing.—I have since seen Mr. Winchester, who said, if it had been left to himself, he should certainly have brought it to our House, but that Mr. Hughes was *recommended* by the Admiralty as a proper Printer . . . They print 2000, 500 of which are on a fine Paper.[1]

One can only hope that before the Strahans lost the series, the printing profits had gone some way to recovering a part of the initial publishing loss.

[1] B.M. Eg. MSS. 2180.

10

Johnson

MOST of Strahan's friends from Scotland, with the notable and wise exception of Hume, were introduced to Johnson. Scotsmen were not unlike the Americans described by William Franklin in a letter to Strahan:

Mr. Stockton, the Gentleman who will deliver you this, is a considerable Lawyer of the Province, & a particular Friend of mine. Give me leave to recommend him to your Acquaintance, and to desire that you would treat him with the Sight of Sl. Johnson, & a few more of your Authors; for we Americans when we get to England, have as much Curiosity to see a live Author as Englishmen have to see a live Ostrich, or Cherokee Sachem.[1]

James Beattie for instance, the Professor of Moral Philosophy at Aberdeen, arrived in London in May 1773 with the hope of securing a pension on the strength of his *Essay on the Origin and Immutability of Truth*, an attack on Hume's infidelity. He called on Strahan immediately, and a week later

Dined together wt. Mr. and Mrs. Hume & Sir John Dalrymple with Mr. Strahan. After tea, I took him aside, and gave him a particular acct. of the state of my affairs. Mr. S. thinks they are in a promising way . . . He says, my Essay has knocked up the Sale of Mr. David Hume's Essays, which he has access to know, being proprietor of those Essays . . . Mr. S. says that nothing ever gave D. Hume so much pain

[1] 18 February 1765: Henkels Catalogue.

as the success of Dr. Robertson's histories; that Mr. Cadel and he (S.) for fear of offending him were obliged to print some Editions of Robertson's histy of Scotland without alteration of date, as Hume could not bear to think that the sale of that work had been so extensive as it really was. Dr. Sam. Johnson called in a little before we left Mr. S's; then Mr. S. and I went to Sir John Pringle's in Pall Mall.[1]

Beattie had already met Johnson through an introductory letter from Boswell; his diary entry serves to show the sort of company that might be met at Strahan's house. Beattie was a constant visitor there during his stay in London. Some weeks after this dinner, Strahan argued against Beattie's going into the Church of Scotland, saying of it:

It is just now divided into two parties, one of which in the extreme is made up of sober pagans, and the other of wild fanaticks. It is a great advantage to the English clergy that they have objects of ambition to make them exert their talents; it is true, he says, those objects are never bestowed on merit, but the view of them keeps up the spirit of the clergy, as the hope of the ten thousand prize in the lottery makes every cobler in the kingdom an adventurer.[2]

Strahan clearly enjoyed introducing his visitors to his lions. Thomas Somerville records that in 1769:

I met with kindness more than hospitable from Mr. Strahan . . . I frequently dined at his house, and was particularly flattered by an invitation to make one in the company of a celebrated literary party at a Sunday's dinner. David Hume, Sir John Pringle, and Dr. Franklin from America were of the number, and a lady, an intimate friend of Dr. Johnson, and a good deal of the conversation related to him and to other literary men . . . [Strahan encouraged me] to think of some scheme of literary employment in London, assuring me of his patronage in such friendly terms as impressed me with a full persuasion of the sincerity of his kind attentions.[3]

---

[1] Walker, op. cit. The Humes mentioned were not related to David Hume.

[2] Strahan was probably echoing the view of his friend Warburton; see p. 118. Young George Strahan had been Vicar of Islington for just a year.

[3] Somerville: *My Own Life and Times*, 1861. I do not know who was the lady, Johnson's intimate friend, who might have dined in this particular company.

Strahan's visitors were very likely to meet Johnson who dined with some frequency at the printer's house. Their early connection had been a financial one, when Strahan had acted as paymaster on behalf of the partners in the Dictionary; and long after their relationship was one of friendship, there are many references in Johnson's letters to Strahan's position as his banker.[1] In 1754 he writes from Oxford asking Strahan 'pray speak to Mr. Millar and supply her [Miss Williams], they write to me about some taxes which I wish you would pay'; and in 1756, asking Richardson for money to settle a debt, he explains, 'Mr. Strahan from whom I should have received the necessary help in this case is not at home'.[2] But Strahan's feelings were not those of a mere financial agent when he complained to Boswell that Johnson 'was in a great measure absorbed from the society of his friends' by the Thrales.[3] To be counted amongst Johnson's friends did not save one from his asperities, and Strahan had his share of the rough side of his tongue. Johnson seems seldom to have assailed him directly but did not hesitate to criticize him to others—over Warburton's letters, for example, or his behaviour as a member of Parliament (p. 192). Strahan deserved his rebukes in these cases, though he would not have relished them; but he could justly have been deeply offended had he known of Johnson's remark to Boswell, 'When I write to Scotland, I employ Strahan to frank my letters, that he may have the consequence of appearing a Parliament-man among his countrymen'. This was a poor return for the trouble of providing Johnson with a free postal service. However, the two men quarrelled only once—the cause unknown—in 1778, the estrangement lasting for a few months.

The connection between them as author and printer or publisher continued. In 1755 Strahan had charged 'the partners in Johnson's 8vo Dict.' the sum of £297 10s. for

---

[1] The last letter Johnson wrote, or rather dictated, was to Strahan, requesting 'whatever portion of my pension you can spare me with prudence and propriety'.

[2] *Letters*, 52, 94.

[3] *Life*, III, 225.

printing 5,000 copies of 70 sheets. In the following year, on 7 January, he noted in his ledger:

Partners in the Rambler

	£	s.	d.
Printing do. 47½ sheets No. 1500 at £1 15s. pr sheet	83	2	6
Corrections and alterations in do.	1	17	0
Copy to print by		10	0
One do. bound given Mr. Johnson		13	0
	£86	2	6

N.B. This Book was all printed off, except the last two sheets, 16 months ago

For his next publication Johnson approached Strahan directly. *Rasselas,* Strahan later told Boswell, was written 'that with the profits he [Johnson] might defray the expence of his mother's funeral, and pay some little debts which she had left'.[1] This was an inaccurate recollection, since the book was written before he knew certainly of her death. Johnson's mother is thought by Malone to have died on 20 or 21 January 1759. On the 20th Johnson—who admittedly knew that she was critically ill—wrote to her, and also in the following terms to Strahan:

Sir, When I was with you last night I told you of a thing which I was preparing for the press. The title will be

The Choice of Life

or

The History of . . . Prince of Abissinia

It will make about two volumes like little Pompadour that is about one middling volume. The bargain which I made with Mr. Johnston was seventy five pounds (or guineas) a volume, and twenty five pounds for the second Edition. I will sell this either at that price or for sixty the first edition of which he shall himself fix the number, and the property to revert to me, or for forty pounds, and share the profit that is retain half the copy. I shall have occasion for thirty pounds on Monday night when I shall deliver the book which I must entreat you upon such delivery to procure me. I would have offered it to Mr.

[1] *Life,* I, 341.

Johnston, but have no doubt of selling it, on some of the terms mentioned.

I will not print my name, but expect it to be known. I am Dear Sir Your most humble Servant

Sam: Johnson

Jan. 20 1759

Get me the money if you can[1]

Johnson appears to have wanted Strahan to act as his literary agent in settling terms with a bookseller. In the event two booksellers, Dodsley and Johnston, as well as Strahan himself, joined in the venture, the partners paying Johnson £100 and a further £25 for the second edition. In April Strahan charged the printing of the book: two volumes, 1,500 copies, 21½ sheets at £1 4s. each—a total of £25 16s.—plus another £2 4s. 6d. for extra corrections. In June he printed 1,000 copies of the second edition at 19s. a sheet, for the sum of £20 8s. 6d. The bill for the two editions was not met until 31 July 1760. The published price of the two small octavo volumes was 5s.[2]

Johnson began to work up his notes of his Hebridean journey as soon as he returned to London in November 1773; by June next year he could tell Boswell that 'yesterday I put the first sheets of the "Journey to the Hebrides" to the press'.[3] The printing was impeded by his spending three months that summer with the Thrales in Wales, although he passed the blame to Strahan. On 26 November he wrote to Boswell:

Last night I corrected the last page of our 'Journey to the Hebrides'. The printer has detained it all this time, for I had, before I went into Wales, written all except two sheets . . . As soon as I can, I will take

<hr>

[1] *Letters*, 124; see Chapman's note on these terms. Strahan provided some money almost at once, for on the 23rd Johnson said he would send Lucy Porter 'a bill of twenty pounds in a few days'.

[2] Reckoning paper at 15s. a ream, the prime cost of the first edition must have been about 2s. 5d., excluding the binding at about 1s. for the two volumes. This would leave 1s. 7d. for discount, overheads and advertising, and for profit.

[3] *Life*, II, 278.

care that copies be sent to you, for I would wish that they might be given before they are bought; but I am afraid that Mr. Strahan will send to you and to the booksellers at the same time. Trade is as diligent as courtesy.[1]

The book was eventually published on 18 January 1775, an octavo at 5s. sewn. Boswell in Edinburgh received a copy that day and 'could not but mention that I had a hidden treasure. But as I had written to Mr. Johnson that I would not let a soul see it till Mr. Strahan's cargo was arrived, I kept it close, although I had many solicitations.'[2] A reprint was issued in February. According to Boswell, 4,000 copies were sold very quickly, but the evidence about the sale is confusing. If there were a run on the first two printings, it would go some way to explain Strahan's apparent dilatoriness in sending to Boswell the 25 copies for his friends which Johnson had promised him. Twelve copies finally reached Edinburgh for this purpose in November 1776, 22 months after publication. Trade in fact had proved a good deal more diligent than courtesy.

Two could play that game, and it was not until February 1777 that Boswell wrote to Strahan about them. After referring to their handsome binding, he went on: 'It is a great performance, and will bear much study. I think, however, that I could write notes upon it, which would improve it. . . . I wish you colud get him to write more.'[3] Strahan did not rise to this fly, perhaps in part because Johnson would have disliked the scheme—as Boswell himself suspected—perhaps because by that time the sale had slowed up. If a new edition of the *Journey* with notes by Boswell had been produced, we might never have had the *Tour;* in which case we can be grateful for this example of what Garrick in another connection called Strahan's obtuseness.

Boswell made no suggestion of writing any such notes when he was in London in the spring of 1775, soon after the publication of the *Journey.* He saw Strahan on a number of

---

[1] *Life*, II, 288.   [2] *Boswell Papers*, 10, 86.
[3] Tinker: *Letters of James Boswell*, London, 1924.

occasions, sometimes at other people's houses but more often, and usually in Johnson's company, at Little New Street. On 25 March he 'went to Mr. Strahan the Printer's, and drank tea, having engaged to meet Sir John Pringle there, where he had dined. The conversation was all of Mr. Johnson and his Journey with me.' Two days later Boswell has a long entry in his Journal about a breakfast at Strahan's.

Called on Mr. Johnson early. He was gone to Mr. Strahan's; found him there and we breakfasted . . . Strahan, of his own accord, urged my coming to the english bar. He said Wedderburn was once in such a style as to apply to him to recommend him in the City; and in what a great situation was he now![1] I liked to hear Strahan argue for this, as Mr. Johnson and I had formerly talked in favour of it, and I was so desireous to come. I liked to hear a fastheaded fellow like Strahan, who had made so much money in London, encourage my scheme. I said my difficulty was that I made now £300 at the scotch bar, and it would be foolish to quit a certainty. Strahan said very well, 'Small certainties are the bane of men of genius and abilities. Are they not, Sir?' JOHNSON. 'Yes, Sir.' Strahan said If he had had £100 a year, he never would have left Scotland . . .[2]

Strahan had taken a poor boy from the Country as an Apprentice on his [Johnson's] recommendation. He asked five guineas from Strahan, I suppose to account of his literary rents and profits, and, speaking of the boy, said, 'I'll give him one. Nay, if one recommends a boy, and does nothing for him, it is not well (or some such phrase). Call him down to me.' I went after him into Strahan's back yard and there I had an example of what I have heard Mr. Johnson profess, that he talks alike to all . . . 'Well, my boy,' said he, 'how do you go on?' 'Pretty well, Sir. But they are afraid I an't strong enough for some parts of the work.' JOHNSON. 'Why, I shall be sorry for it; for when you consider with how little mental power and corporeal labour a printer can get a guinea a week, it is a very desireable business for you. (The words were pretty exactly these; and the little, short, thick-legged, sniveling urchin, as one may say, was shaking himself and

[1] He was then Solicitor-General.

[2] In making use of this passage in the *Life*, Boswell added here 'Mr. Strahan put Johnson in mind of a remark which he had made to him: "There are few ways in which a man can be more innocently employed than in getting money." "The more one thinks of this, (said Strahan,) the juster it will appear." '

rubbing his pockets, while Johnson rolled superb.) Do you hear—take all the pains you can; and if this does not do, we must think of some other way of life for you. There's a guinea.' The creature thanked him, but had not parts enough to do it well.[1]

Courtyard of Mr. Strahan's house, from an original drawing

This delightful scene was drawn by an unknown artist as a woodcut illustration in a four-volume edition of *The Life* published in 1851 by the National Illustrated Library. It is reproduced here, both as an indication of what Strahan's yard looked like, and also as an earlier picture of 'Dr. Johnson's Tree'. The illustration of this, and the accompanying

1 *Boswell Papers*, 10. The boy was William Davenport; see p. 2.

Dr. Johnson's tree in New Street, Shoe Lane

account, appeared in *The Illustrated London News* of 16 March 1861.[1]

In New-street, Shoe-Lane, until within a few weeks, stood an old house, the property of Mr. William Spottiswoode, formerly the residence of his great grandfather, Mr. Strahan, the great friend of Dr. Johnson. Its removal has exposed to public view an old lime-tree,

[1] I owe both these items to the kindness of the late Mr. J. G. Wilson, C.B.E.

151

known by the name of 'Dr. Johnson's Tree'; not that it was planted by him, as it appears to have been a full grown tree in his time, but from the peculiar notice he seems to have taken of it. The Doctor was a frequent visitor at the house. It is related that in some of his particular fits of abstraction the Doctor would go out, regardless of weather, and even without his hat, and would hug this tree for a considerable time, apparently absorbed in his own thoughts and heeding nothing around him. There were then and for half a century after his death several other trees in the same garden, but they have all given way to time and the atmosphere of an increasing town. The house itself, which was built immediately after the Great Fire of London, worn out with hard work, has been obliged to give way to one more vigorous and better suited to the requirements of the day. And even 'Dr. Johnson's Tree' although it has outlived its former associates, is not destined to survive long, its top being near decayed and showing every year less vitality.

Boswell appears to have remained on friendly terms with Strahan although his private feelings toward him were never warm; the printer was of course a useful aquaintance through his intimacy with Johnson. He notes that on Tuesday 16 March 1779 'I then found Mr. Strahan at home, and was pleased with his wealthy plumpness and good animal spirits and his wish to communicate to me all that he knew concerning Dr. Johnson'.[1] But in the same year he wrote to Temple, referring to Sir Alexander Dick's *British Georgick*:

He even desired I would shew it to Strahan; which was a strong indication of what he flattered himself would be *encouraged* by his friends. I evaded his intentions, laying hold of what he declared as to his intending his Georgick only for his son and his descendants, and telling him that to shew it to Strahan who, as poor Garrick said, was an *obtuse man*, would be like shewing family furniture to an auctioneer . . .[2]

In *The Life*, which of course was composed and published after Strahan's death, Boswell speaks handsomely of the printer when he refers to him by name, but tells with some relish anecdotes which put him—slightly disguised as 'an

[1] *Boswell Papers*, 13.   [2] Tinker, op. cit.

eminent printer'—in absurd or contemptible positions. The *wealthy plumpness and good animal spirits* must have been on occasion irritating as well as pleasing to others beside Boswell. He notes in 1783 a visit to Lord Mountstuart: 'merry for a little. He humourously assimilated me to Strahan, as my sword hung aukward. Called it "that Newstreet affair".' Earlier the same day (Sunday, 18 May) Boswell and Mountstuart 'Had a fine laugh at the Story of the Printer from Newstreet', but unfortunately he does not tell the story.

Johnson showed affection at different times for all the Strahan family. His letters to Margaret Strahan are written with real warmth; he called Billy his friend; asked Mrs. Thrale to 'take a little notice' of Margaret Penelope Johnston, Strahan's grand-daughter, at Brighton, as well as asking her to be civil to Margaret Strahan at Bath. But it seems to have been young George Strahan in particular who won his heart. Strahan must have been both irked and flattered by this: flattered that the boy's parts and character had engaged the interest of his famous friend, and irked because the patronage often ran counter to his own plans. As he had told Hall, Strahan apprenticed George to a bookseller as part of his design for his three sons' future—a printer, a bookseller and a stationer. Although George had before him the prospect of part-ownership of the bookselling business, he did not remain an apprentice for long, and in his aversion to the family printing business or to any other form of trade, and in his desire for learning, he found Johnson a powerful ally. After consulting Warton, then Professor of Poetry at Oxford, about a tutor, Johnson wrote to the Reverend Henry Bright of Abingdon: '. . . My young friend after having been some years employed in a shop, is seized with a very strong inclination for scholarship, and is desirous of studying the learned languages, and of going to the University as soon as he can be qualified for academical Lectures . . . I can recommend the young Gentleman as one of uncommon purity of Manners, and Gentleness of Temper . . .'[1] Early in 1763 George was

---

[1] *Letters*, 144·1.

established in Abingdon; he was nearly nineteen and had a
great deal of ground to cover. His belated schooling was
eased by comfort and advice from his distinguished patron,
the more welcome because for some time his father continued
to resent his refusal to become a bookseller. The careful letters which Johnson found time to write to the young man are
delightful; advice about his reading, encouragement over
Latin verses, persuasions to be diligent.

George made sufficient progress in eighteen months to
enable Johnson to place him in University College. 'The
Scholarship', Johnson told Strahan, 'is a trifle, but it gives
him a right, upon a vacancy, to a Fellowship of more than
sixty pounds a year if he resides, and I suppose of more than
forty if he takes a curacy or small living . . . You should fit
him out with cloaths and linen, and let him start fair, and it is
the opinion of those whom I consult, that with your hundred
a year and the petty scholarship, he may live with great ease
to himself, and a credit to you.'[1] George worked hard and
was duly elected to a fellowship, and a richer one than Johnson had foretold: Strahan told Hall in 1768 'George is still at
Oxford, and hath lately got a Fellowship there, which is
worth about £70 a Year, and will ease me a little of the
Expence of his Education'.[2]

In order to be eligible for a fellowship, of course, it was
necessary for George to take Orders. Strahan had evidently
discussed the prospect with Franklin at the time of his son's
admission to the university, for in 1763 Franklin asked, 'Tell
me whether George is to be a Church or Presbyterian
Parson? I know you are a Presbyterian yourself, but I think
you have more sense than to ship him into a Priesthood that
admits no promotion. If he was a dull lad, it might not be
amiss. But George has Parts, and ought to aim at a Mitre.'[3]

This, curiously, is one of the few references that can be
traced to Strahan's religion, and if Franklin were not so
positive one would doubt the Presbyterianism or suspect a

---

[1] *Letters*, 167. [2] *Penna. Mag.*, 13 February.
[3] British Museum Sales Catalogues: Puttick and Simpson, 18 July 1888.

joke. Strahan was married in an Anglican church; his wife
was the daughter of a priest of the Episcopal Church of Scotland and the great-niece of a Bishop of Orkney; and he was
buried in an Anglican church. Neither Boswell nor Johnson
make any reference to his being a Presbyterian. However it is
clear from his advice to Beattie that he took no very spiritual
view of the Church of England; indeed Franklin suggests in
a letter written to him in 1764 that Strahan was an agnostic:

> I enjoy the Pleasure with which you speak of your Children. God
> has been very good to you, from whence I think you may be *assured*
> that he loves you, and that he will take at least as good care of your
> future Happiness as he has done of your present. What assurance of
> the *Future* can be better founded, than that which has been built on
> Experience of the *past?*—Thank me for giving you this Hint, by the
> Help of which you may die chearfully as you live. If you had Christian
> Faith, quantum suff. This might not be necessary;—But as Matters
> are, it may be of Use.[1]

George took his M.A. on 17 April 1771 and in the following year was presented to the living of Islington. Strahan
wrote to Hume two years later: 'My son George is now Vicar
of Islington, with an income of between £300 and £400 a
year; a populous and increasing parish, within half an hour's
walk of my own house. The purchase however cost a good
deal of money, though less than these things usually come
to.' George remained Vicar there until his death in 1824,
although he held other livings: Little Thurrocks in Essex,
which he later resigned, and, after election as a Prebendary
of Rochester, the living of Kingsdown in Kent.

As the young Vicar of Islington and no longer bound by
the celibacy of his fellowship, he could think of marriage. He
took his time and married for love and not for fortune. Johnson told Mrs. Thrale the news: 'Did I ever tell you that
George Strahan was married? It so fell out that George fell in
love with a girl whose fortune was so small that he perhaps
could not mention it to his Father; but it happened likewise
by the lottery of love, that the Father liked her so well, as of

[1] Henkels Catalogue.

himself to recommend her to George. Such coincidence is rare.'[1]

The girl was Margaret Robertson of Richmond, and they were married on 25 June 1778. She was, said Boswell, 'a pleasing woman' in his journal for 4 March 1791. The marriages of his children were much upon Strahan's mind at this time. A year after George's wedding, Margaret Penelope— Peggy—had married John Spottiswoode, on 10 June 1779; it was an important marriage for the future of the business, since two of the Spottiswoodes' sons were to inherit it. Strahan's pleasure at George's marriage turned to disapproval and eventually to an open quarrel with his son when he found that he was outrunning his income and looked to his father to make up his stipend from the profits of the trade he found so distasteful.

Once again Johnson was the intermediary between George and his father, but on this occasion he was not altogether easy about the merits of his young friend's case— 'Your discontent', he told him, 'on many occasions has appeared to me little short of madness.' Fortunately for George, his father and Johnson were upon good terms again after a difference—it seems the only one—between them in the year of his wedding. Strahan was not an easy man to placate and it was six months before he and his son would even meet, after many letters and much advice from Johnson to both disputants. Even so, the reconciliation seems to have been incomplete, for when Strahan drew up his will eighteen months later he felt that George was well enough provided for. He left him 'the perpetual advowson and right of presentation to the Rectory and Parish Church of Cranham' in Essex, but nothing more. The immense wealth of the family business went to Andrew, who was not afflicted with George's discontent and had been pleased to remain a printer.

Johnson dined at Islington with the George Strahans on a number of occasions and grew fond of the whole family. 'I

[1] *Letters,* 592.

hope your dear Lady and dear little ones are all well, and all happy. I love them all', he wrote from Lichfield in the last months of his life.[1] It was in the Islington vicarage that Johnson was persuaded to make his will; and it was to George Strahan that he dictated on 8 and 9 December another will and a codicil to it.[2] By it he bequeathed 'To the Reverend Mr. Strahan, vicar of Islington, in Middlesex, Mill's Greek Testament, Beza's Greek Testament by Stephens, all my Latin Bibles, and my Greek Bible by Wechelius'. More important than these bequests was his entrusting to George the private papers published in 1785 as *Prayers and Meditations.*

George Strahan was strongly criticized for printing amongst the majestic and moving prayers so many random scraps of personal information—Johnson's scruples over his diet at Passiontide, his ailments and the remedies he adopted. It was a justifiable criticism from Johnson's surviving friends, but it can scarcely be entertained in this age of remorselessly complete editions. What is unforgivable is his adjuration in the preface to those who possess sermons composed by Johnson not to 'withhold them in obscurity, but consider them as deposits, the seclusion of which from general use, would be an injurious diminution of their Author's fame, and retrenchment from the common stock of serious instruction'. This was a sentiment George Strahan thought inapplicable to himself, since he never published the sermons which Johnson, according to Mrs. Thrale, wrote for him and of which no trace has since been found.

When Johnson's life was drawing to a close, George was undoubtedly more nearly connected with him than was his father, but the relations between the two older men were still warm. Three months before his death, Johnson had

---

[1] Ibid., 1023.

[2] Hawkins's *Life.* He records that Johnson received his last Holy Communion from George Strahan, and that on 9 December, four days before his death, 'with an effort, he placed himself on his knees, while Mr. Strahan repeated the Lord's Prayer'.

written from Ashbourne to William Strahan, in reply to a suggestion about a new book:

The part of your letter that relates to a writer whom you do not name, has so much tenderness, benevolence, and liberality, in language so unlike the talk of trade, that it must be a flinty bosom that is not softened into gratitude.

It has now pleased God to restore my health to a much better state, than when I parted from London, if my health encreases, indeed, if it does not grow less, I shall hope to concert measures with you, and, by your help, to carry on the design to considerable advantage.

In the mean time, accept, dear Sir, my sincere thanks for your generous offer, and friendly regard. Event is uncertain and fallacious, but of good intention the merit stands upon a basis that can never be shaken. . . .[1]

---

[1] *Letters*, 1006·1, 4 September 1784. The ascription is conjectural but seems valid.

11

Books and Authors

STRAHAN printed a number of famous books in the fifties and sixties, apart from those in which he had an interest as publisher. They included *Roderick Random, Peregrine Pickle,* one of the many volumes of *Sir Charles Grandison* and part of *Tristram Shandy*.[1] Strahan was never a learned printer like Bowyer, despite Hume's flattering compliments, but that he was careful and conscientious is clear from his letters as well as from the volume of work with which he was entrusted. This aspect of his craft may be illustrated by the quotation of another extract from his ledgers, dated June 1753:

	£	s.	d.
Paradise Regained 18mo No 7500			
10 sheets at £6 pr sheet	60	0	0
Correcting do	1	10	0

As the most uncommon care was taken in correcting the above Books, every sheet being carefully read by the Printer, no less than ten times over, he hopes that if they really turn out to be the most correct editions hitherto published (not otherwise) the Proprietors will think him entitled to such a Reward for his Labour as they would have given to a person employed on purpose.

[1] The printing numbers of the last declined from 4,000 for volumes V to VIII, to 3,500 for volume IX. The cost of this last volume at £2 5s. a sheet was £22 10s., plus a charge of 5s. 'for a wooden cut to do'.

Like any good publisher, Strahan went to some pains to be of service to his authors. One of them was Arthur Young, the agriculturist who did so much by his writings to improve the national standards of farming. On 12 May 1770 Strahan wrote to Sir Alexander Dick of Prestonfield, near Edinburgh:

Nothing but an uninterrupted Hurry of Business of one Sort or another could have prevented me from sooner acknowledging the Receit of your very kind Letter.—However I made no Delay in transmitting the Rhubarb Seeds[1] to Mr. Young, whose Letter in Return I herewith inclose to you. It really affords a very pleasing Prospect to see Men of Rank and Fortune apply themselves with so much assiduity to the Study of Husbandry, where there is still such infinite Room for Improvement . . .

Mr. Young purposes to pay you a Visit, as soon as he hath traversed the rest of England. He will be greatly obliged to you for your Countenance and Assistance. You will find him a quick, lively, intelligent Man; but his Abilities you will judge of by his Writings. The Edition of the Six Months Tour is already sold off, and it is now in the Press again. The Demand for such Books is become very general, which is a convincing Proof, that this important Subject is much attended to.[2]

In the following year Strahan had a resounding success with *The Man of Feeling*. Henry Mackenzie had met Strahan through James Elphinston in London in 1766 or 1767 when, in Elphinston's rational spelling, he was 'a prodigy of won and twenty'. Mackenzie in his old age said of his famous novel that 'he wrote *The Man of Feeling* when very young and sent it to his friend Mr. Strahan to print or not as he should think fit: it was of so new a character that Mr. Strahan did not like to venture without the opinion of a literary friend: he confided the MS to a gentleman who took it to Bath where for some time it was mislaid: a Mr. Eccles, a clergyman, got sight of it, was at pains to copy the MS in a blotted interlined manner to give it a genuine air, added notes and actually printed it as his own; he was afterwards

[1] Four years later Sir Alexander was awarded a gold medal by the Society of Arts 'for the best specimen of rhubarb'.

[2] In the possession of Mrs. Dick-Cunyngham of Prestonfield. Young's work was *A Six Months Tour through the North of England*, 1770.

drowned in attempting to save the life of a boy in the Avon, and did not live to bear much of the shame of detection.'[1]

It is doubtful if in fact Eccles ever got so far as to print the work, which Strahan reclaimed for its author. Mackenzie wrote to a friend in May 1771: 'My publishers who are at this season busied beyond measure, were not very attentive to me, so the book was in Edinburgh some days and actually advertised before I knew anything of its arrival.' He must have been mollified by its success. Published in April, the first edition was almost sold out by the beginning of June, and early in August a second edition appeared. Mackenzie was in London again in 1772 when he brought his brother to Elphinston's academy. It was presumably then that terms were agreed for a sequel, *The Man of the World*, which Strahan and Cadell published in February 1773.

Perhaps 1776 was the *annus mirabilis* in Strahan's career as a publisher, with the appearance in the same season of *The Wealth of Nations* and *The Decline and Fall of the Roman Empire*. Gibbon paid his publishers a graceful compliment in his *Memoirs of my Life and Writings*.

After the perilous adventure had been declined by my friend Mr. Elmsly, I agreed, upon easy terms,[2] with Mr. Thomas Cadell, a respectable bookseller, and Mr. William Strahan, an eminent printer; and they undertook the care and risk of the publication, which derived more credit from the name of the shop than from that of the author. The last revisal of the proofs was submitted to my vigilance; and many blemishes of style, which had been invisible in the manuscript, were discovered and corrected in the printed sheet. So moderate were our hopes, that the original impression had been stinted to five hundred copies, till the number was doubled by the prophetic taste of Mr. Strahan . . . The first impression was exhausted in a few days; a second and third edition were scarcely adequate to the demand; and the booksellers' property was twice invaded by the pirates of Dublin.

Hume, to whom Gibbon had sent a copy, was full of

[1] Thompson: *A Scottish Man of Feeling*, London, 1931.

[2] Gibbon earned £4,000 from the first three volumes. He took two-thirds of the profit, which produced for him over £300 for 1,000 copies of the first volume; the printing cost 26s. a sheet per thousand.

admiration and wrote not only to the author but also to Strahan. 'I am very much taken with Mr. Gibbon's Roman History which came from your Press, and am glad to hear of its success. There will no Books of Reputation now be printed in London but through your Hands and Mr. Cadel's.'[1] After complaining that chapter numbers did not appear on every page, and that the references to authorities were printed at the end of the book instead of at the foot of every page—both points being rectified in subsequent editions—Hume went on to compliment Strahan on another publication, *The Wealth of Nations*. 'Dr. Smith's Performance is another excellent Work that has come from your Press this Winter: but I have ventured to tell him that it requires too much thought to be as popular as Mr. Gibbon's.' Strahan replied on 12 April, 'What you say of Mr. Gibbon's and Dr. Smith's books is exactly just. The former is the most popular work; but the sale of the latter, though not near so rapid, has been more than I could have expected from a work that requires much thought and reflection (qualities that do not abound among modern readers) to peruse to any purpose.'[2]

Even so, Smith was paid £500 by Strahan and Cadell for the first edition of the book, which was published on 9 March 1776 in two quarto volumes at £1 16s. in boards. From the second edition, published in 1778 at £2 2s., Smith drew half the profits.[3] Smith wrote to Strahan on 20 December 1777 in terms which have been echoed by many an author: 'Neither you nor Mr. Cadell have wrote me anything concerning the new Edition of my Book. Is it published? does it sell well? does it sell ill? does it sell at all?'

The two men were old friends. Strahan had printed, for Millar, Smith's *Theory of Moral Sentiments* which appeared in 1759, and reached its sixth edition by 1790. Rae prints a letter from Smith wishing to be remembered to Franklin and his son, whom he had met in Scotland, and asking Strahan

---

[1] Hill, op. cit., 8 April 1776. [2] Royal Society of Edinburgh.
[3] Rae: *Life of Adam Smith*, 1895.

to read over his new book and suggest corrections. It was at Strahan's house, probably in September 1761, that Johnson fell out with Smith. 'The first time I met him [Johnson] was one evening at Strahan's,' said Dr. Robertson,[1] 'when he had just had an unlucky altercation with Adam Smith, to whom he had been so rough, that Strahan, after Smith was gone, had remonstrated with him, and told him I was coming soon, and that he was uneasy to think that he might behave in the same manner to me.' All went well for the second Scotsman and Johnson 'was gentle and good-humoured, and courteous with me the whole evening'.

Adam Smith and Strahan were involved in a vexatious situation over David Hume's will. Hume's health had been growing more feeble over a period of years and by 1776 it was giving concern to his friends. Edinburgh was not yet a capital city of medicine and he was urged to come to London for advice; despite the protests of his doctor he did so. He saw Sir John Pringle and then travelled on to Bath, where at first he felt a benefit from the waters. In London he had seen Strahan and undoubtedly discussed with him the final editions of his *History* and *Essays*; before leaving Edinburgh in April he had written to Strahan: 'Last Monday, I sent off by the Waggon, direct to Mr. Cadel, the four last Volumes of my History. I bring up my philosophical Pieces corrected, which will be safe, whether I dye by the Road or not.'

The good effect of the Bath waters was only temporary. In June Hume decided he would prefer to die in his own home and planned to return there. He told Strahan of his intention and expressed his pleasure that work on the new edition of the *History* was already in hand; and added the request which was to lead to so much trouble:

... there is one Request I have to make to you: Before I left Edinburgh, I wrote a small piece (you may believe it would be but a small one) which I call the History of my own Life: I desire it may be prefixed to this Edition: It will be thought curious and entertaining. My

[1] *Life*, III, 331.

Brother or Dr. Adam Smith will send it to you, and I shall give them Directions to that Purpose.

I am also to speak to you of another Work more important: Some Years ago, I composed a Piece, which woud make a small Volume in Twelves. I call it *Dialogues on Natural Religion*: Some of my Friends flatter me, that it is the best thing I ever wrote. I have hitherto forborne to publish it, because I was of late desirous to live quietly, and keep remote from all Clamour: For though it be not more exceptionable than some things I had formerly published; yet you know some of those were thought very exceptionable; and in prudence, perhaps, I ought to have suppressed them . . . As soon as I arrive in Edinburgh, I intend to print a small Edition of 500, of which I may give away about 100 in Presents; and shall make you a Present of the Remainder, together with the literary Property of the whole, provided you have no Scruple, in your present situation,[1] of being the Editor: It is not necessary you shoud fix your Name to the Title Page. I seriously declare, that after you and Mr. Cadell have publickly avowed your Publication of the *Enquiry concerning human Understanding*, I know no Reason why you shoud have the least Scruple with regard to these Dialogues. They will be much less obnoxious to the Law, and not more exposed to popular Clamour. Whatever your Resolution be, I beg you woud keep an entire Silence on this Subject. If I leave them to you by Will, your executing the Desire of a dead Friend, will render the publication still more excusable.[2]

Hume had drawn up a will earlier that year, making Adam Smith his literary executor with a specific request that he should undertake the publication of the *Dialogues*. Smith was reluctant to do so, and accordingly in August Hume added a codicil: 'I . . . leave my manuscripts to the care of Mr. William Strahan, of London, Member of Parliament, trusting to the friendship that has long subsisted between us for his careful and faithful execution of my intentions. I desire that my *Dialogues concerning Natural Religion* may be printed and published any time within two years after my death.' If they were not so published within two and a half years of his death, the copyright in them and in the account of his life was to revert to his nephew David.

[1] As a member of Parliament.   [2] Hill, op. cit.

By this time Hume was back in Edinburgh. Even on his deathbed, he continued to correct his works: 'You will wonder that in my present Situation I employ myself about such Trifles, and you may compare me to the modern Greeks, who, while Constantinople was besieged by the Turks and they themselves threatened with total Destruction, occupied themselves entirely in Disputes concerning the Procession of the Holy Ghost. Such is the Effect of long Habit!'

Strahan replied cheerfully:

This will be a very correct edition, and I will take care it shall be printed accurately and neatly; and what is very encouraging, your *History* sells better of late years than before; for the late edition will be gone some time before this can be finished. In short, I see clearly, your reputation is gradually rising in the public esteem.—A flattering circumstance this, even in the decline of life; and when by the unalterable course of nature, nothing will soon be left of us but a *Name*.— By the bye, does not this almost universal solicitude to live after we close our eyes to this present scene, mean something?—I hope, I almost believe it does. Else why are we, on a variety of occasions, so much interested in what is to pass after our deaths? And do we not, in most of our labours, regard posterity, and look forward to times long posterior to our existence here?[1]

If Hume received this letter, he made no reference to it in his farewell note to Strahan, written on 12 August:

This, Dear Sir, is the last Correction I shall probably trouble you with: For Dr. Black has promised me, that all shall be over with me in a very little time: This Promise he makes by his Power of Prediction, not that of Prescription. And indeed I consider it as good News: For of late, within these few weeks, my Infirmities have so multiplyed, that Life has become rather a Burthen to me. Adieu, then, my good and old Friend.

David Hume

Although the news cannot have been a surprise, we may credit Strahan's sincerity in his reply; even so, he could not resist the temptation, so strongly felt by Boswell also, to

---

[1] Royal Society of Edinburgh, 1 August 1776.

examine Hume's sentiments at the approach of death. Whether the infidel's scepticism would dissolve at the end into faith was a topic of wide interest and discussion. Strahan at least wrote with some grace:[1]

Last Friday I received your affectionate farewell, and therefore melancholy letter, which disabled me from sending you an immediate answer to it, as I now do, in hopes this may yet find you, not much oppressed with pain, in the land of the living. I need not tell you, that your corrections are all duly attended to, as every particular shall be that you desire or order. Nor shall I now trouble you with a long letter.

Only permit me to ask you a question or two, to which I am prompted, you will believe me, not from a foolish or fruitless curiosity, but from an earnest desire to learn the sentiments of a man, who has spent a long life in philosophic inquiries, and who, upon the extreme verge of it, seems, even in that awful and critical period, to possess all the powers of his mind in their full vigour and in unabated tranquillity.

I am more particularly led to give you this trouble from a passage in one of your late letters, wherein you say, *It is an idle thing in us to be concerned about anything that shall happen after our death; yet this,* you added, *is natural to all men.* Now I would eagerly ask, if it is *natural to all men,* to be interested in futurity, does this not strongly indicate that our existence will be protracted beyond this life?

Do you *now* believe, or suspect, that all the powers and faculties of your own mind, which you have cultivated with so much care and success, will cease and be extinguished with your vital breath?

Our soul, or immaterial part of us, some say, is able, when on the brink of dissolution, to take a glimpse of futurity; and for that reason I earnestly wish to have your *last thoughts* on this important subject.

I know that you will kindly excuse this singular application; and believe that I wish you, living or dying, every happiness that our nature is capable of enjoying, either here or hereafter . . .[2]

---

[1] A copy of this letter and a number of Hume's letters to Strahan were borrowed in 1776 by James Hutton, the Moravian preacher, to show to the King and Queen: see Hill, op. cit. Hutton appears to be the only one of Strahan's correspondents who addressed him as 'Billy'.

[2] Quoted by Burton, op. cit. Months later Hume's brother wrote to Strahan: 'You was desirous to know, if my brother had got your letter immediately before his decease. I can inform you he did, and it is now in my possession; but tho' he possessed his facultys, and understanding and cool head, to the last, he was scarce in a condition to answer it, nor the question you put to him: but so far as I can

Hume's death brought Strahan, as well as grief for the loss of an old and distinguished friend, the awkward problem of the unpublished manuscripts. These were sent to him by John Home,[1] the philosopher's brother, in September, with a letter in which he said he would be glad to have news of a decision to publish them. Strahan replied in a firm tone: 'You will see that I there [in letters to the dead man] promise to fulfill his intentions most exactly; a promise I shall most assuredly perform.' His resolution was a little impaired by a letter from Adam Smith in the next post:

My dear Strahan,

By a codicil to the will of our late most valuable friend Mr. Hume the care of his manuscripts is left to you. Both from his will and from his conversation I understand that there are only two which he meant should be published, an account of his own life, and Dialogues concerning natural religion. The latter, though finely written, I could have wished had remained in manuscript to be communicated only to a few people. When you read the work you will see my reasons without my giving you the trouble of reading them in a Letter . . . When you have read it you will perhaps think it not unreasonable to consult some prudent friend about what you ought to do.

I propose to add to his Life a very well authenticated account of his behaviour during his last illness . . .[2]

Adam Smith had no inkling of the furies that were to lash him over the 'well authenticated' account. The public, which comfortably ignored Hume's philosophic works and proved to be totally unconcerned by the *Dialogues* which made Smith so uneasy, was outraged by Smith's panegyric: 'Upon the whole, I have always considered him [Hume], both in his lifetime and since his death, as approaching as

---

[1] David had rationalized the spelling of his surname to accord with its pronunciation, but his brother never followed his example.

[2] This account takes the form of a letter to Strahan describing the last few weeks of Hume's life.

judge, his sentiments with regard to futurity were the same, as when he was in perfect health, and was never more at ease in his mind, at any one period of his life.' Strahan was anxious for reassurance about futurity; see Franklin's letter to him, p. 155.

nearly to the idea of a perfectly wise and virtuous man, as perhaps the frailty of human nature will permit.'

In the meantime Strahan was cautious and perhaps a little nervous. He replied to Smith:

All that I can say just now is that I shall do nothing precipitately . . . I will give the *Dialogues* a very attentive perusal before I consult anybody. I own I did not expect to hear they were so very exceptionable, as in one of his late letters to me he tells me *there is nothing in them worse than what I have already published*, or words to that effect . . . You see by his leaving the Dialogues ultimately to his nephew, in case of accident to me, his extreme solicitude that they should not be suppressed.[1]

Strahan deferred any decision and busied himself with Smith's addition to Hume's Life, which he liked although its shortness puzzled him. He consulted Smith about the advisability of a project 'to annex some of his Letters to me on political subjects.—What do you think of this?—I will do nothing without your advice and approbation; nor would I, for the world, publish any letter of his, but such as in your opinion, would do him honour.—Mr. Gibbon thinks such as I have shown him would have that tendency.' Smith vetoed the plan hastily and wrote once more to Strahan about a 'clamour against the Dialogues' which 'might for some time hurt the sale of the new edition of his works'. Eventually Hume's relations forced the issue. In January 1777 the nephew David and in February the brother John wrote to ask if a decision had been taken over the publication. Strahan replied to David:

As for Mr. Hume's *Dialogues on Natural Religion*, I am not yet determined whether I shall publish them or not. I have all possible regard to the will of the deceased: But as that can be as well fulfilled by you as by me, and as the publication will probably make some noise in the world, and its tendency be considered in different lights by different men, I am inclined to think it had better be made by you. From you some will conclude it comes with propriety as done *in obedience to the last request of your Uncle*, as he himself expresses it; from me it might

[1] Hill, op. cit.

be suspected to proceed from motives of interest; But in this matter I hope you will do me the justice to believe I put interest wholly out of the question. However you shall not, at any rate, be kept long in suspense, as you shall soon have my final resolution.

Strahan's final resolution, as he told John Home in a letter of 3 March, was against publication, and he resigned the copyright to the nephew. His advice was asked on whether the young man should publish the *Dialogues* at once or towards the end of the period mentioned in his uncle's will; they eventually appeared in 1779. One wonders whether Strahan ever felt any uneasiness over his default. The last word may be left with his friend Dr. Blair, who wrote to him on 23 August 1779: 'As to D. Hume's *Dialogues*, I am surprised that though they have now been published for some time, they have made so little noise. They are exceedingly elegant. They bring together some of his most exceptionable reasonings, but the principles themselves were all in his former works.'

12

Domestic Politics

STRAHAN appears always to have been interested in politics
and particularly in parliamentary debate. His letters show
that he was a consistent if occasionally critical supporter of
the various Ministries in power, which were many and short-
lived in the early years of George III's reign. On his accession in 1760, when Britain had achieved under Pitt the great
successes of the Seven Years War, he was determined to
bring about a peace. Pitt was in due course replaced by a
bitterly unpopular Scotsman, the Earl of Bute, who in turn
resigned when the Peace of Paris was concluded in 1763.
The King thereafter had to rely on a succession of Whig
ministers—Grenville, Rockingham, Pitt again as Earl of
Chatham, and Grafton—until in 1770 he found in Lord
North a brilliant parliamentarian and a willing servant.

Strahan's own views were not typical of his milieu. The
City as a whole encouraged the war against the French and
later the Spanish as a means of preserving and extending
overseas markets, and was violently opposed to the King's
peace policy and hence to Bute. Although he was intensely
proud of his country's victories, Strahan supported the
peace, just as in 1771 he was opposed to war over the Falkland Islands. One factor which undoubtedly alienated him
from general City opinion was the form taken by the attack
on Bute—a fierce outburst of feeling against Scotland and
Scotsmen, skilfully fanned and exploited by Wilkes's *The*

North Briton. Strahan was as proud of being a Scot as he was of his commercial success in London, and his resentment reinforced his instinctive fear of the mob violence which Wilkes and the 'Patriots' were to encourage, and led him into the minority of City men who supported with reservations the minister and beyond him the King.

He started to record political intelligence for David Hall, who printed his reports in the *Pennsylvania Gazette.* 'I shall always for the future give you a little Politics, since you desire it', he told Hall in 1759.[1] He possessed marked skill as a parliamentary reporter, not least in his ability to be present at all major debates long before he became King's Printer with an ex officio right of attendance. It must on occasion have been difficult to reconcile the demands of his business with the fascination of the Commons. On 20 January 1764, for instance, he wrote a detailed account to Hall of the debate on the previous day which resulted in Wilkes's expulsion from the House as the author of 'a false, scandalous and seditious libel', no. 45 of *The North Briton;* the debate 'began about five o'clock' and continued until 'the House adjourned (it now being ½ an hour after three in the morning,) till today at noon'.

It was not only in America that his reports were welcomed; Ralph Allen in Bath and David Hume in Edinburgh also enjoyed his long, accurate and detailed accounts of the proceedings. At a time when newspaper reports of debates in Parliament were usually either fictitious or surreptitious, anyone at a distance from London would have been glad of such information. He often duplicated his reports, of course, when describing the same event to different correspondents; for example, on 1 April 1768 he wrote the same excellent report of the riotous scenes at the Middlesex election to Hume and to Sir Andrew Mitchell, the British Minister in Berlin. When he told Hall in 1767 that the latter had an *'exclusive* right' to his political news, he meant as far as other journals were concerned.

[1] APS, 24 March.

Strahan was warmly complimented on his newsletters. 'Nothing can be more agreeable than your political intelligence', Hume told him in 1770. A year earlier Governor William Franklin had written 'Your Letters of political Intelligence, which Mr. Hall publishes in his Paper, afford me, from Time to Time, the best Information we receive of what is doing in Parliament, it containing many interesting Particulars & little Anecdotes, which we have not thro' any other Channel'.[1] 'You can do me no favour more obliging', Robertson wrote to Strahan from Edinburgh in 1767, 'than that of writing me often an account of all occurrences in the debates on this affair' (the Repeal of the Stamp Act). Above all, Benjamin Franklin was anxious to have all the political news Strahan could supply:

Philadelphia, May 1, 1764

Dear Straney,

I receiv'd your favour of December 20th. You cannot conceive the satisfaction and pleasure you give your friends here by your political letters. Your accounts are so clear, circumstantial and complete, that tho' there is nothing too much, nothing is wanting to give us, I imagine, a more perfect knowledge of your publick affairs than most people have that live among us. The characters of your speakers are so admirably sketch'd, and their views so plainly opened, that we see and know everybody; they all become of our acquaintance. So excellent a manner of writing seems to me a superfluous gift to a mere printer. If you do not commence author for the benefit of mankind, you will certainly be found guilty hereafter of burying your talent. It is true it will puzzle the Devil himself to find any thing else to accuse you of, but remember he may make a great deal of that. If I were king (which God in mercy to us all prevent) I should certainly make you the historiographer of my reign. There could be but one objection—I suspect you might be a little partial in my favour. But other qualifications for an historian being duly considered, I believe we might get over that . . .

Strahan first complied with Hall's request for news by sending him mere coffee-house chitchat:

We have lost Fort St. Davids, it seems, in the East Indies . . . The

[1] *Penna. Mag.*, XII, 381.

King of Spain's Death, which is hourly expected, will cut out new
Work for the Queen of Hungary; and enable the gallant King of
Prussia to maintain his Ground with more Facility[1]. . . At home all
is Peace and Unanimity, Mr. Pitt, who has indeed been a singular
Blessing to this Country, proceeds steadily in the Plan he set out with,
and will make us cut a glorious Figure, unless Fox and his Party clogg
his Operations, which yet I hope neither they nor all the Sons of
Corruption will ever be able to do.

That was in 1759. By 1762, with George III on the
throne, Strahan's views of Pitt have changed, as has his own
position. He can now report some first-hand news to Philadelphia.

It is agreed on all hands that a Treaty of Peace is on Foot between
France and us, which will probably take Effect. This will open the
Way for a General Pacification, when every Man may sit under his
Fig Tree in Safety; an Event now much to be wished for.—The
Party Scribblers continue to rail at Lord Bute; but as they have yet
been able to bring nothing against him but that he is a Scotsman, with
very little Effect.[2] They will not wait till his Conduct indicates his true
Character, but think to run him down without giving him a Trial.
For my own part, I am clearly of the opinion, that he means the
Honour and Interest of this Country, and is a Man of unblemished
Integrity; we have therefore much to hope, and little to fear, from his
Administration. I am truly inclined to expect every thing that can
reasonably be expected, as I am convinced his Intentions are pure.[3]—
Mr. Pitt is now nearly forgot, which I soon foresaw would be the
Case; tho' I think his past Services ought ever to be remembered to his
Honour. But his accepting the Pension so readily, and at so critical a

[1] Later, and better informed through his friendship with Sir Andrew Mitchell,
Strahan was to say of the gallant King, 'Mayhap there never existed a greater
Scoundrel'. (To Hume, 1 March 1771.) Pitt's opponent was Henry Fox, later first
Lord Holland, and father of Charles James Fox.

[2] Bute had become Prime Minister in May, with Grenville as Secretary of State;
Pitt had resigned the year before. The 'General Pacification' was effected in February 1763 by the Treaty of Paris.

[3] Writing in 1768 to Sir Andrew Mitchell, Strahan said of Bute: 'The case of this
nobleman is really very singular; divested of power, he retains all the odium of
Prime Minister. Having long since most injudiciously pushed into office, and as
injudiciously retired from the political theatre, he hath ever since exercised the power
of recommending, or rather nominating every succeeding Ministry.'

time, has given a mortal Stab to his Reputation.—At Guildhall, where he was received with enormous Acclamations, I asked him how he liked his Reception? He replied, It was much above any thing he could pretend to merit. I told him, If the Citizens had not thought he deserved it, they had not so highly distinguished him. I observed, that we had been greatly obliged to him for his active and spirited Administration, and I still hoped we should not be deprived of his future Services. He replied, That all our Hopes centred there, *pointing to the King*. The King, said I, is every thing we could wish him; but he is but a Youth, and cannot be supposed fit to conduct the Affairs of this great Nation himself; that must be done by some able and experienced Minister under him. He said, Much depended upon the good Affection of the City. The City, said I, are evidently devoted to the public Service. True, the large Sums of Money now become necessary annually, cannot, at this time, by reason of the length of the War, be raised on such good Terms as at first; but they will be raised, and raised with Cheerfulness too.

I did not then think that this was actually the last Flash of Popularity he was likely to enjoy.—Tho' the very same Evening I afterwards told old Lord Temple, when he was extolling the *Virtue* of his Brother-in-law, the Alliance to which, more than to the *Man*, he said he was proud of, *My Lord, the Ministry have given him the Pension to blast him*, these were my very words: to which he made this memorable Answer, *Sir, we are sensible of this move now*. Tho' I think any body with half an Eye might easily have seen the Drift of it.—He told me also, that Mr. Pitt was first offered the Government of Canada with £5000 a Year, which he refused *because it was a precarious Appointment*; and that two Days after, the Affair was settled as it now stands.— So that it was some Days in transacting, which afforded time enough to foresee all the Consequences.[1]—This is the most material Part of the conversation I had with them at Guildhall. Much more I had, but what I cannot now remember; neither is it material.—The Terms of Peace now talked of, are, that we retain all North America, to be

[1] When Pitt resigned on 5 October 1761 he was urged by Bute and the King to accept rewards for his services; he refused the offices of Governor of Canada and Chancellor of the Duchy of Lancaster, but was induced to accept a pension of £3,000 a year for three lives, with the title of Baroness of Chatham for his wife. As the Court party had foreseen and contrived, he was assailed for 'selling his country'. He vindicated his conduct in a letter to the City of London and in consequence on Lord Mayor's Day, while Bute was hissed, Pitt enjoyed a triumphant reception— the occasion described months later by Strahan.

bounded by the Mississippi; and Senegal; and that Guadaloupe, Martinico, and Grace be restored to the French, with Liberty to fish on Newfoundland. These, if true, do not seem very promising; but I am still hopeful it will be an honourable and lasting Peace.—So much for Politics.[1]

By 1766 Strahan could tell Hall of Pitt that 'I have by no means the best opinion of his Heart and Intentions'.[2] But even from the shadows he could still attract his old supporters; in 1770 Strahan wrote to Hume that 'I went to the House of Lords, in preference to the Commons, as I found your favourite and mine, Lord Chatham, was to be there'. He was sufficiently candid to add that in the debate Chatham's second speech had been a poor one.[3]

Two main topics dominated all Strahan's political letters, as they must have dominated the minds of all thinking men of the time: Wilkes and America. As far as Strahan was concerned the one seems to colour the other, as though the turbulence of the colonists were an exact reflection abroad of the seditious clamours, as Strahan thought them, raised by Wilkes's partisans at home; and to be dealt with in a similar fashion. As a strong believer in the virtues of firm administration, as a self-made man in the midst of creating a very profitable business, and as an instinctive Tory, he was not likely to feel any sympathy for those whose actions, whether so intended or not, were apt to upset his apple-cart. He felt a sort of horror for Wilkes, a sentiment he never abated. His views about the Americans, when war had finally broken out, were just as inflexible but they took very much longer to form. His eventual extremism on the American question contrasts with his earlier sympathy—informed as it was by his correspondence with Hall and his friendship with, almost his veneration for, Franklin—and reflects a slowly mounting exasperation which he shared with his sovereign and with most of his fellow-subjects.

[1] APS, 10 August 1762.
[2] *Penna. Mag.*, 10 May.
[3] Burton, op. cit.

175

His impatience with the Opposition was duly transmitted to Philadelphia. Franklin wrote to him on 8 August 1763:

Dear Friend: I have received here your favour of May 3, and post-script of May 10, and thank you cordially for the sketch you give me of the present state of your political affairs. If the stupid, brutal opposition your good king and his measures have lately met with should, as you fear, become general, surely you would not wish me to come and live among such people; you would rather remove hither, where we have no savages but those we expect to be such. But I think your madmen will ere long come to their senses; and when I come I shall find you generally wise and happy.

Strahan is continually deploring the lack of sufficient firmness in government, but to a different end in respect of his two dominant themes. As for Wilkes, of course, he considered the authorities' weakness lay in not crushing him and his supporters at once; over America, at least in the early stages, he believed that the Government was lax in controlling its subordinates who were thereby enabled to inflame the situation. The latter stricture he extended to the King. He complained to Hall at the time of the Repeal of the Stamp Act that the King was 'not blessed with that share of Fortitude, Courage and Steadiness so necessary to the Maintenance of his personal Authority, and to the due Management of his Servants'.[1]

Strahan's parliamentary reports record only what was the sense of the various speeches. The lack of personal comment and interpretation, or of backstairs intelligence, robs them for us of some of their interest, but it was precisely that lack which made them so valuable to his contemporary readers who were perfectly well equipped to add their own gloss to the bare record. The fact that several of his readers differed in their views on some matters was no doubt another inducement to objectivity. As an example of his skill as a reporter, his account of the debates on the legality of General Warrants is quoted as an appendix.

This is not the place to repeat the story of Wilkes's tur-

[1] *Penna. Mag.*, 7 April 1766.

bulent career which convulsed domestic politics for a decade. In brief, he fled to France rather than appear in court to answer charges of publishing no. 45 of *The North Briton* and his obscene *Essay on Women*; he was outlawed and convicted in his absence. He returned to England in 1768, stood unsuccessfully as parliamentary candidate for the City of London and promptly stood for Middlesex and was elected, though still an outlaw. On April 20 he surrendered himself to the court and was temporarily set free on a technicality, as Strahan indignantly explained to Hall.[1]

The facts I will endeavour to state with brevity and precision. John Wilkes, convicted on two indictments, one for blasphemy, the other for sedition in grossly abusing and giving the lie to his Sovereign, flies from justice and is thereupon outlawed. He attempts once and again to obtain his pardon, but is as often obliged to return into exile. Tired, at last, of his obscurity, depending upon the weakness of administration, and hoping also to avail himself of the confusion and tumult unavoidably attending a general election, he ventures, once more, to return at that critical period; and being desperate, and having nothing to lose, he boldly offers himself as a Representative of the Capital. What unexpectedly followed you already know. But after all, who could believe it, that this very man, who the other day, with fear and trembling, sallied from his retreat; whom we were told any body might secure and bring to justice, and who at length gave public notice of his intention to surrender himself at the bar of the Court of King's Bench; I say, who could believe it, that when this man, so circumstanced, came before them, he was told, that *they did not know him?* He was not *legally* brought before them, as a writ of *Capias utlegatum*, it seems, ought previously to have been issued against him; which the Chief Justice did not choose to order, and the Attorney General, whose particular province it was, did not choose to do. Is not this *passing strange?* But this is not all. The *criminal*, even there, at the tribunal of justice itself, becomes the *accuser*; and in an insolent speech, which to the amazement of all who heard it, he was permitted to make, he charges the Chief Justice himself, to his face, of having *illegally and unconstitutionally* altered the Record . . . in such a manner as materially to affect his case . . . This done, Wilkes is suffered to return home in triumph!

[1] N.J. Historical Society, *Proceedings*, 26 April and 14 May 1768.

This whole proceeding is universally considered by all impartial men as the consequence of a total *abdication of Government*; . . . The secret springs of all this manoeuvre have not yet been discovered. Either Lord Mansfield is afraid of Wilkes's popularity, and does not therefore choose to be active in carrying his sentence into execution, in which case his conduct is dastardly beyond example; or the Ministry[1] mean to protract the matter till the meeting of Parliament, to have their sense of it, and have instructed Lord Mansfield accordingly, in which case he condescends to be their tool. Either way his behaviour has, upon this occasion, been such as gives just cause of deep concern to those who venerate his rare and exalted abilities as a lawyer; and even in spite of these, renders him (I am sorry to say it) the object of general censure—I had almost said contempt . . .

A week later Wilkes was committed to prison, and violent rioting broke out. It lasted for almost a fortnight and culminated in 'the Massacre of St. George's Fields' on 10 May. Strahan continued to Hall:

Wilkes . . . remains in prison. Crowds of people have constantly repaired to St. George's Fields, where the prison stands, and, as the newspapers will inform you, have been very riotous, and some persons have been killed by the military, who were called in to quell the disturbances. How it has happened it is not easy to say, but there has been attempts made, not only by the seamen . . . but by the coalheavers, carmen, &c., to press for an augmentation of their wages, upon the plea of the dearness of the necessaries of life, and refuse to go to work until the masters have agreed to their demands. All this, however, has been done without riot or violence, and hath in appearance no connection whatever with Wilkes or his cause. This matter will, therefore, come to nothing, as indeed I am apt to think will Mr. Wilkes's affair in a very little time . . . The Parliament hath yet taken no notice of him . . . I was in the House yesterday, and perceived several of his well-wishers and abettors look very blank . . . his friends flattered themselves, that some very violent motions would have been made in his behalf before they went upon any other business. . . . As there is not the least colour of reason for complaint on the part of his Majesty, or his Government, or that our liberties are in the least danger, all these attempts to disturb our repose must necessarily prove abortive . . .

[1] Grafton's Ministry. Mansfield was Lord Chief Justice.

Strahan's wishful thinking was soon exposed. In the following year, 1769, Wilkes while serving a twenty-two month sentence of imprisonment was expelled from the House and then re-elected twice; his third re-election was at the expense of Henry Luttrell who was nevertheless declared by the House to be the member for Middlesex. These events were naturally the signal for further rioting and clamour, as well as giving serious cause for concern to many sober citizens. But Strahan had no doubts; nothing which hit at Wilkes could be harmful to the common good. Even so, the uproar must have been unsettling, and it was possibly in a rather wistful mood that he quoted a remark by Wilkes in a letter to Hall in 1770;[1] he says that Wilkes, on being asked how he did, replied, 'I am pretty well, but damnably sick of Wilkes and Liberty'. Strahan's vexation at the weakness of government, as he considered it, was not lessened by events, although he seems consistently to have underrated the strength of public opinion, if not of the Opposition's parliamentary abilities. In 1770 he could tell Hall that the 'faction have, in all appearances, done their worst, and are now at bay, not knowing which way to turn themselves'.[2] He continued:

The Ministry, tho' they have by no means answered the reasonable expectations of the sober part of the publick, and have on many occasions shewn marks of timidity, irresolution and want of concert among themselves, will yet, as far as I can see, or have been able to discover, are [*sic*] likely enough to hold their ground, till some extraordinary event, (such as a foreign war, or a domestic insurrection) of which there is at present not the least apprehension . . . The session is near a conclusion; people are quite tired of the subject [the Middlesex election] and many of the most respectable members of both Houses are gone or going to their country seats; so that you need not expect to hear of anything very remarkable till their next meeting.

Unfortunately none of Strahan's surviving letters touch on the 'printers' case'—the attempt by Parliament in 1771

[1] *Penna. Mag.*

[2] *Booghers Repository*, 1 April 1770. The ministry was North's.

to enforce an obsolete ruling against the reporting of debates by newspapers. In choosing an issue on which they were bound to lose, the Commons showed the same ineptitude that for twenty years had marked all its relations with the public, whatever ministry was in power. In this case the printers concerned were supported by the City authorities; the Lord Mayor's committal to the Tower turned into a triumphal procession and, after the customary rioting, Parliament admitted defeat. Strahan would have been torn between support of the ministry and dislike of the Patriots on the one hand, and on the other his position as a newspaper proprietor who was also a skilled parliamentary reporter. There is no reason to suppose that he ever felt much concern for fellow-printers who found themselves in trouble with the law or the government.

His letters of that year are more concerned with foreign affairs. Strahan would have none of the objections made against the Peace of 1763; he saw no advantages in a continuance of war. He was equally against adventure and in favour of negotiation in 1771 when a sudden quarrel arose with Spain—supported by France—over the Falkland Islands. In January Hume wrote to him: 'This Spanish War is so enormously absurd, unjust, and unreasonable that I think it never had its parralel . . . our Ministry are more afraid of the despicable London Mob than of all Europe. . . . You think we shall have peace: I am glad to hear it; but cannot allow myself to think, that any Chance will save Men so infatuated as our Ministry.'[1]

When Strahan replied to this letter, two months later, the affair had blown over and the Ministry was hard at work persuading the country that they had been wise in not pressing the issue as far as war. In this they had the support of Johnson's *Thoughts on the late Transactions respecting Falkland's Islands* 'in which,' says Boswell, 'upon materials furnished him by ministry and upon general topicks expanded in his richest style, he successfully endeavoured to persuade

[1] Hill, op. cit. It was another eleven years before the North Ministry fell.

the nation that it was wise and laudable to suffer the question
of right to remain undecided, rather than involve our country
in another war'. The pamphlet, which was sold for 1*s*.
through Cadell, was printed by Strahan. The latter sent a
copy to Hume, who told him, when he thanked him for it,
that he thought it 'a good one, and very diverting from the
Peculiarity and Enormity of the Style'.

Strahan's letter of 1 March 1771 to Hume shows him to
be a not uncritical supporter of the Ministry:

> You see I was right in conjecturing that this Misunderstanding
> with Spain would terminate peaceably.—The Occasion of the Quarrel
> I believe with you to be more our fault than theirs. But you will con-
> sider that the Ministry had some factious Scoundrels at Home to
> attend to in the Adjustment of the Dispute, who were abundantly
> eager to find Cause of Blame in their Conduct, and to render them
> odious to the Mob.—Happily, however, they are disappointed, and
> the Accommodation seems to be generally approved.—Approved it
> certainly is by every body who wishes well to this Country, and who
> are sensible how much it imports us to avoid War by every Means in
> our Power, for Reasons sufficiently obvious.—You seem much out of
> humour with the Ministry. Upon my word, as far as I am able to
> judge, they have acted pretty well of late, tho' I must own their
> Timidity regarding our domestic Incendiaries is altogether inexcusable.
> However, bating this great Fault (and *great* I allow it is), Lord North,
> in particular, has acted his Part very well; he speaks with Courage and
> Firmness in the House; and with temper too.—In short, I think he
> gains ground in the public opinion every Day. I firmly believe he
> means well. And I wish the present Ministry to stand their ground,
> purely because they are the *present Ministry*; for, as I told your friemd
> Lord Hertford when I had the Honour to wait upon him, the King
> has changed his Ministers so very often since his Accession, that
> another Change would be almost equal to a Dethronement.[1]

Relief that war had been averted made Strahan optimistic
about the state of affairs in general; he told Hume a month
later that:

> . . . our Trade is really in a flourishing state . . . our Colonies are grow-
> ing very considerable without the smallest fear of a separation from us

[1] Royal Society of Edinburgh.

... from all Quarters of the Globe, wealth is daily pouring into this country, of which you see the most convincing proofs, not only in this Capital, but over the whole Kingdom, in some degree or another ... If the folly and absurdity of the canaille of London doth not receive a check (and a very little matter would effectually do it) it is impossible to say where it may terminate. But in truth it is more contemptible than people at a distance can possibly conceive or believe. The bustle is chiefly, almost solely, in the newspapers.[1]

Strahan had written in much the same strain to Hall some days earlier:

The Peace is now become, in all probability, permanent, both the Spaniards and we having actually disarmed. Fifteen Ships of the Line were ordered the other Day to be paid off; and yet it is intended to keep in Commission a much larger Number of Ships than we had before our late Armament. It now appears pretty evidently that neither the Spaniards nor the French meant in earnest to break with us on this Occasion. Had they really purposed to go to War, we certainly afforded them sufficient Provocation; for our Right to Falklands Islands, which we so totally asserted, is, at best, but very weakly founded, the French having been actually in Possession of them, and at the Requisition of the Spaniards deserted them, three Years at least before the Date of our Claim. But such was the Situation of our domestic Squabbles for Power, and such a Handle had the Opposition made of this Transaction, that the Ministry were under an absolute Necessity of taking up the Matter in so high a Tone, thereby shewing themselves, I am sorry to say it, more afraid of the Mob of London than of the potent Houses of Bourbon ...[2]

The Papers will inform you that our Patriots being unfortunately foiled in all their Attempts to disturb the Government, or to force themselves into Office, are now falling out among themselves ... Whichever Party prevails, it must end in their Destruction. Wilkes himself, with a Perseverance truly diabolical, is indefatigable in acting his Part as a publick Incendiary. But I am convinced his utmost Efforts will be fruitless, and that his Glory is upon the Wain. I have

[1] Hill, op. cit., 25 May 1771.
[2] An echo of Hume, who later returned to the same point. In June he wrote to Strahan of Lord North that 'He bullies Spain and France and quakes before the Ward of Farringdon without' (the ward for which Wilkes was Alderman).

several times observed to you, that all our Grievances and Apprehensions appeared only in our Newspapers. We are indeed in perfect Tranquillity. . . .

In the light of Strahan's belief that public discontent was magnified in the Press, it is ironic that the *London Chronicle*, which he printed and in which he had a part interest, should have been one of the culprits. He told Hume in a letter of 23 July 1771 of a procession through London:

You see our Lord Mayor, after advertising for a fortnight to invite the whole Livery and all the Mob in London to attend him, hath presented another *wise* and *modest* Remonstrance. But whatever they may tell you, I assure you from ocular demonstration, that it made a most pitiful and paltry figure. A number of people were indeed brought into the streets to gaze at him, and the few Aldermen and Common Council-men that accompanied him, but only about a dozen blackguards followed and holloed him.

Yet Hill notes that the *London Chronicle* of 11 July 1771 stated that the procession consisted of about fifty carriages and that it proceeded 'amidst the greatest acclamations of the people'.

Wilkes won his protracted campaign against the authorities. Amidst growing difficulties with the American colonists, the Government could no longer afford the domestic uproar that attended their prolonged refusal to admit that Wilkes was the legally elected member for Middlesex. In 1774 he was returned once more with no opposition from the Ministry; and he ceased to be a diabolical figure in Strahan's correspondence. When he sat down in the evening to 'write politics' to Hall, he tended more and more to describe parliamentary activities as they bore upon the American problem. *Wilkes and Liberty* was a less immediate concern to the Pennsylvanian readers of Hall's paper than their own liberties, and Strahan's letters reflect the shift of interest.

13

American Affairs

THE anomalous relationship between the colonies and the mother country had become dangerously strained as a result of the victories won in the Seven Years War. The conquest of Canada simultaneously removed the colonists' fear of the French and imposed the need of increased revenue for development and administration. Trade had for long been controlled in the interests of Britain but the system was ill-regulated and its effects on the colonies mitigated by efficient smuggling on a very large scale. This lax arrangement could no longer be accepted, and the ministries in power from 1763 onward, without taking into account the growing political and economic vigour of the colonies, tried to raise fresh revenues and to tighten up the existing regulations. In 1764 came the Sugar Act and a year later the Stamp Act, the mild provisions of which caused a storm of protest and an effective boycott of British goods; in consequence it was repealed in 1766. There followed in 1767 new customs duties on paper, glass, lead, paint and tea; once more the Government drew back in dismay at the outcry and in 1770 abolished the duties save for that on tea.

Tea was the commodity which provoked the crucial incident when North permitted the East India Company to send its tea direct to the colonies. Though still subject to the duty, it was much cheaper than smuggled Dutch tea and offered a threat both to the merchants who traded very profitably in the latter and to the shipowners who normally carried dutiable tea from England to the colonies. The extremists who had with ease exploited the pattern of high-handed interference and then vacillation on the part of Britain were now joined by powerful allies: soon there followed the Boston Tea Party, the closing of the port of Boston in retaliation, and in 1775 the first shots when a British force was sent to seize a store of arms at Concord.

Strahan was certainly not ill-informed about American affairs. His correspondence with Hall, his warm friendship with Franklin, his business dealings in various colonies, and his acquaintance with very many Americans on their visits to London, all induced him to sympathize with the colonists. His large interests in the American trade inclined him to a peaceful solution, though the same interests drove him to urge an imposed union when the issue of separation finally came to a head. His eventual rancorous hostility to the separatists derived partly from his earlier disbelief that affairs could ever reach such a pass, and partly from his indignation over the plight of the dispossessed loyalists whom he met in London after they had been driven from their homes in the colonies.

The first important reference to American affairs in a letter to Hall occurs in 1765:

The Stamp Act makes a great deal of Noise, here as well as with you.[1] It hath been mentioned in the Papers lately, that all your Charters, in express Words, subject you to Taxes imposed by the Parliament of England. If so, the People with you seem to have forgot this Clause; but this matter will now be fully canvassed as soon as the Session opens; and then, if I can send any authentic Account of the Debate, or any material Intelligence whatever, you may depend upon hearing from me whether I have any business to write about or not. . . .

. . . I have not seen Dr. Franklin lately; but I dare say he is usefully, I hope successfully employed in your Service. Had his salutary advice

---

[1] Of all the colonial measures enacted by Grenville's Ministry (1763–5) the Stamp Act was particularly resented.

been followed by Mr. Grenville, all this Uproar with you had been avoided, which, however just the Occasion may be, worthless and designing Men will take the Advantage of it, to the great Detriment of honest Men like you. But I hope Matters will now quickly be composed, for most certainly it is the mutual Interest of the Colonies and the Mother Country to agree. . . .

. . . 'Tis a Pity the Parliament did not meet two months ago, and endeavoured to fall upon some Method to stem the Confusion among you before it rose to such a terrible Height. It is true they meet next Tuesday; but then the King is only to make a short Speech, acquainting them with the Birth of another Prince, and the Death of the Duke of Cumberland, and will defer mentioning the Business of their Meeting till after the Holidays. They will then vote an Address of Congratulation and Condolance, issue out the New Writs, and adjourn.—If you ask me; How do you imagine they will proceed in our Affair?—This is indeed a difficult Question; but I suppose they will first assert their Right to impose Taxes on the Colonies, and signify at the same time that upon their humble Remonstrances, that any part of the Stamp Act is particularly grievous, they will be heard, and will have such Redress as his Majesty's Subjects Inhabitants of Great Britain would in a similar Case be entitled to.—If you ask me, how will they enforce this Resolution in case the Colonies will admit no such Power in the British Parliament?—Here I am at a loss again; but I suppose, in the first Place, by sending a number of Armed Sloops to block up all your Ports, and prevent your trading with other European Nations.—But I hope things will not come to this Pass; and that the Wisdom, Policy, and Moderation of the Legislature will quickly find a Remedy for so grievous and dangerous a Wound to the Union, Power, Trade and Security of this great Empire. . . .[1]

A few weeks later, on 11 January 1766, Strahan wrote again to Hall, fulfilling his promise to report the proceedings of the re-assembled House:

You see the King's Speech is very short. I was in the House of Commons when it was read there; and heard, with much indignation, George Grenville make a long, confused, violent, inflammatory Speech, highly censuring the Behaviour of the Colonies in regard to the Stamp Act, calling it downright Rebellion, and proposing to make use of very harsh Expressions towards them in their answer to the

[1] Letter dated 12 December 1765, catalogued by Seven Gables Bookshop.

Speech; but this was overruled, as it would appear to be condemning them unheard. Above twenty members spoke; and almost all of them seemed to be for supporting and adhering to their Legislative authority over the Colonies, and their undoubted Right to impose Taxes upon them. But how they will act when the whole affair, with all the Circumstances attending it, is laid before them, I cannot pretend to say. I hope they will consider it coolly, and with the utmost Impartiality; for nobody can at present foresee all the Consequences that may attend their final Determination in this important matter.—Various Schemes are said to be laid before the Ministry to compose the Difference; but I have not been able to learn any of them that seemed to deserve the least Credit, and therefore I will not repeat them. This only I will say, that I am quite certain the present Ministry[1] wish to do you all possible Kindness, most of them having been strongly against the Act whilst it was under Deliberation last year. I only wish that they may do what they do, frankly, cordially, and heartily, and that before they separate not only this, but every possible Difference which hereafter, as Things are now circumstanced, might happen, will be removed, or prevented; and such a Plan for an indissoluble Union laid, as must give pleasure to every Lover of his Country, and which indeed appears every Day, more and more, to be absolutely necessary in order to prevent the actual Separation of the various Branches of this most extensive Empire. . . .

. . . We now with impatience wait the Issue. How it will be taken up, or in what manner finally settled, cannot be yet so much as guessed at. By much the most satisfactory and most honourable for both sides, as well as the most salutary, safe, and beneficial for the whole British Dominion, would be to unite us together by an incorporating Union, in the same manner as Holland was in 1707, and allow the Colonies to send representatives to our Parliament. This would completely answer every good Purpose to both Sides, and cement us, by insensible degrees, in so complete a manner, as would forever put it out of the Power of any foreign Potentate, or internal Cabal, to separate us. By this very means was Wales long ago, and Scotland more lately, so firmly united to the English Crown, to the amazing aggrandizement of this Island, which but for this had long ago become a Province to France, or some other Continental Power. . . .[2]

[1] Rockingham's Ministry, which had succeeded Grenville's and in two months' time was to repeal the Stamp Act.
[2] Printed in the *Proceedings* of the New Jersey Historical Society.

Strahan's opinions seem to have hardened in the next four years, although on 24 August 1770 he could still tell Hall that he thought 'the Matter now in Dispute between us a mere Bagatelle'. But in a letter of 7 April of the same year he explains how his views and those of Franklin have begun to diverge:

I told you in my last that all the American duties would be repealed, that on tea excepted; which I can now (with *certainty*, I think,) assure you will not be taken off at all, at least this year. I find the Ministry,[1] from the best information, are clearly of the opinion that the Americans must and will submit . . .

. . . It is not easy, I well know, for people to reason coolly, when matters of great moment, in which they are deeply interested, are agitated. But for my own part, I think I have all along considered the affair with the utmost impartiality; and I am still of the same mind I was in, when I told you, in a former letter, that I thought *neither party should stand out upon trifles and punctilios*. Whatever, therefore, your other friends and correspondents may advise, I am strongly of the opinion, that as the affair is now circumstanced, the best way for you to act, is to aquiesce in this same tea duty, which, laying aside the *principle* of the tax, is not worth mentioning, and to trust, with some degree of confidence, in the justice and wisdom of the Parliament for future relief from that, and other more considerable obstructions, under which several branches of your trade now labours. It cannot be, I must insist upon it, it cannot be but they will, in due time, grant you every indulgence that is proper, or that you could wish for. It is their *interest*, it is their *duty* so to do; tho' a variety of accidents and circumstances may now prevent them from fully entering into and discussing your particular concerns. Look round, I pray you, upon your various wants which cannot be supplied from your own internal resources, and consider if you can really subsist and thrive without the protection and manufactures of Great Britain. For my part, I would always have America considered, both by themselves and by us, as a part, or as so many different counties of England—at least, as far as it is practicable so to consider it. Nor do I see anything in the *principle* of this tax (so much dreaded and detested in your side of the water) repugnant to this idea.

[1] North's Ministry, which had been in office for four months.

I am sensible that what I have just now advanced, differs widely from the opinion of our worthy friend, Dr. Franklin. As I most highly esteem him, I am sorry for it. And the disparity of our judgements and means of information is sufficiently obvious. But may I not be allowed to suppose that his warm and strenuous attachment to his native country, and to his friends there, hath in some degree, byassed his sound and perfect and manly understanding, upon which, on other occasions, I could securely depend? Nay, I will venture to tell you (for I always speak my mind to you, as I have done in political matters to some of the greatest names here) that I really think him rather too partial to you, and perhaps too much hurt (tho' not altogether without cause,) with the behaviour of the Mother Country to her children. Having said this much, I will now leave it to time to determine which of us is in the right. It will be no wonder, and I myself shall be heartily glad, if I am found to have been mistaken. . . .[1]

Clearly there was a reaction from Hall to this dismissal of the principle of taxation, for in a later letter that year Strahan takes up the point. After repeating it as his considered opinion that the colonists should pay the tax first, and settle on redress later, he continues: 'I begin to think my Politics now begin to be disagreeable to you. If so, the least hint from you will prevent all further trouble to you on the Head.'[2] Hall apparently did not drop the hint, for Strahan's letters continue to discuss politics. On 1st May 1771 he wrote that 'American affairs have not been so much mentioned of late' and 'I am *sure* the Ministry wish well to America'. The following month he once again propounded to Hall his scheme for 'a complete and cordial union'.

It was stated above that Strahan's increasing irritation at the American demands could be traced to two causes. If not another cause, at least a factor in the growth of his acerbity was his election to the House of Commons as a supporter of Lord North's Ministry, the deficiencies of which were a good deal less apparent to the M.P. than they had been to the stranger in the House. Strahan was a likely man for the Ministry to approach; his principles were 'sound', he could

---

[1] *Booghers Repository.*   [2] *Penna. Mag.*, 7 November 1770.

well afford the expense of election, and as King's Printer he was known not only to Ministers but, more usefully, to the humbler agents of administration, the men who actually pulled the strings. He was returned in 1774 as a member for Malmesbury, which he represented until 1780 when he became M.P. for Wootton Bassett; in both cases he purchased his seat.

In a forecast of the probable results of an election in 1784, the Secretary to the Treasury, John Robinson, marks Wootton Bassett as one of the 'Open Boroughs whose Seats may probably be obtained with Expense', putting that expense at 'suppose 3,000 *l*'. He adds a note: 'Mr. Strahan purchased the last time; probably would again this and has the fairest claim on General St. John, through whom by another agent on the spot this borough is always managed. Strahan has always been, and it is believed always would be steady . . .'[1] Whether he was deterred by his health or the expense, Strahan in the event did not stand for re-election in 1784 at Wootton Bassett or anywhere else.

I am indebted to the late Sir Lewis Namier for an opportunity to examine a notebook which was in his possession. It is one of a couple, clearly Strahan's property since they contain much of his unmistakable handwriting. That which is of concern in the present context[2] is labelled *Parliamentary Characters from the Public Ledger 1779, and The English Chronicle 1780 & 1781*. The notebook, which has been indexed, contains clippings from the two papers describing 440 members; most of the characters are violently anti-Ministerial in tone—the *English Chronicle* in particular was an Opposition journal.

There are two entries relating to Strahan. The first, from the *Public Ledger*, is succinct:

[1] Laprade: *Parliamentary Papers of John Robinson 1774–1784*, London, 1922. In August 1781 Strahan was described by Charles Jenkinson, leader of the King's Friends, as 'a most excellent Member of Parliament'. Add. MSS. 38308 f. 157b.

[2] The other contains scraps of information such as lists of birthdays, and assorted newspaper clippings. The latter include Strahan's obituary of the Dowager Princess of Wales, and Johnson's lines on the death of Levett.

Malmesbury: William Strahan. Bought his seat, and votes constantly with the Minister.

The second, from the *English Chronicle*, is a great deal more cutting. Presumably by 1780 Strahan was a figure better deserving attack than he had been in the previous Parliament.

Wootton Bassett

William Strahan Esq.—Printer to his Majesty, and the parliamentary lacquey of Lord North. This lucky typographer came to London with no other fortune than the ample possession of those characteristic endowments which distinguish the place of his nativity, Caledonian industry, stimulated and aided by true Caledonian cunning. The unremitting exertion of these *excellent* qualifications produced their natural effect in slow but sure gradation, till he was at last exalted to the lucrative employment which he now holds of being printer to his Majesty.—After he had possessed this place a few years, which is said to bring him in an annual income of two or three thousand pounds, he was sent for by the Premier, who gave him to understand, that his Majesty's servants were [not] bestowed offices of considerable emolument, as attended that which he occupied, without a compensation of some kind. The printer, ignorant tho' he be, was not so confirmed a dolt as to misconceive the necessity conveyed in this intimation, and accordingly in the ensuing session, by the proper application of that omnipotent nostrum which palliates every incapacity and every defect, at least in the estimation of English electors, was returned *nefandum dictu*! a Member of the British Legislature. It would be abject and ungenerous to comment upon a man's original situation, and to make these properties the objects of animadversion or ridicule, which exist independent of himself, and for which he cannot justly be amenable, but when this individual so far mistakes his character, and forgets himself, as without understanding, without education, without independence to obtrude himself into a situation where each of these qualities are so eminently necessary, it becomes public virtue, and not personal acrimony, to expose his insufficiency, and to reprobate the ludicrous ambition or despicable interest with which he must have been actuated in so undeserved an exaltation.

Since Mr. Strahan has been in parliament, he has been one of the most useful men in it to his patron and master Lord North. He generally sits two or three rows behind the Treasury Bench, that he may be within the ready nod of his superior in the same honourable service, Sir Grey Cooper. The printer understands the intimation (for what will not long and laborious experience effect?) very readily, and having received his instructions, he comes into the Lobby, and applies to another servant below him, to whom he gives directions for bringing down such of the parliamentary pasteboards as the exigency of the case, or the ostentation of the Premier, may require. Having executed this duty, he takes his seat again, and, if no other work arises, sits very quietly till he is called upon for the mechanical monosyllable in the division. Let no man despair as to his being shut out from the pride of heraldry, or the pleasing implication of splendid genealogy, for Mr. Strahan has lately procured a coat of arms for his carriage. After what has been said, it would be superfluous to add anything respecting the political principles of this member.

Strahan thought this anonymous attack worth preserving, with the characters of most of his fellow-members, in his notebook. The aspersions on his education and intelligence, and the implied account of how he became King's Printer, are very wide of the mark, but there is nothing to show that the description of his activities in the House is inaccurate. He is recorded as having intervened only twice in debates; in 1781, during a discussion of a tax upon almanacs, and in 1783, to inform the House how long it would take to print certain evidence. 'A great politician all his life, in the House he was the printer', observed Namier.

Indeed the only evidence we have tends to demonstrate his laziness—the strictures expressed by Johnson upon Strahan's having 'read newspapers part of the time, and slept the rest', while sitting on an election-committee. 'As an excuse', Boswell continues, 'when challenged by the chairman for such behaviour, [he] bluntly answered, "I had made up my mind upon that case";—Johnson with an indignant contempt, said, "If he was such a rogue as to make up his mind upon a case without hearing it, he should not have been such a fool as to tell it".' However, it was to Strahan that Johnson turned on behalf of Henry Thrale after the latter's defeat at Southwark in the election of 1780, to 'find by enquiry any seat to be had, as seats are had without natural interest'.

Sir Grey Cooper, mentioned in the *English Chronicle* attack, was an important figure in the workings of the North Ministry, so useful indeed to successive Governments that although he first became joint secretary of the Treasury under Rockingham, he retained the post under Chatham, Grafton and North. I owe to Sir Lewis Namier two references to payments made to Strahan while he was an M.P. In 1779, in the Secret Service Accounts, there occurs under the heading 'Occasional Bounties and Expenses paid by Sir Grey Cooper' the entry *Mr. Strahan by order for Secret Services £150*. In the account for October 1780 to April 1781, under a similar heading, there is the note *Mr. Strahan for Woodfall £200*.[1]

There is nothing necessarily sinister of course in such payments. The Secret Service fund was a device for making payments not covered by one of the official Votes. The second payment at least indicates a fee for printing or publishing, presumably something outside the run of the King's Printer's business. It may well have been to Sir Grey Cooper that Strahan wrote in 1771 to suggest that Johnson would make a useful supporter of the Ministry if a seat in the House of Commons could be found for him; the letter is printed by Boswell[2] as addressed to an unnamed Secretary of the Treasury. Incidentally it depicts very clearly the qualities Strahan thought valuable in a member who sat on the Government benches—tractability being the chief.

By 1775, when Strahan had been in Parliament for a year, a final breach with the American colonies seemed to many people almost inevitable. It certainly seemed so to Franklin: although he still had thoughts, when he sailed from Portsmouth in March, of returning in the autumn, he foretold to Priestley a civil war protracted for ten years. Before Franklin sailed, he heard Lord Sandwich applaud *Taxation No*

---

[1] There is an entry in the Rockingham Secret Service Accounts for 19 June 1766 *Mr. Wolfall* [Woodfall?] *by order of his Majesty at the recommendation of Mr. Conway £100*.

[2] *Life*, II, 137.

Tyranny, which was published in March 1775. The sentiments which angered Franklin had already caused irritation
to Johnson, their author, since they had been softened by the
Ministry.[1]

There is no record of Strahan's seeing Franklin during his
last few days in London. Although their political views now
differed widely, they must have parted on good terms, for
Strahan promised to write to him 'every Packet till your
Return, which I still hope will be towards the Fall'. Franklin
was a dangerous man to the Ministry, whether he were in
London or Philadelphia, and correspondence addressed to
him was opened. Strahan might be a vehement supporter of
Lord North, but his letters were not exempt, and copies or
extracts were made and kept.[2] The first, an extract only, is
dated 7 June 1775:

> We begin to expect to hear of the Proceedings of the Congress
> soon.[3] I hope it is composed not of head-strong, violent and unrea-
> sonable Men, but of plain, honest, cool, dispassionate, and impartial
> representatives of the People; more ready to heal than to spread
> Misunderstanding, and perfectly disposed to promote a Reconciliation
> with the Mother Country by every Means in their Power, consistent
> with the Happiness and Liberty of their Constituents.—If this should
> luckily happen to be the Case, I expect to see you quickly return to us
> with the Olive Branch in your Hand, invested with full Powers to
> terminate all Differences upon reasonable and solid Terms.—Believe
> me, I think so well of this Office that I hope it is actually reserved for
> you, and that the successful Conclusion of so important a Treaty will
> crown the Operations of a Life spent in the Investigation of every
> useful Branch of Knowledge, and in the Service of his Country in
> particular. This is truly worthy of your highest Ambition, and I still
> hope to see it gratified in this Respect, however appearances seem at
> present to be against it.'

[1] He passed the alterations in proof and posted them to Strahan from Oxford on
Friday or Saturday, 1 or 2 March; and received a copy of the pamphlet in Oxford
on Wednesday 6 March.

[2] These copies of intercepted letters are amongst the Earl of Dartmouth MSS. in
the William Salt Library, Stafford.

[3] The Second Continental Congress met in Philadelphia in May.

The next letter was thought worth copying in full by the Government agent. It was dated 5 July 1775.

I wrote you the 7th of last Month by the Packet, to which I beg leave to refer. I have since by the Papers and by sevl. of your Friends, heard that you were safely arrived at Philadelphia, & unanimously voted by the Assembly then sitting, one of their Delegates to the Congress, then about to meet. I make no doubt but your Reception among your Friends was abundantly cordial, & I hope you will avail yourself of the great Knowledge you possess, respecting the Matter in dispute between your Country and this, to bring about a speedy Reconciliation . . . If nothing less than a total Renunciation of the Legislature, of all Authority over the Colonies will satisfy them, God knows where the Dispute will end; for I am persuaded this will never be given up here, at least, I see no Tendency towards it. And if the Colonies should actually succeed in their Struggle to be totally emancipated from all Subjection to, or Connection with Britain, it will remain to be seen whether their Liberty & Security will or will not be materially affected by it; Whether it may not throw them under the Dominion of some enterprising Leader among themselves, or leave them a Prey to some ambitious European Power, under whom they may *really* experience all the Evils in the highest Degree, the very appearance of which, & that a very distant one, they now endeavour to avoid. These you may, perhaps, consider as idle and groundless Speculations. I wish heartily they may prove so. But without looking so far into Futurity, the Evils of a Civil War, even for a short Duration, are worthy of some Consideration. Possibly these may still be avoided. *Now* seems to be the critical Moment for America to obtain some permanent Constitution, in perfect Union with the Mother Country, by which her Liberties may be secured and protected by the Laws and Power of the whole Empire, & rendered as permanent in one Corner of it as in another, & every Part of it prove a mutual Protection to each other.

Whether this Course will be taken we shall soon see, when the Resolutions of your Congress are made public. You are a perfect Master of the Subject, & therefore it is happy that you have a Voice in that Assembly, when so much of the Happiness of their Constituents depends upon their Proceedings. But I am somewhat afraid the Voice of Moderation will not now be listened to, & that the Violence of some Men whose Views may not be truly so patriotic as they appear to be, will inflame the Quarrel beyond a Possibility of Accommodation. This I hope you will exert all your Prudence and Sagacity to prevent. For my own part, I have no doubt of the Prevalence of this Country in the End, should hostile Measures be pursued for any Length of Time. But, good God! Where does Victory on either side lead to?— To the immediate Destruction of half, & the ultimate ruin of the whole, of the most glorious Fabric of Civil & Religious Governmt. that ever existed on this Globe. If after we are both weakened by the Struggle, & it terminates in our final Separation, this must unavoidably be the Consequence. However, I still hope better Things, & that perfect Order will arise from the present Convulsions. We are here in a State of the greatest Tranquillity. All Murmurings & Opposition to Governmt. appear only in our Newspapers. I believe the Ministry are quite determined in their Operations, & in the Prosecution of coercive Measures.—I see everybody is learning the Use of Arms with you, but surely it will not be attempted to distress you by Land. Our Navy is our great Strength, & sorry I shall be to see it long exerted against you; tho' if no Steps are taken towards a Reconciliation, I am afraid that must be the Case. Is not this a Situation devoutly to be avoided, if any human means can be devised to prevent it?—But I will not trouble you further on this Subject at present. . . .

So may I prosper, as I wish the Liberty & Happiness of all our Brethren with you, with the same Ardour as I do our own. In this Desire I am sure we are of one Mind, however we may at present differ about the Methods of promoting it. May we quickly be united in Sentiment again; & may your Labours be once more confined to promoting the Arts of Peace, & encreasing the Means of Human Felicity.

I am ever, with the warmest Respect & Esteem, &c.

Will: Strahan

This is the letter of a man in earnest, possibly short-sighted in his hopes that a reconciliation might yet be achieved, but certainly desirous for a settlement to be nego-tiated and not imposed. In his thinking about the American situation, Strahan deceived himself on two points. Misled perhaps by the fact that so much of his correspondence was with traders like himself, he consistently underestimated the force of extreme separatist opinion in the colonies, equating it no doubt with the opposition at home, noisy but ineffective. Secondly, as a Scot who had made his fortune in England, he over-simplified the steps that had led to the Union, exaggerated—many stay-at-home Scots would say—the benefits which the Union had brought to Scotland, and misapplied Scotland's experience to the very different problem of the American colonies. It was perhaps his conviction that an equitable solution could so easily be found, on the Scottish analogy, that produced Strahan's exasperation at what he considered the colonists' wilful refusal to seek an accommodation.

His exasperation would have been even more highly pitched had he ever received the famous letter written to him by Franklin on the same day as the long letter just quoted, 5 July 1775.

Mr. Strahan,

You are a Member of Parliament, and one of that majority which has doomed my country to destruction. You have begun to burn our towns and murder our people. Look upon your hands! They are stained with the blood of your relations. You and I were long friends. You are now my enemy, and I am

Yours, B. Franklin

Franklin never sent this letter and indeed on the 7th wrote to Strahan in his usual friendly fashion, but saying in reply to the printer's counsels that 'Words and Arguments are now of no Use', and that 'all tends to a Separation'. Despite his pleas for moderation to Franklin, Strahan in his heart felt equally that it was too late for argument. Writing on 22 July of the same year to an unknown correspondent, he adopted a more uncompromising attitude.

My opinion has long been fixed, that no total Change of Ministry will take place during the present Reign. And if you will yourself for a Moment consider the Consequences of suffering Men to force themselves into Power by the Methods the present Opposition have taken—by rending the Empire in pieces—you will easily see the Dangers of setting such an Example to future Oppositions. At the same time I cannot allow myself to imagine, that our public Measures would admit of much Alteration, into whatever Hands unforseen

Accidents may throw the Reins of Government. To look back is fruitless and unnecessary. The Question now is, Shall America remain a Part of the British Empire, or not? . . .

As for our Success in America, I have little doubt but by Perseverance, and a proper Exertion of our Naval Force we shall at last bring them to Reason. But if the Temper of that People continue as stubborn and inflexible as by all Accounts it is at present, the Impracticability of penetrating very deep into that Country with any Number of Land Forces we can, with any Convenience, transport thither, may occasion the War to be protracted to some Length.—

But of our final triumphing over their Insolence I entertain no manner of Doubt. By the latest advices from Boston the Troops lately sent out, were safely landed, and in high Spirits. General Gage proposed to march out of the Town on the 14th of last month, and attack the Provincials that besiege him.—And as by the most authentic Accounts, they did not much exceed his Army in Number, tho' they might receive considerable Reinforcements from the surrounding Country by means of Signals they had provided for that Purpose; yet it is not doubted but Gage would be able to put them all to flight. Some indeed think the Matter must be already decided. I am not so sanguine.[1] But I think a good Drubbing will greatly disconcert the Leaders of this Rebellion, who now actually keep their deluded People in that slavish Subjection they with so little Reason apprehend we are preparing for them.—What great Events have been accomplished by the Unanimity of a body of Men struggling against *real Oppression* there are not wanting many Examples in History; but the Effects of the same Unanimity excited by Faction and *imaginary Grievances* remain yet to be seen. . . .[2]

The news of Bunker Hill had reached Strahan by the time he wrote again to Franklin, on 2 August.

It was with the utmost Concern I heard the News of the late Battle at Boston, not only on Account of the Loss on both Sides, but as it widens the Breach, and renders all Hopes of Reconciliation more difficult and more distant than ever . . . I have only therefore to repeat my earnest Sollicitations, that you will exert every Nerve to prevent the farther Effusion of Christian Blood, and to promote a final Settlement of our Differences, such as may leave America every Species of Liberty

[1] The battle of Bunker Hill was fought on 17 June.
[2] John Rylands Library, Eng. MSS. 537–8.

they can reasonably wish for, and Britain the just Supremacy over her Colonies, to which you say yourselves she is entitled and which equally tends to the Happiness and Protection of the whole Empire . . .

Here I will not say we are unanimous, but nearly so, to carry on the War with the utmost Vigour. Great Preparations are making to send more Troops and more Ships with all possible Expedition. The Honour and Dignity of the Crown, as well as the commercial Interests of this Kingdom, are, in the Opinion of the most dispassionate and impartial, all at Stake, and merit our utmost Exertions.—You will doubtless smile at our Credulity, and think that you are able to repel every Force we can bring against you . . .

I hear the Congress are once more to address the King. If they do, and they should propose such Terms as can be deemed in any Shape admissible, a Stop may still be put to this Carnage, and all may yet be well. But as this Address is like to be the last Overture to Accommodation, I hope you have taken care that it is conceived in proper Terms.—Doubtless it would be submitted to your Correction. You know full well the Temper of the People here, and you must be sensible that your Countrymen may have in many Instances mistaken the Voice of Faction for the real Sense of the Nation at large . . . By no means think of insisting upon Conditions to which the British Legislature cannot listen, but come over next October or November, when the Parliament will certainly meet, with such fair and equitable and moderate Proposals as will shew to all Mankind how desirous, how sollicitous, you are to put an End to the Quarrel . . .

Strahan's next letter, dated 6 September, was written in reply to Franklin's pessimistic observations that 'words and arguments are now of no use'. He added, to a sad note, a postscript:

Since writing the above, I have read the last Petition of the Congress to the King, to which your Name is annexed.—It appears to me, to be couched in very loose Terms, neither making any Concessions, or pointing out any feasible Plan of Reconciliation. It plainly appears, indeed, to be written *after* you was convinced that *Words and Arguments were of no Use* . . .

By the way, may it not be justly apprehended, that the People of Property in America, after having put Arms into the hands of the inferior Class, & taught them the Use of them, will one Day find it no easy Matter to persuade them to lay them down again? In my Opinion you have much more reason to dread being enslaved by some of your own Citizens than by the British Senate . . .

The fears which Strahan expressed of the dangers of mob rule were by no means far-fetched in one who had spent his working life in the City. He had seen what Wilkes could accomplish with the London mob at his back; and even worse was to come, with the Gordon riots of 1780. As King's Printer, Strahan perhaps was, and certainly imagined himself to be, an object of attack. Johnson told Mrs. Thrale that Strahan 'had been insulted', and wrote to Boswell that 'Mr. Strahan got a garrison into his house, and maintained them a fortnight; he was so frightened that he removed part of his goods'.[1]

Strahan's last letter to Franklin before the war interrupted their correspondence was written on 4 October, and was very much stiffer in tone.

Though I have nothing new to communicate yet as this is the last regular Packett that is to sail from hence for some time at least, I do not choose to let it go without dropping you a line. I see with Concern that you have accepted the Place of Postmaster from the Congress, a Step of itself which sufficiently indicates your Opinion, that *a Separation will take Place*, the Consequences of which, sagacious as you are, you yourself cannot foresee in their full Extent. That *a Separation* has long been meditated and intended by some People on your Side of the Water appears now to a Demonstration, from the great Preparations that have been made for it, from the gross Misrepresentations of your Committees of Correspondence of what is done on this Side (particularly a long circular Letter in the Carolina Gazette of the 18 July, which now lies before me) from the violent & arbitrary Measures that are taken to *compel* People to sign your Associations, & from the unwarrantable Persecution of all those who hesitate or refuse, or who discover the least Symptoms of Attachment to the British Government . . .

I shall not trouble you farther upon the Subject than just to tell you

[1] *Life*, III, 428, 435. Hill notes that 'during the week when the disorder was at its height Sir Joshua Reynolds' notebook records that he had sittings fixed, among others, for Mr. Strahan'—sittings which had to be postponed until the rioting had been suppressed.

once more, after all that is past, that I am still of Opinion, that the
Ministry of this Country was never disposed to fleece or oppress you,
that this un-natural Civil War has been chiefly, if not wholly, occasioned by our wicked Factions at Home, whose Struggles for Place
and Power have by degrees carried them such daring Lengths, as to
have induced & encouraged you to encrease your Demands much
beyond what you at first dreamt of . . .

I have lately seen many worthy Men who have been forced to
abandon their Homes in almost every part of the Continent, to avoid
Confinement, Confiscation of Goods, & even Corporal Punishment.
These are uniform and consistent in their Accounts of the Tyranny
& Oppression of the leading Powers with you, and give a most lively
& striking Picture of the Miseries of Anarchy which every where
prevails among you, to which any Form of Government (almost) is
infinitely preferable . . .

However you may depend on hearing from me as I do on hearing
from you, when you have Time to write, and when you think it can
eventually answer any good Purpose. I am sorry to differ from you,
toto coelo, in this great Political Dispute; but I can nevertheless sub-
scribe myself with great Truth, Dear Sir,

Your affectionate humble Servant,
Will: Strahan

Strahan had evidently expressed similar opinions to his
old friend Robertson, who replied to him on 6 October 1775,
'I agree with you in sentiment about the affairs of America
. . . The struggle will be long, dubious and disgraceful . . .
It is lucky my American History was not finished before
this event. How many plausible theories that I should have
been entitled to form, are contradicted by what has now
happened!'[1]

Lacking Robertson's peculiar consolation, Strahan had
become thoroughly angry about the situation when he wrote
to Hume on 30 October—the more so, perhaps, because
Hume was a strong supporter of the American cause. 'I am
entirely for coercive Methods with these obstinate Madmen'; he added gloomily that 'At present I believe we have

---

[1] Stewart, *Life.*

totally lost America', but put his hopes in the belief that 'they cannot subsist without Trade'.[1]

Next year he was more cheerful about the progress of the war. On 10 June 1776 he wrote to Adam Smith:

> You would see by the last Gazette, at the same time, what Havock our Navy was making among their Shipping, no less than 70 and upwards of their Ships having already fallen into our Hands. If we proceed at this Rate we shall soon make them weary of opposing themselves to the Strength of Old England, which I hope will still prove triumphant over all her Enemies, Domestic as well as Foreign.[2]

But the war, from the British point of view, went from fiasco to disaster. Strahan was in a chastened mood when next he wrote to Franklin. The latter was then American Minister in Paris, living at Passy where his lively interest in his old craft led him to install a printing press. Soon after he heard the news of Cornwallis's surrender at Yorktown, Franklin re-opened the correspondence with his old friend. He wrote to Strahan on 4 December 1781, after some general salutations:

> A strong emulation exists at present between Paris and Madrid, with regard to beautiful printing. Here a M. Didot *le jeune* has a passion for the art, and besides having procured the best types, he has much improved the press. The utmost care is taken of his presswork; his ink is black, and his paper fine and white . . . I will send you a sample of his work when I have an opportunity.
>
> I am glad to hear that you have married your daughter happily,[3] and that your prosperity continues. I hope it may never meet with any interruption, having still, though at present divided by public circumstances, a remembrance of our ancient private friendship. Please to present my affectionate respects to Mrs. Strahan, and my love to your children. With great esteem and regard, I am, dear Sir, your most obedient and humble servant. . . .

France was of course at war with Britain, and the letter

[1] Hill, op. cit.
[2] Royal Society of Edinburgh.
[3] Margaret Penelope Strahan married John Spottiswoode of Spottiswoode on 10 June 1779.

took some time to reach Strahan who did not answer it until
27 May 1782.

I am happy to hear there is so great an Emulation upon the Conti-
nent for the improvement of the Art of Printing, and I hope it will
continue. Here all our Pressmen are spoilt by the hasty and slovenly
Manner in which our numerous Newspapers and Magazines are
printed; nor is there the least Encouragement for any one to carry the
Art to any farther Degree of Perfection. I am now too far advanced in
Life to think of it; but I shall be much obliged to receive from you a
Sample of Didot's Performance in that Way, as you kindly promise me.

I rejoice to see that you do me the Honour still to retain a Remem-
brance of our ancient private Friendship, and in the present Prospect that Public Circumstances will not much longer divide us. That
Event I long for, I will own, with no small degree of Impatience;
sincerely hoping, that no Success on either Side, however flattering,
will induce us to protract this unnatural War, which tends only to
strengthen the Hands of our mutual Enemies, who are at the same
time Enemies to the Liberties, civil and religious, of all Mankind.[1]

Inclosed I send you a Copy of the Bill to enable His Majesty to
conclude a Peace, &c., with the Amendments as it passed the House
of Commons last Friday. These Amendments, if I am not misin-
formed, were suggested by yourself; so it is plain that here is no Impedi-
ment to the accomplishing so necessary and so desirable a Work. Of
the good Disposition of his Majesty's present Ministers, you have
already had ample Testimony . . .

I begin now to flatter myself that we shall soon meet again. Mean
while you have my best Thanks for your good Wishes, so kindly
expressed in your last, towards my Family, who are all well (my Wife
excepted who is now at Bath for the Recovery of her Health) and
remember you with wonted Esteem and Affection. You will find your
Wife[2] the same plain honest Girl she was when she made choice of you

[1] Military operations in North America had ended with Cornwallis's surrender
at Yorktown in October 1781; the flattering success to which Strahan alludes was
Rodney's defeat of the French fleet a month before. In November 1782 a preli-
minary treaty was signed with the United States, followed in 1783 by the Treaty
of Paris between Britain, the United States, France, Spain and Holland. Strahan
voted against Shelburne's peace proposals, 18 February 1783, in respect of France
and Spain.

[2] His daughter Peggy. Franklin made a habit of jocularly calling the daughters
of his friends 'wife'; see Van Doren, op. cit., p. 662.

about 20 Years ago, and myself writing at the same Desk where you first found me at a still more distant Period.

With further Particulars I will not now trouble you, hoping to have an Opportunity of writing again.

I remain with the greatest Esteem and Respect, Dear Sir, Your most obedient, and affectionate humble Servant

Will: Strahan[1]

The two men continued to correspond. There is a letter of Franklin's to his 'Dear Friend' asking him to find work for the bearer, one Meyer, who had worked in his press at Passy and was 'a good compositor, understands Latin, French, and German, and has the character of an honest man'. Franklin amused himself by writing two 'typographical' letters,[2] the first on 16 February 1784 when the younger Pitt was struggling to form a majority in the Commons, after the collapse of the Fox-North coalition ministry:

Those places (of power), to speak in our old stile (brother type) may be good for the CHAPEL but they are bad for the masters, as they create constant quarrels that hinder the business. For example, here are two months that your Government has been employed in *getting its form to press*, which is not yet fit to *work on*, every page of it being *squabbled*, and the whole ready to fall into *pye*. The *founts*, too, must be very scanty or strangely *out of sorts*, since your *compositors* cannot find either upper—or lower—case letters sufficient to set the word ADMINISTRATION, but are forced to be continually *turning for them*.

And on August 14, 1784:

I remember your observing once to me, as we sat together in the House of Commons, that no two journeymen printers within your knowledge had met with such success in the world as ourselves. You were then at the head of your profession, and soon afterwards became a

[1] Letter in the possession of Miss Madeline Hodge.

[2] When he wrote to Andrew Strahan in 1786, after the death of his father, Franklin referred to these letters. 'A Friend of mine tells me he has seen mentioned in a Scotch Magazine a late letter of mine to your Father, in typographical Terms, which he much desires to see. I do not find that I have any Copy of that Letter. I think indeed there were two of the same kind. If you can furnish me with Copies of both, you will much oblige me. B.F.'—APS.

Member of Parliament; I was agent for a few provinces and now act for them all. But we have risen by different modes. I as a republican printer, always liked a form well *planed down,* being averse to those *overbearing* letters that hold their heads so *high* as to hinder their neighbours from appearing. You, as a monarchist, chose to work upon *crown* paper, and found it profitable; while I worked upon *pro patria* (often indeed called *foolscap*) with no less advantage.

They did not meet again, however. When Franklin left France in 1785 to return to America, he crossed by the packet from Le Havre to Southampton and spent four days there, from the 24 to 29 July, waiting for his ship to Philadelphia. Several of his friends, as well as his son, came down from London to see him; but his old friend and fellow-printer had died a fortnight before.

14

The Inheritance

WILLIAM Strahan died in his house at New Street on Saturday 9 July 1785 in his seventy-first year. He was still King's Printer and at the head of his trade, although no longer a member of Parliament. His obituarist in *The Lounger* observes that, from the spring of 1784, 'tho' without any fixed disease, his strength was visibly declining; and though his spirits survived his strength, yet the vigour and activity of his mind were also considerably impaired. Both continued gradually to decline until his death.'[1] However, he retained sufficient vigour of mind to commission with Cadell, shortly before his death, Hawkins's life of Johnson, to preface a collected edition of his works.

His wife Margaret, whose health had given Strahan so much concern, survived him by less than a month: she died on 7 August in her sixty-sixth year, 'a lady', said the *Gentleman's Magazine*, 'whose goodness of heart and tenderness of disposition endeared her to her family and all her acquaintance'.

Strahan's affairs were in good order, as his immaculate accounts would lead one to suppose. His estate was worth £95,000, and included his share in the King's Printer's Patent, in the Law Patent, in the *Public Advertiser* and in the *London Chronicle*. His will had been drawn up a year

---

[1] He was buried in St. Faiths and not in his parish church of St. Brides.

before. It is dated 2 July 1784, and appoints Andrew Strahan and Thomas Cadell his executors. To his wife he left
that share of his personal estate as laid down by agreement dated 19 July 1738 'wherein and whereby I obliged
myself to be made a freeman of London . . . in contemplation of my marriage with my present wife'. He willed that
this statutory disposal of his personal estate in favour of his
wife should stand, despite 'the Act of Parliament for em-
powering freemen of London to dispose of their personal
estate'.

To his elder surviving son George he left only the perpetual advowson to the rectory of Cranham in Essex; he
doubtless considered that with this and the living of Islington he had provided well enough for a son who had shown
so marked a distaste to the printing house or to trade. But
to Andrew he left the land and buildings 'in Little New
Street Shoe Lane in the parish of St. Bride', as well as some
land in Norfolk of which 'I and John Windus Gentleman
are seized or possessed in equal Moietys'. He also left
Andrew £5,000 and the residue of his real and personal
estate—in fact, the family business.

To his surviving daughter Margaret Penelope Spottiswoode he left £5,000 free from any control by her husband
John Spottiswoode, she to enjoy the interest for life, the
capital then to pass to her children. To his grandchildren
William and Margaret Penelope Johnston, the children of
his dead daughter Rachel, he left £5,000 each. He remembered the children of his long-dead sister in Edinburgh by
leaving annuities of £50 each to the two girls and of £20
each to the sons, to be forfeited in the case of the latter if they
were to mortgage the annuities. His only other relative, his
brother-in-law James Elphinston, was left an annuity of
£100, together with £100 in cash and £21 for mourning.

He left varying amounts to his business associates: £100
to Charles Eyre; £500 to Thomas Cadell and £100 to his
wife Elizabeth 'to be laid out in any pieces of plate she shall
choose which it is my desire shall be retained and kept in

memory of her husband's and her own friend'. He left small annuities to the children of old friends in Scotland—John George Wishart of Edinburgh, Patrick Maxwell of Dundee —and to William Preston, then his overseer and subsequently a partner in the business with Andrew;[1] and £100 to Richard Yorke 'my late apprentice and present Journeyman'. To his domestic and household servants he left a year's wages and £5 each; to the poor of St. Brides £100; and £1,000 to the Stationers' Company, of which half the interest was to be paid—and so still is—to five poor journeymen of English blood, and half to five poor Scottish journeymen. All this was a far cry from his humble beginnings in the London trade, with a wages bill of less than £5 a week. He could claim to have earned by intelligent industry every penny of his fortune, and to have avoided both extravagance and parsimony in the use that he made of it.

'In lapidary inscriptions a man is not upon oath', and obituaries are distinguished more by their praise than their discernment. Nevertheless some sentences from *The Lounger* deserve quotation. They come from the issue of 20 August 1785:

His mind, tho' not deeply tinctured with learning, was not uninformed by letters. From a habit of attention to style, he had acquired a considerable portion of critical acuteness in the discernment of its beauties and defects. In one branch of writing himself excelled, I mean the epistolary, in which he not only shewed the precision and clearness of business, but possessed a neatness, as well as fluency of expression which I have known few letter writers to surpass. Letterwriting was one of his favourite amusements. . . .[2]

In his home there was none of that saucy train, none of that state or

---

[1] Preston had been apprenticed to Walter Ruddiman in Edinburgh and came to London in 1760 at the age of 20, becoming a compositor in Strahan's office. He was, says Timperly, 'promoted to the reader's desk, then to the superintendence of that vast concern'.

[2] According to Forbes's *Life*, Beattie had said so much the same same thing that one wonders if he wrote the obituary. 'Mr. Strahan was eminently skilled in composition and the English language, excelled in the epistolary style, had corrected (as he told me himself) the phraseology of both Mr. Hume and Dr. Robertson.'

finery, with which the illiberal delight to confound and to dazzle those who may have formerly seen them in less enviable circumstances. No man was more mindful of, or more solicitous to oblige, the acquaintance or companions of his early days . . . At his table in London every Scotsman found an easy introduction, and every old acquaintance a cordial welcome . . .

Nichols speaks of Strahan in terms borrowed from the obituary in the *Gentleman's Magazine*; he was entitled to do so since he almost certainly wrote the original notice himself.[1]

The good humour and obliging disposition, which he owed to nature, he cultivated with care, and confirmed by habit. His sympathetic heart beat time to the joy or sorrow of his friends. His advice was always ready to direct youth, and his purse open to relieve indigence. Living in times not the purest in the English annals, he escaped unsullied though the artifices of trade and the corruption of politics. In him a strong and natural sagacity, improved by an extensive knowledge of the world, served only to render respectable his unaffected simplicity of manners, and to make his truly Christian philanthropy more discerning and more useful.

One of the recipients of his beneficence broke into verse. This was John Noorthouck 'of Barnard's Inn, Gentleman', to whom Strahan left an annuity of £20. An indexer and corrector of the press,[2] Noorthouck had probably worked for Strahan; according to Timperley, he 'both loved and revered him'. The verses appeared in the *Gentleman's Magazine*, and in their lumbering gait show at least that their subject could inspire a true affection.

FAINT SKETCH OF A CHARACTER

Attempted on the Loss of a Much Respected Friend

If industry and knowledge of mankind,
   Could prove that Fate is not always blind;
   If wealth acquir'd could prompt a gen'rous heart;

---

[1] *Literary Anecdotes*, III, p. 390.

[2] A Liveryman, he was paid £80 in 1780 by the Stationers' Company for indexing some of their records. Blagden, op. cit.

To feel new joys its blessings to impart;
Lament with me such worth should be withdrawn
And all who knew his worth must weep for STRAHAN!

In business, which became his pleasure keen,
Though not enough the tradesman to be *mean*:
Social and frank, a zealous friendly guide,
With safe advice, and ready purse beside,
And far above the *littleness of pride*:
Pride that, exacting homage, meets, in place
Of true respect, contempt beneath grimace.

A breast thus warm could not with coolness bear
Those base returns the good must sometimes share;
Sincere himself, his feelings stood excus'd,
Never by one man to be twice abus'd:
For natures alter not; the leopard's skin
Is stained without as hearts are stained within.

Numbers whose private sorrows he reliev'd,
Have felt a loss, alas! but ill conceiv'd;
He's gone! and those who miss him never will
Find equal excellence his place to fill.
Thy darts, O Death, that fly so thick around,
In *such a victim* many others wound.

Of Strahan's earliest friends and correspondents, only
Franklin was still alive. He wrote from Philadelphia to
Andrew Strahan on 6 May 1786:

I condole with you most sincerely on the Departure of your good
Father and Mother, my old and beloved Friends. Your consolation
will be that you have been a good and dutiful Son, and that their
Memory will be respected by all who had the Happiness of being
acquainted with them.

Remember me affectionately to your Sister Spottiswoode, and your
Brother George. You mention that their Children are well, but say
nothing of the Children of your Sister Johnson. I feel myself interested in what relates to any of your family, and shall be glad to hear
also of the Welfare of those Children. . . .[1]

It remains to note briefly what befell Strahan's family, if

[1] Letter in Fordham University Library.

we share Franklin's interest in it. George remained Vicar of Islington, where he died on 18 May 1824. His hearse 'drawn by six horses, was followed by five mourning coaches . . . and by those of the Lord Chancellor and several private friends anxious to show their esteem for so worthy a man . . . Most of the tradesmen of the town [Islington] had their shops entirely closed.'[1] His widow died in 1831. Their two daughters had been married on the same day, 23 July 1812; Margaret to Freeman W. Eliot and Isabella to W. Rose Rose.

Franklin could have been reassured about the welfare of the Johnston children. William, who went into the army, rose to the rank of General, while Margaret Penelope married Sir Alexander Monro.[2]

Andrew Strahan inherited the private printing business as well as the share of the King's Printer's Patent, and proved to be as active and successful as his father had been. He too became a member of Parliament, though rather a restless one; between 1796 and 1820 he represented Newport, Wareham, Carlow, Aldeburgh and New Romney. Fanny Burney describes him as having 'the appearance of a very worthy, sensible, unpretending man, well-bred and good-natured'. His interests extended to the paper trade; he was instrumental in starting John Dickinson in life as a stationer, and by his gifts and loans enabled him to found the great business that bears his name today.[3] Andrew Stahan died in 1831, leaving an estate of 'more than a million of money', according to Timperley. He had retired from active direction of the business in 1819.

He was succeeded by two of his nephews, the eldest and youngest sons of his sister Margaret Penelope and John Spottiswoode of Spottiswoode. Robert, the younger of the two, died in 1832 but Andrew Spottiswoode lived until 1866, becoming in his turn a member of Parliament, for

[1] *Gentleman's Magazine*, 1824, I, p. 473.
[2] Ibid., 1809, in the obituary of James Elphinston.
[3] Joan Evans: *The Endless Web*, London, 1955.

Saltash and then for Colchester. He married Mary, the daughter of Thomas Norton Longman, and had two sons, William and George Andrew. When these sons in due course inherited the business, it was formally divided into the two parts in which it had always functioned. The Patent with all its rights and privileges was exercised by William Spottiswoode as a partner in Eyre and Spottiswoode, the firm which is still the Queen's Printers as well as general publishers. The private printing—William Strahan's original business —fell to the share of George Andrew Spottiswoode, as a partner in Spottiswoode and Company, now Spottiswoode Ballantyne and Company.

The Queen's Printers have removed some hundreds of yards, but the London offices of Spottiswoode Ballantyne were still, until 1964, in Little New Street where William Strahan lived and worked more than two hundred years ago. He wrote with more truth than he knew when he told his old friend Hall in 1753: 'Indeed I never dreamt of extending my Business so far; but truly it has come to me without my seeking, and I don't dare baulk it, especially as I have Posterity who are likely to live long after me.'

Appendix: A Parliamentary Report

IN January 1764 Strahan reported to Hall in detail the debate in the House of Commons leading to Wilkes's expulsion as the author of no. 45 of *The North Briton* (New Jersey Historical Society, *Proceedings*, 1849). A month later he wrote to Ralph Allen an account of the debate on the legality of General Warrants. It was under such a warrant—'general' because it named no specific persons or charges—that Wilkes and the printers of *The North Briton* had been arrested in 1763. Between then and the debate Wilkes had been freed on the strength of his parliamentary privilege, and he and the printers had succeeded in recovering damages for wrongful arrest and wrongful seizure of papers.

P. C. Webb was Treasury Solicitor, Robert Wood under-Secretary of State.

... I should have sooner done myself the Honour to write to you, but that I had nothing particular to trouble you with, and waited the Issue of the Debates in the House of Commons in regard to the Seizure of Wilkes's Person and Papers, by virtue of a Warrant from the Secretary of State.

On Monday this Debate was opened by reading another Letter from Wilkes; and then several Witnesses were examined as to the Behaviour of the Messengers at his House. Beardmore, his Attorney, in particular, gave a circumstantial (and evidently a partial) Detail of what happened on his Commitment to the Tower, and the steps taken to obtain a Habeas Corpus in order to [*sic*] his Release. After this, Mr. Webb, in his Place, gave a very full Account of the whole Transaction, from which it appeared that Mr. Wilkes was treated with proper Respect and Decency, that his Papers were offered to be sealed up in the presence of Lord Temple, who happened to be at his House when he was seized, or any other of his Friends, that on his Commitment to the Tower, tho' an Order was given that no Person should have access to him, that Order was reversed next Morning; and that no Obstruction whatever was given to his obtaining his Habeas Corpus. Mr. Wood next stood up, and in a very genteel manner acknowledged the Share he had in the affair, for which he had no Apology to make, as he imagined he was, in so doing, discharging the indispensable Duty of his Office. It was now near Eleven, when a Motion was made to adjourn, which passed in the negative, 379 to 31. They then proceeded to read authentic Copies from the Records of all the Warrants that had been issued by Secretaries of State for a Century past; but this dry and unentertaining Business soon disposed the House to adjourn, which they did about twelve.

From this night's Debate I plainly saw that the Ministry did not intend to bring the main Question to a Decision, and that the Opposition, on the other hand, meant nothing more than by pushing the matter as far as they were able, to make a Handle of it to raise a Cry against the Administration. This was so very obvious throughout the whole Altercation (for it deserves not the name of an honest Debate) that I own it hurt me exceedingly to see the Great Council of the Nation so uselessly and so factiously employed, whilst many of our most material and most urgent Concerns were suffered to be neglected. Mr. Pitt's Behaviour more particularly disgusted me. The Observations he made, and the Objections he raised during the Examinations, were apparently frivolous and insincere, and most unworthy of the high Character he once sustained with all honest men. I will not trouble you with Instances of this, tho' I could give you many, because I wish, in Gratitude for his former Services, they could be utterly forgotten. I will only say, I think his whole Conduct, since he gave up the Seals, is of a Piece; exceedingly factious, with repeated, tho' unsuccessful, attempts to regain his Popularity, which I am now more than ever fully persuaded is irretrievably lost . . .

Next day (Tuesday) the House proceeded in hearing the Warrants read, among which was one issued by Mr. Pitt himself, when Secretary of State, ordering the Sailors and Passengers of a certain Ship to be brought before him to answer to the *Premisses*, tho' no Charge whatever was mentioned in the Warrant. To this Mr. Pitt readily pleaded Guilty, and with much affected Contrition and Submission threw himself upon his Country. He insisted likewise that Mr. Wood (of whose Honour and Fidelity he had had, he said, repeated Experience whilst in Office) stood there his Fellow Criminal, and that they ought both to submit to the Justice of their Country. Mr. Wood replied to this, that he did by no means look upon himself in the Light of a Criminal; that what he had done he thought it his indispensable Duty to do; and that he only waited the Sentence of the House upon his Conduct, from whence he would not depart till they had pronounced it. It was now near two in the morning, when it was proposed to put this Question: *That a General Warrant for apprehending and seizing the Authors, Printers and Publishers of a Seditious Libel, together with their Papers, is not warranted by Law.* This gave rise to a fresh Debate; after which another Question was put, viz: *That this Debate, and the further Consideration of the matter of this Complaint, be adjourned till this Day at twelve o'Clock;* which was carried in the negative, 207 to 197. Then this last Question, amended by inserting the Words *Friday morning next* instead of *this Day at twelve o'Clock,* was agreed to without a Division. It was then moved, *That the Complaint against Robert Wood, Esq, a Member of this House, for a Breach of Privilege of this House be discharged.* Upon which it was again moved to adjourn; which, upon a Division, passed in the Negative, 208 to 184. And then the Motion for discharging the Complaint against Mr. Wood, Mr. Webb, and the Managers, was agreed to without a Division. Then the House adjourned till Friday, it being now half an Hour after Seven in the Morning. The Speakers of chief note this Day were, the Attorney General, Mr. Grenville, Mr. Wilbraham, Mr. Wedderburn—Mr. Pitt, Sir William Meredith, Serjeant Huett, Thos. Townsend, Col. Onslow, Mr. Beckford, and Mr. Mawbey— Mr. Pitt spoke 10 or 12 times.

On Friday they accordingly resumed the further Consideration of this Matter, when both Sides exerted themselves to the utmost in mustering their whole Forces, so that the House was very full. Many excellent Speeches were delivered, which did more Honour to some People's Talents than to their Candour and Integrity. At length the Question was proposed: *That A General Warrant for apprehending and seizing the Authors, Printers, and Publishers of a seditious and treasonable Libel is not warranted by Law, although such Warrant hath been issued according to the Usage of Office, and hath been frequently produced to, and so far as appears to this House, the Validity thereof hath never been debated in the Court of King's Bench, but the Parties thereupon have been frequently bailed by the said Court.* Upon this a very warm Debate arose, which terminated in putting the previous Question, *That this Debate be adjourned till this Day four Months;* which, upon a Division, was carried by a very narrow majority, 232 to 218. The Reasons for dismissing the Question in this manner are sufficiently obvious. Many and great Inconveniences would attend the explaining the precise Power of a Secretary of State. In all Governments there is lodged *somewhere* Powers not warranted by Law, to be exercised upon great and critical Occasions, such as times of open Rebellion or dangerous and secret Conspiracies; and as under our Constitution, which admits of greater liberties to the Subject than the best Republic that ever existed, every Minister exercises this Power at his Peril, we have nothing, in my humble Opinion, to apprehend from the Abuse of it. This I am fully persuaded every Member in the Opposition were duly sensible of, notwithstanding their violent Declamations to the Contrary. Those who spoke this Day, in the Order in which they spoke, are as follows:

Attorney General	Lord Frederic Campbell
Mr. York	Mr. Shelly
Attorney General	Lord Granby
Lord North	Mr. Charles Townsend
Lord George Sackville	Dr. Hay
Colonel Burgoyne	Mr. Richard Webb
Mr. Nugent	Mr. Dowdeswell
General Conway	General Townsend
Mr. Stanley	Mr. Fuller
Mr. Hussey	Lord Barington
Charles Townsend	Mr. Thos. Townsend
Lord Barington	Mr. Eliot
Mr. Wilbraham	Mr. Thos. Townsend
Sir Francis Delaval	Lord North
Mr. Pitt	Mr. Barre
Mr. Grenville	Mr. Shiffner

In this manner hath this important Affair been composed for the present; and I hope the remainder of the Session will go on pretty smoothly; at least, I see not any new Matter for the Opposition to take up that will answer their Purpose. 'Tis high time, you will doubtless think, that the Legislature should seriously set about settling our new Conquests, and improving by all other Means the late Peace, which, bad as it may by some People be represented, appears more and more every Day to be a very great and seasonable Blessing to this Kingdom.

Tomorrow Mr. Wilkes's Trial for being the Author and Publisher of the *North Briton* comes on before Lord Mansfield at Westminster, the Issue of which I am in little Pain about, as the Jury is Special, and the Proof strong and clear . . .

Index

Gibbon, Edward, 8, 40, 161, 168; *Decline and Fall*, 51, 161
Glasgow, 4, 51, 77, 105
Goldsmith, Oliver, 38; *Vicar of Wakefield*, 41
Gordon, Ann, George, Isabella and William, jun., 98, 207
Gordon, William, sen., 4, 98
Gordon Riots, 200
Grafton, Richard, 125
Grand Magazine, 104
Grenville, George, 170, 173n., 185n., 186, 187n., 215
Griffiths, Ralph, 103

Hall, David, 11, 60, 66, 67, 68, 69, 70, 71–9, 92, 93, 100, 117, 131, 137, 153, 171, 175, 183, 188, 201, 212, 213; Franklin's employee and partner, 62 et seq.; Franklin's successor in business, 89; orders goods from S, 73; orders books from S, 77 et seq., 84, 90; financial dealings with S, 73 et seq.; punctual payments, 68, 73, 79; cannot return to Britain, 87–8; death, 91: Letters to S, 89, 91
Hall, William S, 91, 94, 96
Hamilton, Archibald, 121
Hamilton, Gavin, 44–5, 54, 78
Hart, T., 6
Hawkesworth, John, 112, 139–140
Hawkins, Sir John, 22, 157n., 206
Hertford, Lord, 46, 114–15, 181
Hills, Henry, 125
Hitch, Charles, 16, 22, 26, 37n.

Hodges, James, 16, 37n.
Hollis, Thomas, 130
Home, David, 168–9
Home, John, 166n., 167, 168, 169
Hughs, John, 124
Hume, David, 5, 8, 19, 43, 105, 114, 118, 120, 131, 133, 143, 144, 161, 171; on copyright, 134; literary earnings, 44–5; and Rousseau, 48–50; and Warburton, 118–19; his will, 163–4: Letters to S, 19, 43, 46, 49, 51, 52, 53, 54, 56, 57, 58, 115n., 119, 134, 135, 162, 163–4, 165, 172, 180, 181; to Millar, 44, 48; *History of Great Britain*, 43, 47, 50, 51, 54–5, 163; *Essays*, 44–5, 50, 51, 143, 163; *Dialogues on Natural Religion*, 164, 167–9
Hutton, James, 10, 166n.

Innys, William, 21
Insurance, 65, 75–6

Janssen, S. T., 16
Johnson, Job, 28, 74
Johnson, Samuel, 2, 7, 8, 9, 22 et seq., 30, 37, 38, 39, 42, 56, 104, 118, 119, 120n., 130n., 133, 136, 143 et seq., 155, 193, 200, 206; on boarding schools, 93; on copyright, 134; on discounts, 32–3; and Elphinston, 23; and Adam Smith, 120, 163; and S as printer, 24–5, 146–8, 181, 194; and S as banker, 25, 145,